Nelson Mandela once said, "Educatior
ful weapon to change the world." I firmly believe in this. Still, I
believe even more in a Christ-centered education, which seeks to
train academically capable children and adolescents, and above
all, human beings who are compassionate and with firm convic-
tions to face a constantly changing society. We are convinced that
when the life of a teacher, a principal, or a school owner is transformed by the Word of God, the lives of the children who are
under his influence will be touched in the same way. This book
shares how Christian partners journey together to serve, train, and
inspire school leaders in low income countries.

Nelsa Zolezzi, director of Desarrollo Cristiano of Peru

We face a terrible crisis of values daily, but at ADRA Peru, we
share the same effort with Edify, transforming the lives of many
children through education with Christ-centered values. For this,
I thank God for the ministry of Edify. I invite you to enjoy this
publication, and I am sure it will be a great blessing. The won-
derful stories of transformed lives of students, teachers, and educational promoters are very inspiring. I am a witness of their
generosity, commitment, and their love for the children of Peru
who need to live with hope and purpose.

Plinio Vergara, general director, ADRA Peru

The world we live in results from the people and organizations
that came before we did. It is not perfect, and we are sure that it
is not close to the ideal world we would like to pass on to future
generations. That is why Edify and organizations like Sinergia
FLT decide to equip educational leaders' minds, hearts, and hands

to create learning experiences in the real world for real people. Readers of this book will find a sign of God's grace on every page.

Guillermo Yan Alfonso MA, director of leadership development at Sinergia FLT

Edify's well-researched book clearly articulates a burning social crisis in many less developed countries—lack of access to basic education for large numbers of young people in the low-income segment. This book offers a credible, sustainable solution—the Edify model of low-fee independent schools. Edify's model wisely incorporates not only education that informs the mind but a value-based curriculum that helps transform the mind and the heart. Therefore, I highly recommend this book to all those who are working to create a better world in the education space within less developed societies.

Tim Kreutter, cofounder of Cornerstone Development Africa

Quality education is a basic human right but does not occur in many developing countries. Edify has supported education programs in twelve countries with low-fee independent Christian schools, and their impact cannot be overemphasized, as voiced by many stakeholders in this book. I have known and worked in the field with Chris and Makonen; they are men I admire greatly for their great love and support for the underprivileged. This book will serve as a blueprint for many others to increase access and quality of education and technology, and in so doing, promote the work of our Lord Jesus even further.

Tony Fosu, CEO, Sinapi Aba Savings and Loans Ltd., Ghana

Educational inequality sets children on very different paths, regardless of their talents, work ethic, and innate potential. A lack of access to high-quality, affordable education can even set nations on different trajectories. Thankfully, there are courageous school entrepreneurs. This book shows how low-fee Christian schools are creatively addressing poverty and unleashing educational opportunities. I have seen this inspiring work firsthand. In this informative and inspiring book, you will learn of the impact of investing in children and how this investment can fill entire communities with hope.

Peter Greer, president and CEO, HOPE International, author, *The Gift of Disillusionment*

Makonen, Bettina, and Chris have done excellent work in presenting the role of low-fee independent schools in this book. These schools create access to quality education for children living in poverty. Edify's work to help over ten thousand such schools improve and expand a Christ-centered education in twelve developing nations around the world is commendable. I applaud their spirit to share all they have learned with any organization seeking to transform disadvantaged children's lives through Christian education.

Michael D. Epp, senior vice president, Global Association of Christian Schools International

An extraordinary revolution of low-cost private schools is sweeping the developing world. Set up by entrepreneurs, these schools serve the poor better than any public alternative. This timely and inspirational book catalogues Edify's journey to work alongside these schools, providing capital and other assistance to enable them to flourish and prosper. It is essential reading for all those who want to understand this grassroots approach to sustainable and scalable development.

Professor James Tooley, vice-chancellor (president),
University of Buckingham, England

Some of the greatest heroes in the emerging world are local, faith-driven entrepreneurs building low-fee independent schools designed to educate the poorest children in their communities. These market-driven schools provide access and quality education to low-income working families at prices they can afford. For more than a decade, Edify has been a leader in helping these inspiring business owners improve their schools, become sustainable, and share Jesus with millions of young students across the globe. No one does it better.

Dale Dawson, founder and CEO of Bridge2Rwanda

PATHWAY

TO FLOURISHING

GODLY
NATIONS

Low-Fee Christian Schools for
Children Living in Poverty

Makonen Getu, PhD, Christopher A. Crane, and
Bettina Gomez-Garcia

This book is dedicated to the proprietors, leaders, teachers, and students of low-fee independent schools.

CONTENTS

FOREWORD

This book is a valuable reference for those interested in learning and addressing deep and persistent education inequality in developing regions. In this book, Makonen, Chris, and Bettina provide a remarkably insightful compilation of unique approaches and experiences in establishing and scaling a global network of Christ-centered, low-fee independent schools.

There have been many attempts by education leaders to create well-functioning low-fee independent schools around the globe. Indeed, not all low-fee independent schools are created equal, nor do they operate in the same manner and yield similar results. I have been blessed to visit Edify schools, meet teachers and proprietors, and talk with students and parents. This book details Edify's distinctive and bold journey of creating a pathway to flourishing Godly nations.

When institutions, structures, and programs lack cohesion, sustainability is compromised, and failure is unavoidable. This book explains how Edify demonstrates an exceptionally high level of cohesion in its overall operating model. From establishing and promoting a Christ-centered character development curriculum to training quality teachers and administrators as well as from integrating digital learning solutions to devising innovative impact assessment practices, Edify has looked at all facets of its operating model to ensure a high level of overall cohesion.

Among many great facts, the best thing I keep witnessing is that Edify continues to revisit all identified elements of its operating model to seek possible ways to improve and stay current with the fast-changing environment and rapidly advancing learning technology. We know too well that it is not just a few things that could possibly make a school run well in a community; all components need to work in harmony to sustain a good school for decades and centuries.

This book is a must-read, particularly for those who do not want to reinvent the wheel or repeat previous mistakes that numerous education organizations and leaders have made. Many school systems developed in the last century do not have a fully positive impact on economic development today. Many classroom activities do not lead to the students' development of cognitive and metacognitive skills necessary to tackle the problems in the workplace today and tomorrow. Educational datasets merely showing the increase in hours of schooling or enrollments in a sizable system often fail to warrant the return on investment in skill development and socioeconomic attainment. Many students who diligently spend time memorizing facts for high-stakes exams often do not become lifelong, active learners who can make a positive difference in themselves and others in today's hyperconnected world. Most of all, it is extremely difficult to find mass education programs that help those hardworking, intelligent students to grow into becoming Christ-centered, twenty-first-century leaders.

In this book, Makonen, Chris, Bettina go into the details on how to put it all together to help generate future Nelson Mandelas and MLKs. In Edify's unique model, there is an incentive for all constituents to excel, and at the same time, all participants are held accountable. Edify also constantly strives to leverage the latest analytical data models to vividly show the evidence of its progress in both quantitative and qualitative measures.

In short, this book explains what it takes to develop a sustainable model that addresses the ever-widening education gap between developed and developing regions. In fact, helping students grow their knowledge and faith in Jesus Christ while preparing to tackle the challenges of the twenty-first century and creating jobs for themselves and others is exactly what I would look for in today's schools. Edify is making tremendous progress in such endeavors.

For years to come, many schools in low-income countries still may not have functioning toilets, while many students may come to school hungry and not have access to twenty-first-century digital learning resources. Therefore, the education gap may continue to widen. Brookings Institute indicated that it might take more than a hundred years for the developing regions to catch up and bridge the gap. I strongly believe we can certainly accelerate the improvement process, and we must. This book sheds light on how to do precisely that.

Paul Kim, PhD
Associate Dean and Chief Technology Officer
Graduate School of Education
Stanford University

ACRONYMS AND ABBREVIATIONS

ACD	Authentic Character Development
ACSI	Association of Christian Schools International
ADI	Agape Development Initiatives
AEAD	Association Evangelique d'Appui au Development
AIDS	Acquired Immunodeficiency Syndrome
AMO	Apacienta Mis Ovejas
APRENDI	La Associacion Pro Ensenmanza y Desarrollo Integral
AWANA	Approved Workmen Are Not Ashamed
CCE	Christ-Centered Education
CDI	Career Development Institute
CLA	Cornerstone Leadership Academy
CLASS	Computer Lab Access for Sustainable Schools
COVID	Coronavirus Disease
CTTO	Christian Transformation and Training Officer
DAI	Development Associate International
DC	Discipleship Club
DFID	Department for International Development

DR	Dominican Republic
EEGRP	Edify Early Grade Reading Project
EFA	Education for All
EVASUE	Evangelical Students and Graduate Union of Ethiopia
GDP	Gross Domestic Product
GPE	Global Partnership for Education
GSMA	Gropue Speciale Mobile Association
HIV	Human Immunodeficiency Virus
HLC	Hippocamps Learning Centers
ICT	Information and Communication Technology
ILO	International Labor Organization
IFC	International Finance Corporation
IPM	Integrated Program Model
ISO	International Organization for Standardization
ISTM	Inter-Generational Transformation Ministry
LFIS	Low-Fee Independent School
MDG	Millennium Development Goal
MFI	Microfinance Institution
NGO	Non-Governmental Organization
PTA	Parent and Teacher Association
SDG	Strategic Development Goal
SAT	Sinapi Aba Trust
SME	Small and Medium Enterprise

SMILE	Stanford Mobile Inquiry-based Learning Environment
SPTWD	Society for Promotion of Tribal Welfare and Development
STC School	Transformation Committee
UK	United Kingdom
UN	United Nations
UNESCO	United Nations Educational, Scientific, and Cultural Organization
UNICEF	United Nations Children's Fund
US	United States

ACKNOWLEDGEMENTS

Several people have contributed to the production of this book. We wish to acknowledge them and appreciate their contributions.

We start with the school proprietors, leaders, administrators, support staff, teachers, and students of Edify's partner schools. We thank them for the time, knowledge, stories, and data they shared with us through interviews and reports. We thank them particularly for the testimonies given in Chapter 8. We are encouraged by their passion and determination to open and operate low-fee Christian schools that give access to a quality and Christ-centered education to children living in poverty under very challenging socioeconomic conditions. This book would have not been written without their noble participation in the global effort to bring a solution to the education crisis.

Our appreciation also goes to the Edify staff at all levels: the field officers, country directors, regional vice presidents, senior leadership team members, and board members have all contributed to the success of Edify's program. We especially thank Tiger Dawson, CEO and president of Edify, for his encouragement, support, and comments he rendered us from the inception to the end of the writing project. The Christian Transformation and Training Officers (see Appendix 1) have contributed to gathering data and compiling the voices from the field in their respective countries of operation. We thank Reuben Thiessen, Storm Godwinson, Andy Johnson, and Godwin Fiagbor for their contribution to the EdTech chapter, Dorcas Adwoa Aidoo and Peter Amfo to the Christ-centered training chapter, and Abigail Oteng-Yeboah to the IPM and Impact Assessment chapter. We also appreciate Julie Walton and Meghan Stock for the compilation of the loans and training charts, respectively.

Moreover, we thank Mike Hamel, author, and Professor James Tooley, vice-chancellor of University of Buckingham, for their reviews and comments on early drafts.

Last but not least, we want to recognize and thank Edify's partners for their support to the implementation of the program: the lending partners (see Appendix 2) have delivered the loan products and services to partner schools in their respective countries on behalf of Edify. The training partners (see Appendix 3) have delivered the training products and services. The financial partners have not only generously given the funding necessary for making the provision of these critical products and services possible but also by supporting and encouraging Edify through field visits and prayers. We thank them for the invaluable role they have played and are playing in boosting Edify's effort to improve and expand a sustainable Christ-centered education with the aim to raise servant leaders who will build flourishing Godly nations.

INTRODUCTION

"Education is the most powerful weapon which you can use to change the world."

— Nelson Mandela

We agree that education is often a child's one chance in life to escape poverty. However, hundreds of millions of children living in Africa, Asia, and Latin America have difficulty accessing a school providing an education that prepares them for life. Education Ministries in developing nations are often seriously under-resourced when it comes to educating all their children. Public (government) schools are often in short supply and ineffective. There can be overcrowded classrooms of a hundred or more students, corruption, bureaucracy, dangerous gangs, and inadequate facilities. Public school teachers are often absent or otherwise not teaching. The executive director of a large microfinance organization (MFI) in West Africa calls public schools "football [soccer] academies." When asked why, the ED explained that when teachers were absent, the children were sent outside to play.

These multiple public school problems result in students not learning to read, write, or do simple math has been termed the "global education crisis." Female students are vulnerable to teenage pregnancies out of wedlock and forced child marriages. Their children will likely be uneducated and mired in poverty for life. Lack of critical thinking skills puts them at risk of being regularly cheated as well as misled by corrupt politicians with false promises. The future portends hundreds of millions of people struggling with skills insufficient to earn their way out of poverty. Many men and women will be much less productive than they could have been for their communities and nations. Many of those who drop out early do not go beyond secondary school education. They will likely be relegated to manual labor in high heat and humidity for life, starting in their early teenage years.

The book is about the role of low-fee independent schools (LFIS) providing access and quality education to children living in poverty and Edify's program in helping such schools to improve and expand a Christ-centered education sustainably. The schools educate children of working poor families who can afford to pay fifty cents to one dollar per day per child. Remarkably, if these schools have 250 or more fee-paying students, are fully financially sustainable without government subsidies or donations from anyone!

This Book's Audience

This book is for (1) those who seek to help many more disadvantaged children in Africa, Asia, and Latin America receive a good education, so they can provide well for their families as adults; (2) it is for those who believe in coming alongside a homegrown solution that is already flourishing, schools that have commonly been started by disadvantaged people educating children in their own disadvantaged communities; (3) it is for those who think it is possible for edupreneurs (school entrepreneurs) who, in order to achieve academic excellence, must ensure teachers are present and teaching well to provide better education at their for-profit schools than government bureaucracies.

Although this book contains principles for anyone interested in wishing to improve and expand LIFS, it is especially intended for Christians who wish to impart Christ-centered morals and values that will guide the children to become caring and responsible adults.

For those ideologically opposed to free market schools that give parents a choice between public schools where academic performance is poor and those which "make a profit off the backs of the poor from charging fees," this book may be of little interest. And profits only occur after years of subsidizing losses while the school grows to a student enrollment of 250 or 300, which finally allows positive cash flow. Many school proprietors are motivated from a sense of mission to provide good education to their children or others in the community rather than profits.

We applaud those who seek to improve education by governments. We sincerely wish them success. Countless billions of US dollars from Western donors have gone to improving public schools for decades in developing nations. Alas, far too often there is little to show for it. We believe that public school education quality has continued to decline in many nations despite massive amounts of donations. In many of the twelve countries where Edify operates, we often are told that most public school teachers send their children to LFIS. Such schools, by the way, ease the burden of under-resourced governments from having to educate all children. According to the renowned LFIS researcher, Professor James Tooley, 50–70 percent of school-going children in developing countries are in LFIS, thus freeing up resources for educating the remaining children.

Whenever the authors have heard criticism of LFIS, it is invariably about inputs and not outcomes. The criticism may be that LFIS teachers are unqualified or young or paid less, yet students score higher on national examinations. An enthusiastic young teacher who is present every day can often achieve better results than a credentialed teacher with 30 years of experience who is absent or perfunctory. The criticism that LFIS facilities are sometimes inferior to government schools is true, but the children achieve higher scores. The criticism that LFIS do not meet all the myriad of government requirements is sometimes true, but neither do many government schools.

International Security

The world faces future serious problems if high percentages of emerging country populations continue to enter the workforce woefully unprepared. The number of children leaving schools and entering the labor market without the necessary skills has been growing globally. Schools are failing to prepare young people for gainful employment. As a result, the global youth unemployment rate has grown to alarming proportions with varying degrees across countries. If a high percentage of the job-seeking youth in the world continue to be unskilled and unemployed, society will face great risks of their being recruited into criminal activities and terrorism from lack of hope and alternatives. Such terrorism will likely be widespread and cause national as well as global insecurity and instability. There will be endless antisocial behavior and criminal activities rendering security and socioeconomic development difficult. Conversely, if most children obtain good literacy and numeracy skills, they can go further in their education, get good jobs, some in the knowledge economy, and transform their lives and make meaningful contributions to their nations. With better education and increased youth employment, societies are likely to maximize productivity and resource utilization for their communities and global trade.

In Africa, Asia, and Latin America, LFIS are contributing to the optimization of their abundant resources and enhancement of personal and social transformation by offering quality education with skills that generate employable people. This will contribute to peace and security in their respective regions and global stability.

One Partial Solution

LFIS are one solution currently mitigating the global education crisis. They have the potential to make a dramatic difference in the future. LFIS are providing access to quality education to hundreds of millions of children living in poverty. We will discuss how Edify's program is helping such schools to improve and expand a Christ-centered education sustainably. Edify is a registered 501(c)3 charitable organization in the US. At the time of the publication of this book, Edify partners with 12,000 LFIS in educating 3,400,000 children. Edify does not start schools or own schools. It assists local Christian school proprietors in what they have already been doing.

Some governments in developed countries, as well as many governments in emerging nations, have educational bureaucracies struggling to hold school administrators and teachers accountable to provide a good education to children living in poverty. However, LFIS edupreneurs, often disadvantaged people living in disadvantaged communities, are better able to ensure teachers are present and teaching. Studies show that children in most LFIS regularly score higher to significantly higher on national examinations than children in more crowded public schools with 70 to 100 students per classroom.

We will discuss the history and rationale for the emergence of LFIS, and why Edify was formed to serve them. We will explore the Edify model and delineate how Edify's products and services consisting of Christ-centered training, loan capital, school management training, and education technology are implemented. Also discussed is the quality and content of the education delivered by the LFIS and the stakeholders (school leaders, teachers, and students) involved. Of the approximately 180,000 teachers and leaders at 10,875 Edify partner schools, 44,500 received training and $39.8 million was loaned to LFIS through local MFIs by the end of September 2021. The loan repayment rate was 98 percent. Many more classrooms and other infrastructure were constructed that allowed many more children to obtain a life-transforming education.

Edify assists Christian schools to help children become beacons of the love of Jesus to build flourishing Godly nations. With Edify's support, LFIS impart to children principles taught by Jesus of love overcoming hatred, peacemaking overcoming violence, integrity overcoming corruption, and servant leadership overcoming self-serving leadership.

Opportunities to Scale Affordable Education

Edify leaders have developed innovative rapid scaling models. During 2020–2022 the pandemic caused governments to close all schools in many countries where Edify operates. This caused school edupreneurs to turn to online training searching for ways to continue educating their students, staying solvent, and developing plans to reopen when governments allowed. This online methodology caused many more LFIS pursue partnerships with Edify.

Edify doubled the number of children impacted in 2021 as compared to 2020. With the newly developed innovations to scale rapidly, Edify is likely to benefit tens of millions of children cumulatively in the future.

Edupreneur Voices

This book offers voices from the field that highlight the views of school edupreneurs. In their own words, they express and share their thoughts about the transformative impact Edify's program had on their respective schools.

Governments and LFIS

We discuss government regulations and attitudes toward LFIS. With Peru as a case study, we see regulations and standards LFIS are expected to follow, and the difficulties many of them face in meeting these requirements. It shows how Edify works to help them achieve the required compliance.

Governments can empower more children being educated and getting a better education, while saving tremendous amounts of government money from having to build so many more schools and paying so many more teachers who might be absent much of the time.

We conclude with thoughts and suggestions for the way forward. Most of the recommended pathways apply to all those involved in the promotion of education, including NGO education service providers, churches, donors, impact investors, national governments, and microfinance service providers. The recommendations are proposed in the spirit of strengthening and boosting the role and contribution of the LFIS sector in the provision of access, quality education, morals, and values among children living in poverty.

Thank you for reading this book. We invite you to join this exciting and fulfilling effort in any way you choose to bring quality Christian education to children who otherwise will likely be relegated to dire poverty their entire lives. Edify will share all it has learned with any individual or organization wishing to expand and improve a Christ-centered education. Such education is truly profound and brings long-lasting transformation.

1

GLOBAL EDUCATION IN CRISIS

*"Speak up for those who cannot speak for themselves;
ensure justice for those being crushed. Yes, speak up for
the poor and helpless, and see that they get justice."*

— Proverbs 31:8–9, NLT

The international mandate of enhancing education was given to the United Nations Educational, Scientific, and Cultural Organization (UNESCO). The Universal Declaration of Human Rights, which was adopted in 1948, stated: "Everyone has the right to education. Education shall be free, at least in the elementary and fundamental stages. Elementary education shall be compulsory."[1] In 1990, the Declaration on Education for All (EFA) was adopted at the World Conference on Education for All in Thailand, whereby 155 countries and representatives from 150 organizations agreed to universalize primary education and massively reduce illiteracy by the end of the decade.[2]

Despite the measures taken during the last 30-plus years at both global and national levels, 263 million children are still out of school. About a quarter of the children in low-income countries attend non-state schools. The 250 million children who are in school are not learning, and learning outcomes in both government and private schools are extremely low.[3] Studies also estimate that 91 percent and 87 percent of primary school-age children in low-income countries will not achieve minimum proficiency levels in reading and math, respectively.[4]

The global education crisis and disparity between countries have been further. Over 1.6 billion students globally have seen their education disrupted by COVID-19 over the past year. The learning poverty rate in low- and middle-income countries was 53 percent (9 percent in high-income countries), which meant more than 50 percent of the ten-year-old children could not read and understand a text. The figure was close to 90 percent in Sub-Saharan Africa. The pandemic caused the learning poverty rate to go up to 63 percent.[5] According to UNESCO, "close to half the world's students are still affected by partial or full school closures, and over 100 million additional children will fall below the minimum proficiency level in reading as a result of the health crisis."[6] In their 2020 study, Cordeiro and others stated that whatever progress was made between 2015 and 2020 "came to a grinding halt and some countries experienced regression."[7]

In a global crisis such as this, low-income countries and low-income social groups suffer the most. So much educational injustice exists between the haves and have-not countries at a global level and between social groups within countries. The former enjoy more access and higher quality education while the latter are relegated to lesser access and lower quality education.

The authors believe it is a great social injustice that millions of children living in poverty in developing nations have either no school available to them or only a public school run by the government where it is difficult to receive the reading, writing, and arithmetic skills to work their way out of poverty. This book explores an education alternative that is affordable, even to low-income families, so those children can live a life not mired in debilitating poverty, but rather they can develop their innate talents to be productive for themselves, their families, and their community. Before discussing this alternative, let's look at the state of education today and the aspirations of governments for education in their countries.

The Millennium Development Goals (MDGs) were succeeded in 2015 by the Sustainable Development Goals (SDGs). The 17 SDGs were initiated and signed by 193 United Nations member states at the UN Sustainable Development Summit in New York in September 2015 as part of the 2030 Agenda for Sustainable Development.

The SDGs exceed the most concise MDGs, which has led to some criticism. The MDGs were defined as relative, quantified, and time-bound, while the SDGs have been seen as vast and idealistic. The 17 SDGs are: 1. no poverty; 2. zero hunger; 3. good health and well-being; 4. quality education; 5. gender equality; 6. clean water and sanitation; 7. affordable and clean energy; 8. decent work and economic growth; 9. industry innovation, and infrastructure; 10. reduced inequalities; 11. sustainable cities and communities; 12. responsible consumption and production; 13. climate action; 14. life below water; 15. life on land; 16. peace and justice and strong institutions; and 17. partnerships for the goals.

The second goal under the MDGs focused specifically on ensuring children everywhere, boys and girls alike, would be able to complete a full course of primary schooling. Goals under the SDGs included a broader range of targets. The overall target for a goal was to ensure inclusive and equitable quality education and promote lifelong learning opportunities for all.

While this chapter recognizes the positive achievements[8] that have been made since the UN Sustainable Development Summit, the chapter aims to show briefly how the world has failed to achieve the intended objectives and how global education is in a state of dire crisis.

Failures

The international community promised to provide universal primary education at the 2000 World Education Forum in Dakar, Senegal, where world leaders made commitments to education and our world's most valuable resource—children. But a decade later the basic human right to education for all is still denied. Despite the countless summits, high-level meetings and high-blown rhetoric, progress toward the United Nations' Education for All goal of universal primary education by 2015 has been disappointing, and as the Global Monitoring Report ominously cites, "We are heading steadfastly for an avoidable failure."[9]

Bishop Desmond Tutu, honorary chair of the Global AIDS Alliance, and Dennis Van Roekel, president of the National Education Association, made the above statement in 2010 in their call to serve the world's children with reference to the 263 million children who were out of school then. The number of out-of-school children school has gone down since then, but the overall crisis has continued to worsen.

The commonly held belief has been that by increasing access, nations will see higher levels of educational attainment and, as a result, higher levels of GDP per capita will be achieved. However, despite the above few visible successes, the various global education initiatives seem to be lagging well behind in the aim of the stated goals by 2030. Neither the expected economic growth nor the improved learning outcomes have materialized. The development and education community has been pursuing a false peak on the summit of eradicating global poverty. The most notable one is the failure in the improvement of the quality of education.[10]

Below is a summary of the failures/challenges spelled out by the Sustainable Development Goals Report of 2019. It admits refocused efforts are needed to improve learning outcomes for the full life cycle, especially for women, girls, and marginalized people in vulnerable settings and that the "learning environment, the capacities of teachers and the quality of education" fail to keep pace with the goals.[11]

- In 2017, 263 million children and youth aged 6 to 17 were still out of school, and more than half of the children and adolescents were not meeting minimum proficiency standards in reading and mathematics.
- In 2015, an estimated 617 million children and adolescents of primary and lower secondary school age—more than 50 percent—were not achieving minimum proficiency levels in reading and mathematics. Of these, about two-thirds were attending school but were not learning in the classroom or had dropped out school.

- Some 750 million adults—two-thirds of them women—remained illiterate in 2016. Half of the global illiterate population lives in South Asia, and a quarter live in sub-Saharan Africa.
- Many developing countries still lack basic infrastructure and facilities to provide effective learning environments. Sub-Saharan Africa faces the biggest challenges: at the primary and lower secondary levels, most schools have limited or no access to electricity, the internet, computers, or drinking water.
- Globally, little progress has been made in the percentage of primary school teachers who are trained: it has been stagnating at about 85 percent since 2015. The proportion is lowest in Sub-Saharan Africa (64 percent).

The Present Crisis

The global education big push championed by UNESCO and other organizations to promote universal primary education (UPE) has not only failed to meet the expected goals fully as presented above but also the way the programs have been delivered by the institutions managing their delivery has resulted in a global learning crisis.

The global education crisis has been recognized by the international community, particularly during the last three to five years to the extent that new initiatives have started being undertaken and advocacy mechanisms been put in place. One of the most recent events related to the international gathering of September 18, 2017, which was attended by global education leaders and leaders of France, Malawi, Senegal, Norway, the United Kingdom, Australia, and Tanzania. At that gathering, heads of states of government, business leaders, foundations, and civil society discussed the issue of approximately 264 million children and adolescents not being in school and only one in twelve young people in low-income countries being on track to gain secondary level skills.[12]

According to UNESCO, 617 million children and adolescents worldwide are not achieving minimum proficiency levels in reading and mathematics. This is said to signal "a learning crisis," which could threaten progress toward the United Nations Sustainable Development Agenda. The United Nations Secretary-General Antonio Guterres stated: "Investing in education is the most cost-effective way to drive economic development, improve skills and opportunities for young women and men, and unlock progress on all 17 Sustainable Development Goals. Financing education is indeed the best investment we can make."[13]

Some of the manifestations of the global learning crisis resulting from the failures in achieving the education goals stated in the various global treatise, declarations, and programs could include the following:

Deteriorating Quality of Education. Academic performance and quality of education, including cognitive skills, have deteriorated to below par and are unfit for purpose. This has resulted, partly due to the limited infrastructure, in teaching and management capacity; lack of discipline and accountability; incentives and poor salaries received by teachers; shortage of textbooks; overcrowded classrooms; the continued application of a conventional rote teaching methodology; and lack of adoption of education technology.

More importantly, the crisis related to quality of education and academic performance has resulted from the lack of focus on the quality of education. Most of the global initiatives, including the MDGs, focused on quantity and not quality of education. There has also been limited focus on accountability both within and outside schools. According to UNICEF, "In placing the emphasis upon assuring access for all, these instruments mainly focused on the quantitative aspects of education policy."[14]

The COVID-19 crisis has brought about another serious dip in the quality and performance of global education. For much of the 2020 academic year, more than one billion students worldwide were out of school due to COVID-19.[15] In the majority of the world, the pandemic's impact on education proves to be severe for the most vulnerable populations. According to UNESCO, school closures lead to a host of short-term issues, including loss in learning, poor nutrition, confusion, stress for teachers, and unprepared parents for distance learning.[16] When interruptions in education arise, increases in food insecurity follow suit as students lack access to discounted, healthy nutrition. Further, reliance on distance technology and parents to conduct their education deprives students of their already few educational opportunities. Not only do parents sacrifice their jobs to stay at home with their children and, therefore, face financial insecurity, but many lack the ability to respond to the educational needs of their children. For example, in Uganda, homeschooling is nearly impossible as approximately 50 percent of the women who stay at home with their children are illiterate.[17]

Disparities in learning also increase when children have to rely on technology. This is proven in Sub-Saharan Africa as 90 percent of students lack access to household computers while 82 percent have no internet access.[18] Such a lack of access to technology also inevitably produces negative impacts on teachers as they are unequipped to communicate and respond to the needs of their students.

While the short-term effects of COVID-19 are identifiable, long-term impacts of the pandemic are on the horizon. Specifically, with students being out of school, UNESCO predicts a sharp rise in dropouts as more students will be expected to work due to the economic shock of the pandemic.[19] Other long-term outcomes of the school closures prove detrimental to the well-being of children. The United Nations expects higher reports of early marriages, recruitment of children into militias, sexual exploitation of girls and young women, teenage pregnancies, and child labor.[20] When schools shut down, students not only lose the opportunity to learn but also the nutrition and protection that schooling provides.

Mass Unemployment. The 2020 ILO report on global employment trends for youth reports 267 million young people aged fifteen to twenty-four are not employed, being educated, or trained. In some developing countries, about two-thirds of the working age youth are either unemployed or trapped in low-quality jobs. In the six countries surveyed, this stood at 60 percent, while in Liberia, Malawi, and Peru the figure exceeded 70 percent. In continental Africa youth unemployment constitutes approximately 70 percent of national unemployment.[21]

This results from the failure of the education system to produce employable graduates. The curriculum and teaching system do not reflect the economy, nor do they consider the needs in the labor market. Upon completion, the students are not prepared for employment and enter the labor market with mismatching skills and remain unemployable. The modern industrial sector, which already has a limited absorptive capacity, has difficulties finding candidates with the right skills. Agriculture, the main employer, is also in a similar situation.

A 2020 poll of 40,000 youth in 150 countries revealed at least a third feel unprepared to enter the workforce. The research exposes the serious disconnect between education and employment and elaborates where the pathway falls short, thereby calling to bring the workplace into the classroom and vice versa. The education system has, to a great extent, failed the youth and the economy in every developing country by not investing enough in quality education.[22]

Mass Social Wastage. Despite the surge in the number of children going to school, the world, particularly the developing world, has become a place where an increasingly growing number of young people are being turned into a mass social wastage. Several factors have contributed to this phenomenal social wastage. For instance, the massive number of youth who have not been able to attend school and the massive number of youth who drop out of school for various reasons is a major reason. Other reasons include failure in exams, an inability to pay school fees and other related expenses, pregnancy among girls, and parental decisions to withdraw their children because of domestic needs. Even students who pass their exams at primary and secondary levels often leave schools because of lack of space. In low-income countries, about 50 percent of primary students drop out of school.[23]

The streets in towns and villages are filled with youth who are idle or underemployed, demoralized and suicidal, or resorting to drug and alcohol abuse, prostitution, violence, crime, and social unrest, thereby endangering their lives and the lives of others. To cite an example, one of the contributors to this book visited some low-fee independent schools belonging to the Kenyan Independent Schools Association (KISA) in Western Kenya. One of these schools was run by two retired teachers, both women, who moved back to their village of origin and built houses of higher standard. The school was small and didn't make money. When asked why they wanted to run a school after retirement, the two women said:

> The village is full of young boys and girls who have dropped out of school and have nothing to do and nowhere to go. They are idle, frustrated, and desperate. They are into drinking and smoking harmful substances. They are busy creating menace both day and night by robbing and breaking into homes to steal any stuff that comes their way in order to keep going with their bad habits. Because we live better and have more electronic gadgets that can be sold easier and faster, we have been targets of repeated burglaries. We have opened the school to take them away from the streets, marketplaces, and bars and keep them busy making life more meaningful for them. This way, we keep ourselves as well as the community safe and at the same time create a better future for them. In all honesty, the immediate reason was our own selfish interest of protecting our lives and property.[24]

On the one hand, by not giving opportunity to all children and by not retaining them to completion, the education system continuously turns the youth into a development liability and not a development asset. The youth not only become a burden to their parents but also to their communities and nations.

The high rate of unemployment, employment in mismatching jobs, and disguised unemployment not only drive the youth into despair and crisis but also make it difficult for parents to see value in sending children to school. This also drives societies to losing the valuable skills of the youth, which forfeits stronger productivity growth that would have been achieved had these young people been employed at their appropriate level of qualification.[25]

Demography. Increased population growth means increased pressure on social infrastructural facilities with implications on social interventions such as education. Population growth happens through increased childbirth, which means more young people (about 50 percent of the world's population is under the age of twenty-four, and it is a higher percentage in many developing nations) and an increase in the school-going population. This means more schools, more classrooms, more textbooks, more teachers, and more money.

Where the population and economic growth rates do not match, i.e., where the economic growth rate lags behind the population growth rate, financial constraints render the provision of these inputs difficult. As a result, more students often have to be put in fewer classrooms, use fewer textbooks, and are taught by fewer teachers. This leads to overcrowded classrooms, high student-teacher ratios, high student-book ratios that results in poor quality education and low academic performance (for both teachers and students alike), high rates of staff turnover, high rates of dropouts, and limited opportunities for continued education and employment. Herein lies the devastating effect of population growth on education, particularly in parts of the world where the growth rates are high.

The latest global population statistics indicate the world population has grown from 5 billion in 1987 to 7 billion in 2011, and the UN believes this will reach 9.7 billion by 2050. UNESCO records that 97 percent of the population increase happens in the developing world. Africa is considered the fastest growing continent: its population is expected to double by 2050.[26]

Significant increases in poorly educated and unemployed young people are a prescription for civil unrest. Worse, with little future prospects, they are susceptible to recruitment by gangs or terrorist groups.

In regard to the impediments to educational growth caused by population growth, the UNESCO thematic study, for example, found out that:

> In the Sub-Saharan Africa, the Arab States, and somewhat less in Southern Asia the achievement of universal primary education has been hindered by the growth and age-structure of populations. Efforts to increase primary enrollment ratios have had to work against a rapidly growing population. Thus, despite significant increase in enrollment, the number of out-of-school children did not decline correspondingly.[27]

Educational achievements lag behind in Africa, and with the direct correlation between population growth and educational difficulties, the population explosion is likely to take the current crisis in schools to explosive proportions, undermining the quality of education even further.

In Africa, the only place on earth with a youth bulge (40 percent of the population is under age 15 and 70 percent under age 30), where population growth is the fastest and youth unemployment most rampant, a demographic time bomb is to be expected. Referring to the general issue of youth bulge, Justin Lin, World Bank's chief economist, writes, "If a large cohort young people

41

cannot find employment and earn satisfactory income, the youth bulge will become a demographic bomb because a large mass of frustrated youth is likely to become a political source of social and political instability."[28]

Moral Decline. The moral crisis in schools has been rampant with far-reaching damage on education and school life. Yet it is one of the problems that receives little attention by the international community dealing with education. The widespread undiscipline, disrespect, irresponsibility, substance abuse, bullying, class absence, sexual immorality, early pregnancy, violence, including beating of teachers, school fights, and school shootings and killings are serious indicators of the deterioration of moral standards in the education sector. These have had devastating effects on school security and safety and the quality of education and academic performance. The problem has been aggravated by the lack of value-based education as part of the curriculum. On the contrary, this seems to have been discouraged by policies that restrict religious education that is meant to teach students the essentials of moral ethics.

Donor Funding to Education. Despite increased investments in basic education, large gaps still hinder progress toward the achievement of the SDG targets by 2030. According to the Global Education Monitoring Report published by UNESCO, overall global aid to education has stagnated since 2009, growing approximately 1 percent. The share of education fell from 10.7 percent of total aid in 2007 to 7.1 percent in 2017. Moreover, donor money doesn't seem to go to countries most in need. In 2015, for example, 32 low-income countries, of which 25 were in Africa, received only about 19 percent of total aid to education and 23 percent of aid to basic education during 2005–2015.[29]

A general fear perpetuates that the SDG 4 targets might be compromised in the event that donors don't increase their contribution as pledged in connection with the declaration of the SDGs. Although aid to education reached a record high, fetching US $15.6 billion in 2018, UNESCO estimates that global aid likely to fall by US $2 billion from 2018 to 2022, entailing a 12 percent drop as a result of the pandemic. UNESCO now fears the funding gap to achieve SDG 4 in poorer countries risks increasing to US $200 billion annually due to COVID-19 if urgent action is not taken.[30]

As an attempt to redress this trend, UNESCO Director-General, Audrey Azoulay, cautioned and appealed to the world:

> Just as aid to education seemed to have recovered its lost momentum, the COVID-19 pandemic threatens to take us back several years. Faced with the havoc wreaked by the pandemic, aid to education will arguably be more important than ever before. Countries will need additional funding to respond to the pandemic, and education must be prioritized both in terms of aid and domestic allocations to avoid a setback to our global education goal, SDG 4.[31]

Corruption. According to the 2018 Corruption Perception Index published by Transparency International, most corrupt countries are in the developing world. On a scale of 0–100 (100 being the least corrupt country), most African countries scored below 40, whereas all the developed countries scored at least a 70.[32]

Corruption has become an increasingly growing impediment to building nations and achieving human flourishing. Although in various degrees, it permeates the fabric of societies in the entire world and causes far-reaching socioeconomic consequences. Jean-Marie

Hyacinth writes, "Linked with drug trafficking, money laundering, illegal trade of arms and many other forms of criminality, corruption is harmful to economic growth."[33] The Transparency International Report, *Exporting Corruption 2020*, stated, "Money lost to foreign bribes creates significant economic repercussions, triggers unfair competitive advantages and results in fewer public services for the people who need them most."[34] One UNESCO meeting on tax evasion, for example, recorded "between 4 and 10 percent of global corporate income tax revenues were lost annually, which translated to between $100 and $240 billion. The loss of corporate income tax was more strongly felt in developing countries."[35]

As one part of the fabric of society, education is no exception and has been susceptible to corruption. While education serves as a means of developing personal integrity and accountability, it can also be eroded, and its advancement impeded by corrupt practices. The Education for All Monitoring Report in 2015 noted corruption accounts for a large loss of resources for education. By 2015, Nigeria and Kenya lost a combined total of $69 million of education funding over a period of two years due to corruption.[36]

The pursuit of unlawful economic and political gains by people involved in the designing and implementation education policies and programs and the allocation as well as procurement of resources have marred the access to quality of education. Corruption in the procurement of school resources and nepotism in the hiring of teachers and the falsification of research results for personal gains have been practiced in the education system. Transparency International asserts:

> Corruption not only distorts access to education but affects
> the quality of education and the reliability of research

findings. From corruption in the procurement of school resources and nepotism in the hiring of teachers to the buying and selling of academic titles and the skewing of research results, major corruption risks can be identified at every level of the education and research system.[37]

Summary

The global education sector in developing countries is in crisis. By keeping tens of millions of children out of school, by failing to improve the quality of education, and by producing "unemployable" youth, the education sector turns much of the young generation into a liability rather than an asset to sustainable and holistic development and nation building. This is a crisis that is only expected to be deepened by the decline in funding going to education and the lack of focus on improving education quality. As Jean-Marc Bernard states, "The substantial reduction in the external aid to education, and more specifically basic education, coupled within countries, is expected to have a large negative impact on basic education in Global Partnership for Education in developing countries."[38] The global education system is at a worrying crossroads.

Despite the myriad global summits, accords, declarations, policies, and donor as well as government financial investments made during the last two decades, the world education problem and the moral decline surrounding it is persistent and still with us. It has not gone away. It is likely to grow deeper.

2

LOW-FEE INDEPENDENT SCHOOLS AND EDIFY'S RESPONSE

"The world we have made as a result of the
level of thinking we have done thus far creates
problems we cannot solve at the same level
of thinking at which we create them."

— Albert Einstein

Einstein's quote implied the global education crisis cannot be solved by using the same methods and ideas that created it. That's why Edify offers a different approach centered on low-fee independent schools (LFIS). This chapter presents the definition and history of LFIS, why many parents prefer LFIS to public (government) schools, and why Edify chooses to support LFIS.

Definition of LFIS

Historically, the main providers of education have consisted of governments, religious establishments, NGOs, and private entrepreneurs in both developed and developing countries. Where the government system is perceived to be inadequate, small-scale entrepreneurs and a range of non-governmental organizations have stepped in to provide schooling for those who cannot afford the high fees of the elite schools but are able and prepared to spend a significant proportion of income on lower fee schools.[1]

Before public schools started emerging in the early seventeenth century and became commonplace in the nineteenth century, the main education providers were non-governmental bodies consisting of churches, mosques, temples, communities, and parents. Non-public schools existed and operated for a long time prior to the emergence of public (government) schools, the evolution of which "has drawn from the form and approaches of non-state precedents."[2]

UNESCO classifies all non-public education, i.e., all schools owned and managed by organizations/individuals other than public authorities, as private.[3] Non-public schools could include schools owned and run by not-for-profit (NGOs and religious institutions) and for-profit organizations and entrepreneurs.

According to James Tooley:

> Schools that are run by proprietors [entrepreneurs] are classified as for-profit. In the event they exist, this classification could also apply to schools run by education companies. This is not to say that these proprietor-run schools make large or even any surpluses. It is simply to indicate that if any surpluses are made, then these are available to the person who owns the school to use as he or she wants. This often includes reinvesting in the school but could also include for personal use. Typically, for-profit schools do not have any external source of funding other than student fees, (except they can raise outside capital, to be repaid if loans, or

on which dividends need to be paid if provided as equity). All other management types are classified as non-profit. Under non-profit management, any surpluses made are only available to be used in the school. Non-profit management can also readily solicit funding from outside bodies, which they do in order to supplement income from student fees.[4]

Conventionally, private schools have provided elite and privileged education to children from high-income social strata, often located in low-density and privileged areas. In developing countries, however, a new "brand" of private schools has evolved during the last two or so decades. They are variously presented as "low-cost," "low-income," "affordable," "budget," and "low-fee" schools.

Edify uses the term "low-fee independent schools" for three simple reasons:

1. The term "private" connotes expensive, elite schools. "Independent" clarifies that these schools are not managed by the government.
2. The terms "low-cost" and "low-income" are less precise as they describe costs and incomes, respectively, and do not distinguish between the supplier and buyer. The terms "affordable" and "budget" are also controversial as many clients often struggle and find it difficult to meet their fee obligations. Knowing whether the fees are always "affordable" and to whom this applies is difficult.
3. On the other hand, the term "low-fee" is more precise in that the fees charged by these schools are often lower than conventional private schools and sometimes even what some government schools cost. The fees usually vary between $5

and $25 per month. Pauline Dixon puts the average fees in Hyderabad and in Nigeria at 5.5 percent and 13 percent of minimum wage, respectively.[5] High-income private schools in Ghana, for example, cost $100 to $200 per month, with a few charging much more.

What are these "low-fee" independent schools and how do they operate? What role do they play in the education sector? According to the groundbreaking initial research undertaken by James Tooley in China, Ghana, India, Kenya, and Nigeria, these schools are often located in slums and shanty towns, metropolitan slums, peri-urban areas, and poor rural areas. The research showed:

> The vast majority of school children were found to be in "budget" [low-fee independent] private schools. . . . In the poor urban and peri-urban areas of Lagos State, Nigeria, 75 percent of the schoolchildren were in private schools. In the peri-urban district of Ga, Ghana, the figure was 64 percent, while in the slums of Hyderabad, India, 65 percent of schoolchildren were in private, unaided schools.[6]

By definition, therefore, low-fee independent schools are not learning institutions for school children from wealthy families in wealthy areas. They exist to provide access to education to children living in poverty in marginalized areas and neglected areas such as slums, shanty towns, and informal settlements.

Who runs low-fee independent schools? The definition of the term given above delineated two sets of low-fee independent schools: for-profit and non-profit that both charge fees. The latter are often owned by NGOs, churches, or mosques. The for-profit ones are owned and run by individual proprietors as for-profit social businesses.

The proprietors are often low-income men and women (e.g., retired teachers, pastors, social entrepreneurs, or parents in need of a good education for their children) and usually come from within the disadvantaged communities where the schools are located. Some are motivated by profit-making in that they see a demand and then start educating children in their neighborhood as an income-generating (business) activity. Very often they start with a few children and use their living rooms, verandas, or community/church halls. Social mission is the motivation for others. These groups treat their engagement as a calling and do so out of national or religious responsibility. It is the poor teaching the poor. Often the motivation is a mixture of profit and social mission.

Edify's support focuses on for-profit, low-fee independents schools because the likelihood to ensure success and sustainability is often greater with privately owned businesses than those owned by NGOs and churches. For many individuals who own schools, if they do not provide a good educational service, they will not be able to feed their family. Parents are unlikely to keep their children in a poor performing school that charges fees. There is significant incentive and accountability for school proprietors to diligently educate the children entrusted to them.

The proliferation of low-fee independent schools in developing countries has been phenomenal in the last two decades and is likely to continue unabated in the future. Bagnay recognizes that non-state provision of education is a significant provider in many developing countries and likely to grow further.[7] The World Bank records that between 2000–2018, enrollment in primary private and public schools grew by 73 percent.[8]

Why is there a rapid growth of such schools across the developing world? In most instances, the low-fee independent schools appear to have emerged in response to the failure of the public education system to provide access to educational facilities or quality education to children in poor and remote areas.

In the words of Tooley:

> Individual entrepreneurs . . . recognized the desire of poor parents *like them* to have a decent education, saw the problems of public education, and decided that the best way forward might be to start a school. They took a risk, started small, scoured around for teachers and buildings, experimented with what worked, found that parents liked what they were doing—or changed things around until parents did—and their schools grew and grew. Others saw what they were doing and thought it seemed a neat way to help their community and make a little money as well—sometimes conversely. And individual parents . . . anxiously aware that not all was well for their children in government schools, calculated that they would just about afford the private school [LFIS] gave it a try, found it worked, and told others about their success.[9]

Why Low-Income Parents Choose LFIS

Why do poor parents choose to send their children to LFIS? Why don't they send them to government (public) schools where education is "free"? There are several reasons. Some of the common ones include the following:

Access. As pointed out earlier, 58 million school-aged children are still out of school.[10] Lack of access to educational facilities is one major reason. This is particularly true in slums and marginalized areas of many developing countries where government schools are either non-existent or inadequate. Such places are often deprived of government educational facilities. And the nearest schools are often hard to reach because of distance as this involves transportation expenses where there is transport and physical fatigue and security problems when children have to walk. "In this case, even if parents would prefer government schools, they send their children to private schools because there is no government option,"[11] says Baird in reference to India.

As a result, even parents who would have preferred to send their children to public schools have no choice but to use fee-paying independent schools. LFIS often operate in poor and marginalized communities where public schools do not exist or are inadequate. Therefore, they create learning opportunities for poor children who otherwise would not be able to go to school because of distance and related costs.

In Mathare Valley, the oldest slum in Nairobi, for example, where 70 different schools were engaged in the provision of education among the poor and marginalized, only three were run by the government. In other words, the children in the 67 low-fee independent schools would have not had the opportunity of accessing education had these not existed in the area.[12]

Girls' Education. In most developing countries, fewer girls go to school than boys. A World Bank report estimates that in 2018, 55 percent of global population of children out of school (58 million) were girls.[13] Despite the improvements made during the last decade, gender inequality is still prevalent. UNICEF lists some key reasons why girls lag behind boys in access to education:[14]

- Parents want girls to help with domestic responsibilities, including taking care of siblings, and boys are given preference when choices have to be made.
- Early marriage, sexual harassment, and violence in and out of educational settings tend to constrain girls from going to school.
- Teenage pregnancy adversely affects girls' education.[15]
- School systems are often not empowering for girls, nor are they sensitive to their special needs through curricula, guidance, and counseling services as well as facilities (such as toilets that are not appropriately situated or separate).

However, even when parents are committed to educating their daughters against the odds, the lack of or inadequate access to educational facilities within easy and safe reach puts girls at a disadvantage.

Parents are often unwilling to send their daughters to school in scenarios where they have to walk long distances because transportation is expensive, and walking is dangerous. Parents fear their daughters could be attacked, abducted, or raped on the way to and from schools.

They also fear sending them to public schools because there is poor discipline, attention, and sometimes school violence. Girls may be impregnated and abused. Both cause damage as they result in expulsion from school and in poor performance, respectively.

An alternative choice comes in low-fee independent schools, which are established by social entrepreneurs within the communities, and the schools often operate within easy-walking distance. In many instances, the proprietors are known by both parents and students. Several of them also provide bus services to children who come from relatively far places.

Therefore, parents choose LFIS because they offer better proximity, discipline, attention, safety, and security, and they present themselves as a solution to the problems faced by girls. They also choose LFIS because the put high value on the character formation their children attain in these schools.

Quality of Education. In public schools, teacher absenteeism, lack of discipline, and overcrowded classes are some of the main reasons that cause poor learning, low pass rates, high dropout rates, and poor academic performance.

Government schools often have trained teachers, many of whom hold teacher training college or university degrees. However, they fail to have the impact they are desired to make on the quality of education children should receive. The two main reasons for this are the high level of absenteeism and the lack of motivation among teachers.

Tooley says:

> Parents with meagre resources still sacrifice to send their kids
> to private schools [low-fee independent schools] because the
> private owner does something that is virtually impossible
> in government schools: replace teachers who do not teach.
> Government teachers in India and Africa have jobs for life,

just like American teachers. Many sleep on the job. Some don't even show up for work.[16]

Because of absenteeism, classes are not run as efficiently as they should, resulting in students receiving fewer effective learning hours per day than normal. Government schoolteachers are often out doing other businesses to complement their incomes. Even when they are at school, teachers in government schools are not necessarily teaching the classes assigned to them. Other times they might tend to focus on the few best students. Lack of accountability and demoralization are rampant, and government schools too often fail to offer quality education that students deserve.

According to the UN, "It is much harder to get motivated teachers to impart real learning skills." Solving the incentive problems to keep teachers and other workers in government schools motivated proves challenging.[17]

Why are absenteeism and indiscipline so widespread in government schools? Some of the common reasons are:

- Teachers are unionized and, therefore, difficult to fire. They treat their job as life-long and fear no consequences.
- Supervision in public schools is inadequate to ensure discipline in relation to attendance and lesson plans, which are two critical factors in ensuring that students receive quality education. Often non-performing teachers are not disciplined.

The government education system seems to be more concerned with the number of children registered in school and less about the quality of education that is delivered. Yet "it is not just going to school but learning something while there that matters."[18]

Moreover, due to inefficient practices and corruption in regard to the distribution of resources (curricula, textbooks) and the construction of new schools, government schools are far from being able to deliver quality education to the satisfaction of parents.[19]

In describing the situation in Ghana, Adei writes, "Our policy makers do not show concern that most children have no future because public basic education is in crisis. . . . Teachers in public schools are simply not teaching; contact hours are less than 40 per cent of what is expected and the quality of education in terms of the three Rs (i.e. arithmetic, reading and writing) were at their lowest."[20] According to Adei, the major causes were poor supervision and management at the school level and centralization of decision-making under a bureaucratically inefficient and self-serving Ghana Education Service, which are lessons that could apply more generally to other countries.[21]

In low-fee independent schools, teachers' attendance is closely supervised, lesson plans are regularly checked, performance is monitored and appraised, classes are less crowded, students are given better attention, and tutorial services lead to better pass rates and academic performance.

In their study, "The Aggregate Effect of Schools Choice: Evidence from a Two-Stage Experiment in India," Karthik Muralidharan and Venkatesh Sundararaman characterize the situation in India as follows:

> We find that the main operating difference between
> private and public schools in India is that private schools
> pay substantially lower teacher salaries (less than a sixth of
> that paid to public school teacher), and hire teachers who

are younger, less educated, and much less likely to have professional teaching credentials. However, they hire more teachers and have smaller class sizes and less multi-grade teaching than public schools. Using official data, as well as data collected from direct observations conducted during unannounced visits to schools, we find that private schools have a longer school day, a longer school year, lower teacher absence, higher teaching activity, and better school hygiene.[22]

In terms of academic performance, the authors hold that "Cross-sectional evidence finds that students in private schools significantly outperform their counterparts in public schools, even after correcting for observable differences between the characteristics of students attending the two types of schools."[23]

A World Bank impact evaluation of a low-cost private school (LFIS) program in the Sindh province of Pakistan carried out in 2013, made the following conclusion:

Low-cost private schools [LFIS] in Pakistan are proving very successful at attracting students—boys and girls—and teaching them effectively for less money than it costs to run a government school. Some of the lower costs come from hiring teachers who receive lower salaries than government schoolteachers, but this doesn't appear to be hurting the quality of education. On the contrary . . . students did substantially better on tests than children whose only option was a government school.[24]

Very often more students in low-fee independent schools pass class and national exams than those in government schools and have better chances to go further in their education, including entering university. This is not because low-fee independent schools are better equipped or have better teachers. On the contrary, they have less qualified teachers and poorer facilities than government schools. The main reason is that students get better attention, care, and tutorial support by the teachers. The proprietors who are the private owners of low-fee independent schools are on site and make sure the teachers are present and teach diligently by closely monitoring their movements and whereabouts.

The proprietors recognize that poor academic performance means a bad reputation, which leads to withdrawal of children, resulting in a loss of business. So they keep a close eye on their teachers to ensure high levels of accountability and responsibility are maintained. When a teacher is sick a substitute conducts the class. Non-performing and undisciplined teachers are fired or reprimanded. As a result, teachers work harder and achieve better outcomes.

Apart from its relevance to improving academic performance, maintaining good discipline means students have role models of responsibility in the teachers who are present and accountable for doing a good job rather than role models of people who show a lack of caring by absenteeism, striking, and not being diligent in their work.

Student discipline is also relatively better in low-fee independent schools than government schools. Students are not allowed to go out of school during school hours or loaf around on school grounds as they wish. This is important for families as it ensures safety and prevents children, particularly girls, from resorting to practices that can put their well-being and education at risk during school hours.

The poor "are abandoning public education. It's not good enough for their children. And they have found a superior alternative."[25] With better discipline in place, students learn, focus, perform better, and make better academic achievements. This is what parents want and serves as another reason why they send their children to low-fee independent schools.

Moreover, low-fee independent schools engage parents more actively in the education of their children. First, parents are given reports and asked to go through their children's assignments and homework and give feedback on a daily basis. Second, parents are engaged in school events and activities as well as decision-making processes, including fixing school fees. These make them feel they have a chance to influence school practices.

Parents also like that they have easy access to teachers and headmasters in low-fee independent schools. Because teachers and headmasters are always at school, the parents can easily get in touch with them when they have concerns or want feedback. This can be difficult in government schools.

Furthermore, class sizes are often smaller in low-fee independent schools than in government schools, and parents feel their children get better attention and higher learning outcomes in class as a result.

Employability. At least five factors enhance employability: academic scores, higher education, critical thinking skills, computer skills, and English language skills.

Under normal conditions, academic scores and higher education are likely to be closely linked. The higher the grades that students score, the greater the chance to remain in school and continue to the next level in their academic pursuits.

Under normal conditions, such students have no reason to drop out of school, which means higher rates of retention. The combination of higher academic scores and higher education, in turn, mean graduates have better employment opportunities in the labor market.

Critical thinking skills are about clear communication, problem solving, logical reasoning, creative analysis, generating and critiquing arguments, and making sound judgments also contribute to employability.

How students are taught in class and the level of education (the higher the better) determine the extent to which they acquire these skills. The more innovative, creative, independent, and the participative teaching methodology applied by teachers, the greater the opportunities for developing critical thinking skills.

In a non-threatening environment that allows students to think freely without fearing to make mistakes, students work on independent projects, dialogue, and reason instead of memorizing facts just to pass exams and receiving information passively. Thus, they are likely to develop critical thinking skills. These are important components of most professions that employers often seek to find in the candidates they recruit.[26]

With facts readily available from the internet, memorization of a great many facts is no longer as important in the workplace as being able to find relevant facts, create with facts, collaborate with facts, and synthesize facts.

Critical thinking skills not only strengthen employability, but they also contribute to the increase of GDP more than access. In their study, Hanushek et al. found that "while increasing access appears to increase GDP by 10 percent, improving cognitive skills as measured by progress on international benchmark assessments can increase GDP by 25–30 percent."[27] Where low-fee independent schools offer a more engaging and non-threatening teaching approach, they are likely to constitute relatively better places for students to acquire critical skills than government schools.

It goes without saying that in this day and age computer skills are highly associated with employability. Although not sufficient, computer skills have become a necessary component of all professions. Such skills are likely to boost learning outcomes and academic performance (high scores and pass rates). In most cases, particularly at the primary level, low-fee independent schools offer such services better than government schools. Low-income parents, therefore, prefer to send their children to schools where computer labs are available (more on this in a later chapter).

In most developing countries, speaking and writing good English are seen as key factors in passing national exams, succeeding in higher education, finding a good job, and developing a career. To use an expression by a proprietor in Ethiopia, "English is gold."

Christel DeHaan, a German-born American businesswoman and philanthropist who founded Resort Condominiums International, was very involved in educating children living in poverty in Mexico. She told Chris Crane of research she commissioned on the value of learning English. If two children live in dwellings next to each other in a Mexican slum, with identical socioeconomic demographics, but one speaks English at age eighteen, the lifetime income of that person will be triple the one who only speaks Spanish.

Moreover, English is the language of internet communication, and children can have great difficulty developing good computer skills without good English skills. Low-income parents, therefore, value the opportunity for their children to learn to speak English, and they find that low-fee independent schools do a better job at this than government schools.

Best Value for the Money. Education is an important investment for poor families, and they want to get the best for the financial sacrifice they are making. They tend to be highly aspirational. Better education means better paid employment, and that means better income security for parents as they expect future financial support from their educated children. Their children are also likely to marry better educated people, so they will be able to provide a better education for their children. They want their children to live a life better than theirs.

As demonstrated above, parents perceive that LFIS are more likely to create better opportunities for better career development and do whatever it takes, including taking school fee loans, to place their children in such schools. The authors have been told by parents and others in developing nations that any disadvantaged family who can afford to send their children to a low-fee independent school will do so. They have also stated public school teachers almost always send their children to low-fee independent schools.

Parents also find LFIS more flexible in terms of fee payments and uniform requirements than government schools. This is very important for many low-income parents, and particularly those whose earnings come from casual employment, as flexibility gives them opportunity to pay in small amounts when they get money.

Moreover, public schools are not as fully "free" as they are often perceived. The truth is the various "hidden costs" parents incur are not far less than the fees they pay in LFIS. Costs in government schools are often 50–70 percent of those paid in LFIS. The small differences that might exist in certain cases become insignificant because of the better value in LFIS.

Low income and poor families choose to educate their children in LFIS rather than "free" government schools because of the poor and declining public education resulting from "the lack of teacher accountability, strong unions (which contribute to teacher complacency and lack of motivation to teach), poor facilities, high pupil-teacher ratios, and poor management."[28]

Conversely, LFIS offer better conditions for safety (proximity and lack of violence), discipline (students and teachers alike), higher academic performance, and employability, which enables them to get best value for their investment. The key in all this is the performance of LFIS because without achieving high academic grades, students have no chance of staying in school, passing national examinations, and going for further studies to acquire employable skills (computer, critical thinking, and English).

The difference in the quality of education between government schools and LFIS often makes choosing LFIS compelling. As Tina Rosenberg argues: "In the United States, private school is generally a privilege of the rich. But in poorer nations, particularly in Africa and South Asia, families of all social classes send their children to private schools."[29]

Why Edify Supports LFIS

Some of the reasons why Edify supports LFIS include the following:

Education is key to personal and national development. "Education is an indispensable key to, though not a sufficient condition for, personal and social improvement . . . education can help ensure a safer, healthier, more prosperous and environmentally sound world, while simultaneously contributing to social, economic, and cultural progress."[30]

The general global view is that education has an inherent quality of generating better citizens, families, communities, and nations. By producing a useful citizen, education can, therefore, "enhance a society's ability to overcome poverty, increase incomes, improve health and nutrition, and reduce family size."[31] It is estimated that for each additional year of education, the lifetime income of a person increases by 10 percent, and women with a senior secondary education have 2.2 children whereas women without a senior secondary education average 6.1 children. According to the Center for Global Development, "No country has ever achieved continuous and rapid growth without reaching an adult literacy rate of at least 40 percent."[32]

In any society, and particularly in developing societies where opportunities for self-development are limited, education serves as the gateway to personal development, empowerment, and well-being. To use Nelson Mandela's words, "It is through education that the daughter of a peasant can become a doctor, that the son of a mine worker can become the head of the mine, and that a child of farmworkers can become president of a great nation."[33]

Education opens the door to overall human flourishing and nation building. Through education, people gain knowledge and skills, which give them the ability to gain employment or start their own business, thereby creating value and a livelihood for themselves and others. They become creative, innovative, and productive.

As better-educated citizens run their own businesses, they become job creators. As they generate wealth through productive employment and business, they give financial support to their extended families and pay income tax to the state, thereby contributing to family well-being and national economic development. Increased income often translates into increased purchasing power in that people will be able to invest in the improvement of housing, nutrition, health, education, water, and sanitation, thus elevating their standards of living. People are able to enjoy increased abundance and live longer. This enhances effective demand, which is likely to boost production and other economic and service activities that lead to national employment and economic growth. Moreover, as they participate in state administration, they are likely to contribute to the improvement of national efficiency and governance, including accountability.

Educations is also a social equalizer, as stated by the nineteenth-century American educator Horace Mann: "Education . . . beyond all other devices of human origin, is a great equalizer of the conditions of men. . . . [It's] the balance wheel of the social machinery."[34] Even in the twenty-first century, education enhances equality, in general, and gender equity in particular, because "access to education is the sine qua non for effective participation in the life of the modern world at all levels."[35]

In societies where women are oppressed and marginalized because of traditional and cultural practices and economic injustices, education enables more women to participate in government, business, law, medicine, and other walks of life. More women become aware of their rights and become empowered and participate in decision-making processes and policies that affect their destiny. "Education is one of the most important means of empowering women with the knowledge, skills and self-confidence necessary to participate fully in the development process."[36] They also become effective contributors to the educational and general well-being of their children, including keeping household food security. "A child whose mother can read is 50 percent more likely to live past age five."[37]

Education not only increases human capital but also enables people to develop inter-personal communication and cross-cultural skills that enable them to relate to and serve others. They become aware of their rights and obligations to others and acquire skills that will enable them to live peacefully with and serve others. As more are involved in productive engagement, crime and anti-social behavior are likely to decline in communities.

In their paper, "Greed and Grievance in Civil War," Paul Collier and Anke Hoeffler, find that a 10 percent increase in school enrollment decreases the likelihood of a country to experience a conflict by 3 percent, while an increase in male enrollment led to a significant decline in the duration of conflict.[38] According to the GPE 2012–2013 highlight, "Education is a way to move forward and rebuild. Focusing on education in fragile states promotes peace-building and conflict and mitigation and fosters economic growth. The re-establishment of education systems in fragile states can provide a visible sign of a return to normalcy."[39]

Education also helps people acquire knowledge and skills needed for sustaining the environment. An educated population is better prepared to understand the connection between environment and sustainable development and is likely to make positive contributions toward its preservation.[40]

Without denying the importance of other equally important interventions, Edify believes education is critical to the building of nations in which people lead dignified, empowered, decent, and harmonious lives. Edify's overall belief is that education produces better individuals, which leads to better families/households, which leads to better communities, which leads to better nations, and which ultimately leads to a better world, more peaceful and productive, for all people.

In short, education is a powerful tool of personal and national development and herein lies Edify's primary reason for engaging in the promotion of educational opportunities and good values among poor children in developing countries through the provision of financial and technical support to LFIS.

LFIS play a major role in the education sector. LFIS are an important factor in the provision of educational services to children living in poverty. LFIS deserve support for numerous reasons.

First, as pointed out above, LFIS are large in number and constitute an industry in their own right. The conservative estimate of LFIS operating across the developing world is between 500,000–700,000.[41] According to Tooley, extrapolating from the research he has done in India and West Africa, at least 300,000 such schools are in India and 100,000 are in Anglophone West Africa.[42] According to the International Finance Corporation (IFC), private enrollment during the last 10 years increased from 15 percent to 40 percent in Ghana, Kenya, Nigeria, Senegal, and Uganda with much of this due to LFIS.[43] These numbers mean that LFIS cannot be ignored.

Second, they provide educational services to a large number of students, particularly those living in poor and marginalized areas. In several countries, these schools are estimated to educate 50–70 percent of the primary school students in urban slums. In his latest book, *Really Good Schools,* Tooley estimates an average of 70 percent of the children in the developing countries are educated in low-fee independent schools.[44]

These proportions convincingly indicate that LFIS are key contributors to global education in general as well as the education of people living in poverty in particular. In a world where governments are increasingly failing to fully meet the educational needs of millions and millions of children living in slums and other neglected areas, and where conventional private schools are focusing on providing for children coming from wealthier and elite families, the LFIS have emerged as the best alternative for people in poverty to educate their children. Without the service of LFIS, millions of children living in poverty would be out of school.

Third, LFIS make major contributions to the achievement of the Sustainable Development Goals, particularly those related to primary education and gender parity. As such, they complement the efforts made by national governments in achieving their MDG commitments related to education: universal primary education and gender parity.

Fourth, LFIS create employment for many trained or untrained young teachers as well as school leaders, who would have been idle or underemployed and become a liability instead of an asset to society.

Fifth, once registered and part of the formal economy, many LFIS contribute to national wealth generation through the income tax they pay, the materials purchased, and the people employed as they build and expand their educational facilities.[45]

LFIS offer a financially sustainable solution to the educational crisis. Edify recognizes the importance of charity in relief and emergency cases. As a development tool, however, aid given in the form of "handouts" has, at times, done more damage in developing countries than good. Charity and official aid have not solved poverty but sometimes bred perpetual dependency. In the words of Bob Lupton, charity can be "toxic,"[46] and the Zambian economist Dambisa Moyo claims official aid is "dead."[47] Edify believes in a "hand-up" approach, where local potential is unleashed with full force. In this regard, business that results in wealth generation is a more powerful means of sustainable and independent development than charity or official aid.

The LFIS are social businesses run by female and male entrepreneurs/proprietors in pursuit of wealth generation and social mission by offering educational services that are vital to personal and national development. Because they are privately owned and the risks are borne only by the owners, the proprietors endeavor to manage and utilize scarce resources as efficiently as possible to generate profit that will enable them to support their families and continue delivering education on a financially sustainable basis without relying on charity.

The proprietors create employment opportunities for themselves and generally pay government taxes and stimulate growth, thereby contributing to poverty alleviation and non-dependence. In most cases, government schools do the opposite—they do not generate wealth. They consume wealth and rely on external aid and government budgets, thus remaining in perpetual dependency.

One of the factors behind the education crisis facing the developing world is the dependency of the Education for All on external aid as well as the subsequent failure of donors to honor their global commitments during economic recessions. When government and community schools are built or operated, fully or partially, with money donated by public or private donors, they often never become financially sustainable. Free money often results in operating inefficiencies, unaccountability, and lower quality education for children.

Edify chooses to work in partnership with Christian LFIS that offer a Christ-centered education and strengthen their efforts. Their business approach to education and development is a more sustainable solution, relying on income generated locally. Theirs is a local initiative with local resources and represents a new approach to an old problem, while the government's approach is an attempt to solve a problem using the methods that created it. Edify offers these schools loans to build more classrooms and improve educational facilities that create conducive physical learning environment for children living in poverty.

LFIS are constrained from playing their role in education to the fullest. Despite their popularity and increasingly growing contribution to education and development, LFIS are everywhere faced with multifaceted obstacles that undermine their ability to do more and better. There are several major constraints:

1. *There is a general misperception of what LFIS are.* They are often confused with the conventional meaning and practice of private schools, which exist only to serve rich children. This sends the wrong message. LFIS are often motivated by social mission as well as earning a living for the proprietor. They don't serve the rich nor do they attempt to make profit at any cost. Although they recognize that making profit is necessary for sustainability and expansion, LFIS serve low-income children and their fees are, in most cases, determined with parental participation.

2. *In many countries, government policies, standards, and practices disfavor LFIS.* Getting registration licenses is often expensive, bureaucratic, or impossible.[48] The practice of nepotism and "discrimination" in these and other cases, such as training opportunities, is rampant and demoralizing for many proprietors of LFIS. The same goes for getting building permits, land title deeds, and access to land needed for expansion.

3. *Access to loan capital is limited or non-existent.* Many of the LFIS operate in informal settlements, which leave most of the proprietors unable to provide collateral. Moreover, most LFIS lack a track record to show to financial service providers. Unlike government schools, which receive international aid, LFIS receive virtually no external financial aid. The only exception known to the authors is a pair of chains of schools numbering 150 or more schools. The lack of access to capital has constrained the proprietors from investing in infrastructural facilities needed for further expansion, increased outreach, and a conducive learning environment.

4. *By offering relatively higher remuneration packages, both government and elite private schools make it difficult for LFIS to recruit trained teachers.* LFIS cannot afford to pay their teachers as high as the unionized teachers in government schools. The inability to offer attractive remunerations means LFIS are often unable to recruit trained teachers. However, national exam scores indicate that a young, enthusiastic, untrained teacher who is faithfully present in the classroom often leads to greater student learning outcomes than trained teachers with thirty years of experience who may be absent from the classroom a high percentage of the school day. However, LFIS staff turnover can be high, causing

irregularities and occasional disruptions in teaching and team cohesion. Teachers move for greener pastures at government schools or for further studies.

5. *Edify finds that most of the proprietors of LFIS have very limited skills in human and financial resources management.* Management structures and practices, as well as accounting systems in most LFIS, are rudimentary and far from meeting the basic requirements needed for running profitable social businesses. The inability to install computer labs and offer computer training and e-learning opportunities has also constrained the capacity to attract more students.

6. *Very often, proprietors of LFIS are excluded from national policy consultations and policy-making processes and, therefore, are unable to contribute and influence issues related to education.* This is exacerbated in contexts where the proprietors lack associations or any avenue through which they would be able to discuss issues, share information, learn from one another, and express their joint views.

The combined effect of the above constraints faced by LFIS has made it difficult for them to unleash their full potential and take their contribution to the next level. Edify seeks to help LFIS overcome these shackles, so as to enable them to play their rightful role in educating children living in poverty. This is, therefore, another reason why it chooses to partner with LFIS.

Values are critical in sustainable transformational development. Values and worldviews (paradigms) are intertwined and mutually influence each other. "As he thinks in his heart, so is he" (Proverbs 23:7). We often tend to think as we are taught and act as we think. The way we think and act emanate from our values which, are determined by our worldviews. These are often passed on, built, and reinforced by different means, and are learned in families, communities, schools, faith institutions, and schools.

Edify strongly believes our values determine our character, how we perceive ourselves and others, and how we position ourselves in society. As a Jesus-centered organization, Edify believes faith is the foundational pillar of transformed lives and that it comes from hearing the Word of God. The earlier that children are taught and rooted in Jesus-centered values, the stronger will be their roles in building transformed families, communities, and nations of integrity, honesty, transparency, accountability, mutual care, love, peace, harmony, and stability.

Edify believes it is nearly impossible to achieve sustainable, beneficial, and transformational development without change agents rooted in the values taught by Jesus:

- Love to overcome hatred
- Peacemaking to overcome violence
- Integrity to overcome corruption
- Servant leadership to overcome self-serving leadership

This is why Edify chooses to partner only with LFIS whose proprietors are followers of the values and principles of Jesus and who are committed to offer a Christ-centered education as part of their curriculum.

Edify's Program

As documented in his book *A Dream and a Coconut Tree: Transforming Education for the Poor,* Chris Crane established Edify in 2009, four years after he attended a conference of the Templeton

Foundation in 2005, at which James Tooley shared his research findings. The presentation below provides a brief description of Edify's program composition and outreach.[49]

Vision: flourishing Godly nations

Mission: to improve and expand sustainable Christ-centered education globally

The three key components of Edify's program consist of the following products and services:

- Loan capital: to improve and expand school facilities
- Training: to equip school leaders and teachers to develop sustainable Christ- centered the data education technology: to enhance learning outcomes and employability

These products and services are demand-driven and contextually reviewed to reflect the potential and requirements of the partner schools.

In terms of geographic coverage, Edify serves in eleven countries in Africa (Burkina Faso, Ethiopia, Ghana, Liberia, Rwanda, Sierra Leone, and Uganda), Latin America (Dominican Republic, Guatemala, and Peru) and India (Northeast India). As of October 2021, the program in Northeast India has been discontinued due to local policies and practices that made operations impossible. At the same time new programs have been initiated in Panama (December 2021) and El Salvador (February 2022).

Summary

Private schools in general and LFIS in particular emerged to fill the gap that was created in the education sector. LFIS are expanding rapidly in the developing world. LFIS were founded by parents to be a better place for quality education to provide their children better opportunities for higher pass rates, further (higher) studies, and employment.

LFIS are able to present themselves as a better alternative than their government counterparts because they ensure a high level of teacher accountability, better discipline, safety, lower student-teacher and lower student-class ratios, better attention to students, better tutorial services, computer skills training, English language skills, and active parental participation. Conversely, the government schools were, in most cases, overcrowded and suffered from a lack of teacher accountability, poor management, high pupil-teacher ratios, and limited or no parental involvement. These resulted in low pass rates and higher dropout rates. (It must, however, be pointed out that this doesn't mean all LFIS are great and all government schools are bad. There are good, successful government schools, and some LFIS do not perform well. However, in general and on average, the authors have seen LFIS do better than government schools and are more conductive places for children to learn).

The main rationale for Edify's support to LFIS lies in its recognition of the critical role education plays in bringing about sustainable personal and national transformation, on the one hand, and how LFIS bring a financially sustainable, free enterprise solution to the education crisis facing the developing world, on the other. LFIS play a substantial role in the education of large numbers of children in disadvantaged communities who otherwise would have never had the chance to go to school. However, LFIS often lack the resources to unleash their full potential.

Edify's mission is to provide loan capital, Christ-centered training, curricula, and education technology to LFIS to boost their ability to expand educational facilities and improve the quality of and access to education for children living in poverty in such a way that they become employable, servant leaders.

3

LOAN CAPITAL FOR EDUCATION AT LOW-FEE INDEPENDENT SCHOOLS

This chapter will present the dynamics surrounding the Edify loan regime, including its role, methodology, terms, outreach, and repayment as well as show the power that capital plays in helping low-fee independent schools to sustainably strengthen their ability to increase access and improve education for children living in poverty.

Access to Quality Education

Children are at the heart of Edify's program. Edify works to develop and transform children from a young age so they can be transformed in their own lives and become effective catalysts for national and global change. Edify believes transformed people contribute to human flourishing and greater peace and stability in the world.

Whatever Edify does in supporting low-fee independent schools (LFIS) is, therefore, to create a favorable environment that will maximize the learning/development outcomes of students in school and create opportunities for those outside school. Like all the other products and services, the loan capital is provided with this ultimate objective in mind. Edify provides access to capital through demand-driven loans to low-fee independent schools to expand or improve facilities, thereby increasing access to education for people living in poverty.

Many LFIS are constrained from enrolling as many children to meet demand because of limited physical capacity. This results mainly from a lack of access to capital. To address this constraint, Edify provides loan capital to its loan partners (local microfinance institutions and commercial banks) for onward lending to school proprietors. The three main uses for the loan capital are school buildings, computer labs/education technology, and transportation.

School Buildings: Physical Learning Environment

A school building can have a significant positive or negative effect toward fostering a productive learning environment. Classrooms that are dark, uncomfortable, crowded, and noisy or where the teacher is far away from the students can be a disincentive for them to learn or continue with their studies. Designing schools from the viewpoint of the student is important to ensure all or most of their needs are met.[1]

At present, there is a global recognition of the connection between a school's physical environment and learning outcomes. An effort is made both in developed and developing countries to design and remodel school buildings to make them more conducive to learning and to mirror workplaces of today and the future by using digital learning.

In the world of LFIS, the effect of school buildings on learning is often negative for reasons of both quantity and quality. With regard to *quantity*, this relates to the inadequate supply of educational facilities and its effect on enrollment. While low-fee independent schools are popular and create access to disadvantaged children in poor communities, they are unable to meet the demand because of physical limitations. They do not have the capital needed to build new schools or add new classrooms easily and quickly. School proprietors often do this incrementally.

They are also constrained by a lack of land and, even if land is available they are unable to purchase land because the costs, in urban slums for example, are often prohibitively high. There are also often problems with land registration, which inhibit investment in school buildings. In some countries, such as Ethiopia where land is owned by the state, purchasing land is prohibited. Land is leased and acquired through auction, which is competitive and often beyond the reach of the owners of low-fee independent schools. This is particularly so in urban areas where land is scarce.

Edify's loan capital helps school proprietors create more access for children in poverty through the expansion of infrastructural facilities. Various options make this possible. The most common ones include:

- Proprietors build new schools, add new classrooms, or complete unfinished constructions.
- Some proprietors also use the loan capital to buy land for future or existing expansion.

Each of these means that proprietors are able to create more space for more children in their communities, which can lead to increased enrollment, and therefore fewer children out of school in the communities served.

The *quality* aspect relates to the inadequacies of existing educational facilities and the effects on the learning outcomes of students. Edify finds that important factors include classroom size, thermal comfort, light, noise, and other facilities:

Classroom Size. The physical size of classrooms is one of the factors that affect the quality of learning. In America or Britain, for instance, we expect classrooms to accommodate around 30–40 students, plus have space for the teacher and some storage. An ideal size for a class with 30 students would be up to 50 square meters. One commentator observes: "It is . . . not recommended to have a classroom with an area of less than 40 square meters, unless it is known that there will never be more than 20 pupils in the room."[2]

The classrooms in many low-fee independent schools are smaller than the standard size described because sometimes such schools operate in residential houses, church halls, or other facilities not specifically designed for educational purposes. Or when purpose-built classrooms are used, scarcity of investment funds leads to the creation of smaller than desirable classrooms. Classrooms are consequently cramped, with little or no space for group work activities, free movements, etc. In addition, the furniture (desks) in the classrooms is not only inadequate for students to sit comfortably but also not easy to move around to facilitate easy group activities.

The classrooms fall short of playing their role as an important tool for facilitating the delivery of effective education for all students through creative ways, and group participation is rendered difficult by the lack of adequate space. Many low-fee independent schools also lack storage facilities, a staffroom for teachers, and canteens, which impact learning outcomes in various ways.

Thermal Comfort. Four major components influence thermal comfort: humidity, temperature, ventilation, and radiation. In addition to the quality of the teacher and parental input, thermal comfort is an important factor influencing students' and teachers' health and performance in classrooms because a student may not be ready to learn if they are overwhelmed by the heat, humidity, or lack of ventilation in the classroom. Poor ventilation, particularly in cramped classrooms, causes drowsiness, lack of concentration, or headaches, which affect the comprehension and motivation of students. Poor air quality also causes absences (teachers and students alike) and impedes student achievement. Children still developing physically are more likely to suffer from bad air quality.[3]

One study showed "students in classrooms with higher outdoor air ventilation rates scored 14 to 15 percent higher on standardized test scores than children in classrooms with lower outdoor air ventilation rates."[4]

Many LFIS have poor ventilation. In many instances, windows are narrow or inadequate in number, and often only on one side, thus not allowing cross-ventilation and with no overhangs to prevent the sun from heating the exterior walls so the walls do not heat up and re-radiate the energy onto the students. Moreover, roofs are not high enough above the student level, so the roof does not as easily re-radiate the sun's energy onto the students; ridge vents are not provided in gable roofs to allow the heat to escape rather than being trapped; porches and breezeways with seating are not provided to allow students to study outside the classroom on the most extreme days.[5]

Light. A study of 751 primary students in seven schools in Blackpool (UK) showed light was one of the six influential factors impacting children's learning.[6] Light affects concentration, test scores, and on-task behavior. Lighting is critical to student learning and performance. Studies show lighting plays a direct role in improved test scores, increased on-task behavior, and increased ability to concentrate. . . . Students with the most daylight in their classrooms progressed twenty percent faster in math and twenty-six percent faster on reading tests than students in classrooms with the least amount of light.[7]

Many low-fee independent schools have poor or no lighting for illumination in the classrooms. This is particularly so in rural schools where reliance on natural lighting is most common for two reasons: either they are not connected to electricity supplies or the use of electricity is expensive or intermittent. This is far from being adequate for proper learning. When windows have to be closed due to rain and when the skies are cloudy, it gets too dark to read and write in the classroom, rendering effective learning difficult.[8]

Noise. Noises that come from outside and inside classrooms impede the learning process and the mental development of children. As research shows, "Students in noisy buildings performed below their peers who in quieter conditions on both standardized tests and reading development. Noisy buildings are also associated with speech problems. Students constantly exposed to noise have more headaches, stomach troubles, and changes in mood and anxiety, so overall health can be affected."[9] The absence or the reduction of noise enhances learning performance.

Some low-fee independent schools are often located near roads with busy traffic, marketplaces, and in overcrowded neighborhoods.

They also have small schoolyards and classrooms in one big hall with no walls and very poor partitions where everybody talks loudly like in an open marketplace. This makes hearing and concentration very difficult for children in general and those with learning disabilities and hearing impairment in particular. Younger children also are relatively more affected. As a result, the overall student learning suffers.

Other Facilities. Such facilities as water, toilets, canteens, sport/playgrounds, etc., also affect learning outcomes. The lack of and poor quality of toilets, for example, affect girls in particular to the extent that they are likely not to attend classes when they have their periods.

Many of the LFIS lack such facilities and those which happen to have them rarely provide separate toilets for boys and girls. Very often they lack locks and do not offer privacy for girls.

According to one researcher, "For many girls, the lack of privacy, safety and proper facilities are barring them from an education. Without a toilet, the open-air alternative leaves them open to attack by snakes, or sexual assault by male peers and adults. Even if there are latrines available, the lack of segregation threatens sensitive gender differences."[10]

Regarding both quantity and quality aspects, therefore, it is evident from the above descriptions that proprietors of low-fee independent schools have a great need for capital investment to expand the size of their school buildings to provide more access to children not going to school and improve the quality of existing facilities to establish favorable learning environments and maximize student-learning performance. The Edify loan capital enables proprietors to achieve that.

Maintenance. The appearance and conditions of school buildings also affect enrollment. Buildings and classrooms with mud floors and poor windows, doors, desks, and paintings do not attract parents and teachers or students. Many low-fee independent schools have these problems. They need capital for maintaining and restoring buildings and classrooms to meet acceptable standards. This will keep parents, teachers, and students satisfied and improve learning outcomes. Part of the Edify's loan capital is, therefore, used for maintenance purposes.

Science and Computer Laboratories

Another main role of Edify's loan capital plays is in developing science and computer labs. There are three main reasons why low-fee independent schools invest in the development of these two types of labs:

1. *Science and computer labs serve as a marketing tool.* Parents want their children to have the opportunity to learn computer skills and experiential science from an early age. Because many of the clients of low-fee independent schools cannot afford to have computers at home, they choose schools that offer computer lessons. Having science and computer labs enables schools to become more competitive in attracting and retaining students.
2. *Commitment to improving learning outcomes.* Many low-fee independent schools also invest in science and computer labs as part of their strategic commitment to improve academic performance. As children use computers, they access information and broaden their general knowledge and exposure, and their English language skills improve. Children

also increase their interest in science subjects and learn better as they experiment in science labs. These practices contribute to the improvement of academic performance, including passing national exams and becoming more employable, which improves the reputation of low-fee independent schools that invest in science and computer labs and results in increased enrollment.

3. *Meeting government requirements.* In the Dominican Republic, for example, a school cannot legally offer schooling through twelfth grade without computer, biology, and chemistry labs.

Transportation

Most LFIS are located within the communities of their students and often within reasonable walking distances. Because of their popularity, they also attract students from both near and far places. However, many of the low-fee independent schools lack transportation or have an inadequate fleet of vehicles. This limits their ability to create access to those children from relatively far places who find walking tiring and unsafe. To address this, they can buy vans or buses so that they can transport students. Hence the demand for capital is met through accessing Edify's lending services.

Having adequate and safe transportation services enables the low-fee independent school to increase their enrollment and revenue resulting from it, on the one hand, and from the bus operations, on the other. It also enables them to improve student safety, timely arrival, and overall attendance.

The ultimate goal of Edify's loan capital is to enable low-fee independent schools to increase access to create more opportunity for those are out of school to enroll and to improve the learning environment for those who are in school so students get the best possible education. Edify's loan capital builds the means (infrastructural facilities) to achieve the end: quality education.

Non-Physical Aspects: Learning Culture

Edify strongly believes in the critical role the physical learning environment plays on the quality of education students receive in school. Equally, if not more important, is the human factor. The teaching skills, styles, and personalities of teachers delivering the learning and the pedagogical tradition they follow also affect the quality of education either negatively or positively.

Edify is particularly interested in student-centered learning. The Center for Development and Learning, for instance, notes that "in a learner-centered school, education is done 'with' instead of 'to' students. Students feel connected in a learner-centered school; the student, his classmates and his teachers are partners in the learning process."[11] In other words, the teaching puts the students first, and the focus is on students' needs, abilities, interests, and learning styles. The student's voice is acknowledged as central, and the teacher plays a facilitator's role.[12]

Edify seeks to develop motivated learners and to incorporate experience with classroom learning to improve creativity, critical thinking, and retention. According to Galindo, typical learners retain 10 percent of what they hear, 20 percent of what they read, 50 percent of what they see, and 90 percent of what they do.[13]

Edify believes traditional teaching techniques often have a negative impact on student learning as they often are teacher-centered, one-sided, passive, and threatening in nature, thus causing restraint on student creativity and critical thinking. Edify finds such an approach as disempowering and rather encourages low-fee independent schools to practice student-centered approaches and facilitates training for their teachers to equip them with facilitative and participative tools.

In partnership with both local and international learning organizations, Edify enables schoolteachers to adopt a more student-friendly, non-threatening, empowering, facilitative, participative, and learning-by-doing culture to create freedom for innovative and critical thinking.

Rote learning (or teacher-centered learning) is then replaced with creative ways in which students work individually and in groups, and the teachers interact with them instead of lecturing at them; in addition, games are sometimes used as vehicles for learning. This allows students to learn more from what they see and do and less from what they hear. The students become active doers and not passive hearers in classrooms. Moreover, the students remember more what they learn from doing than what they learn from hearing.

Student-centered learning also allows for all the students in the classroom to learn as opposed to the traditional teaching method whereby teachers focus on the few top students. In this way, not only is learning maximized, but the students also develop team and communications skills and exercise freedom with discipline, not just discipline without freedom.

Regarding other traditional practices, Edify encourages and trains both teachers and proprietors not to condone rote memorization in all situations. It also seeks to avoid corporal punishment, caning, and the carrying of sticks by teachers, as all these impede student learning and creativity and are illegal in many countries we work in. Although some proprietors say parents sometimes complain that the school should be caning their children, this is a practice Edify expects to be removed in the schools it supports.

Edify also encourages and equips proprietors with knowledge and tools for recruiting, selecting, developing, and retaining quality teachers to ensure the low-fee independent schools are able to deliver quality education that is in the best interest of the students.[14]

Lending Methodology

Now that we have shown the role of Edify's loan capital in promoting education by creating conditions for increased access and improved quality of education through low-fee independent schools, we turn to the discussion of the lending methodology applied. How are Edify's loans provided?

Although Edify provides loan capital, it is not a microfinance institution and therefore doesn't directly lend money to school proprietors. The provision of loan capital is implemented through a lending methodology that has two main features: small and medium enterprise (SME) loans and lending through partnership.

SME Lending. The tradition followed in microfinance is that clients are given loans as individuals or group members. The groups consist of solidarity groups (often four to eight members) and village banks (twenty-five to thirty-five members), also called trust groups or community banks by some MFIs. These constitute the group lending methodology, which aims to accommodate new clients and small loans mostly for retail activities and operate on the basis of peer guarantee in place of collateral. Loan cycles are short (four to six months), and repayments are often collected on a weekly basis. Despite the recent move to provide SME loans by regulated institutions, group lending has been and remains the dominant methodology in the microfinance industry.[15]

Both by their size and nature of business, LFIS are small and medium enterprises. Group lending, either in large or small (solidarity) form, is probably out of the question for these types of borrowers. They are much more complex organizationally and larger operationally requiring larger loans and longer terms. SME lending is, therefore, the most appropriate methodology to meet the needs of low-fee independent schools.

Lending Through Partnerships. The second feature of Edify's lending methodology relates to its application of the partnership model. Edify does not establish offices in the countries of its programs. This is an expensive undertaking and not an ideal way of facilitating the development of sustainable local initiatives. Moreover, Edify recognizes that the local partners know and relate to the local contexts better. Instead of competing with local institutions, Edify partners with and strengthens them.

In the pursuit of this purpose, Edify identifies and signs contractual agreements with like-minded, high-quality, and reputable local partners with a good track record, through which its financial services are delivered to the low-fee independent schools. The arrangement takes different forms: The local lending partners receive loans at subsidized interest rates by Edify for three to five years that are repayable in local currency. The local implementing partners then lend Edify's capital to the low-fee independent schools usually at agreed below market rates. The lender then recycles the money to more low-fee independent schools to continue financing the building of new educational facilities and improving existing ones.[16]

The Edify loan capital is given on a 50-50 matching arrangement, which means for every Edify-loaned dollar the lending partners put their own local capital. The Edify loan capital is given as a loan guarantee. This is also done on a 50-50 basis. In the case of the latter, there is no interest or transformation fee paid to Edify. Wherever an interest is paid to Edify, the interest income doesn't go to Edify. Rather, it supports the transformation and training activities in the countries concerned. In some cases, particularly when they are not yet financially sustainable, Edify supports implementing partners to strengthen their lending capacity by paying for the recruitment of a loan/credit officer for a shorter period of time

The following section will describe how Edify selects lending implementing partners and how they put Edify's loan capital in use with reference to criteria, terms, outreach, portfolio, repayment, processes, and monitoring activities.

Criteria for Selecting Implementing Partners. How does Edify select its implementing partners? Before Edify starts a program in a new country, a comprehensive feasibility study is done to assess the socioeconomic landscape: policy and regulatory frameworks, microfinance industry, etc. Discussions are held with potential partners. The choice of lending partners is made on the basis of such studies and subsequent discussions.

What are the lending criteria that implementing partners are required to fulfill to have access to Edify's loan capital? Edify requires that local lending partners must:

- Share Edify's vision and mission as well as values.

- Have a good track record and reputation regardless of their size and length of experience in microfinance/lending operations.
- Have sound governance and leadership structures.
- Be prepared to lend to Christian schools.
- Demonstrate operational and financial sustainability.
- Have experience in lending to schools.
- Be willing to take part in training to manage schools better as well as sharing costs, facilitating, and setting up such events.
- Provide dedicated loan officer(s).
- Allow Edify to do due diligence and verification.
- Allow Edify to call a third party to audit, the costs of which are covered by Edify.
- Provide to Edify data and profiles of schools receiving loans.
- Allow Edify to visit schools and facilitate such visits when necessary.
- Provide reports on loan distribution and sustainability.

Loan Terms. The duration of Edify's loans is determined by the size of the loan. So far, this has varied between 12–36 months. In the countries we work in, a new classroom typically costs about $5,000 to build, although costs vary from $2,000 to $12,000. The term for this size of loan is usually 24 months. The loan duration for loans above $5,000 goes up to 36 months. As the classroom usually takes 2–4 months to complete and won't generate any income for 1–6 months, low-fee independent schools are given a grace period of 1–3 months by the lending partners. Although the lowest and average loan sizes are $2,000 and $6,000, respectively, there are cases where schools borrow up to 4–5 five times the average amount.

Edify's loans are subsidized, and the implementing partners are encouraged to charge LFIS reasonable rates. As mentioned above, the implementing partners generally charge below market rates with contextual variations. Interest rates are highly dependent upon the underlying inflation in any given country and vary between countries (usually 10–15 percent above inflation). Other factors include costs of delivery incurred by the lending partners, which vary depending on level of efficiency.

Marketing. How do low-fee independent schools know about the services Edify provides through its implementing partners? There are two main ways: deliberate promotional efforts made by the lending partners and word of mouth.

The lending partners promote the education finance product and services as part of their overall programs through media (mainly radio and newspapers), leaflets/brochures, and billboards. In some instances, they also approach low-fee independent schools to tell them about the product. They also use churches and other local associations to disseminate information about the availability of the products. Moreover, many of the low-fee independent schools get to know about the products through word of mouth. In some cases the proprietors themselves share the information with one another when they meet in their regular association meetings.

Processes. How are applications submitted, processed, and then approved or rejected, so money can be disbursed and repayments collected? The lending partners have institutional structures and related infrastructures stretching from central to regional to branch to satellite offices. Traditionally, their lending processes start at the lowest unit (satellite) and are completed at the central offices, depending on the loan amounts involved as the different offices have different approval levels.

In the case of Edify loans, a different setup occurs. Since they are all SME loans, they are approved at head office levels and handled by a manager fully dedicated to managing Edify's lending operations. Loan officers and branch managers might be involved in marketing, distributing, and collecting application forms for onward transmission to the managers dedicated to Edify loans, but they are no involved in the approval process.

Once received, the managers scrutinize and appraise the loan applications on the basis of feasibility and sustainability considerations and then submit them to a loans committee with recommendations for further examination. The committee is the ultimate approving/rejecting authority.

Once the approval is made, loans are often disbursed within a week. At the same time the branch and satellite offices concerned are informed, and they start taking responsibility for the collection of the repayments. Subsequent loans are given only to schools found on improving.

Outreach

How many school loans (single and repeated alike) have been given out to schools under Edify's lending program? Also, how much has been lent over the last ten years? The description below sets out the answers.

Between 2010–2011, Edify operated in the Dominican Republic and Ghana. Rwanda was added in 2012 and then Burkina Faso and Liberia in 2013. Peru and Guatemala were included in 2014, Ethiopia in 2015, Northeast India in 2016, Sierra Leone in 2017, and Uganda in 2019.The latest additions are Panama (December 2021) and El Salvador in February 2022. These two are included in current study.

Number of Loans

Between 2010 and September 2021, a total of 5,753 loans were given in the 11 countries of operation. The country breakdown is shown in Table 1 below.

Table 1: Cumulative Number of Loans Given as of September 30, 2021 (Edify's Fiscal Year)

Country	Starting Year	Number of Loans
Dominican Republic	2010	1,725
Ghana	2010	1,438
Rwanda	2011	315
Burkina Faso	2013	294
Liberia	2013	717
Peru	2014	353
Guatemala	2014	52
Ethiopia	2015	43
Northeast India	2016	11
Sierra Leone	2017	98
Uganda	2019	707
Total		5,753

Source: Edify Data Base

Loan Portfolios

The table below shows the cumulative loan amounts given in each of the eleven countries where Edify provided services between 2014–2021.

Table 2: Cumulative Loan Amounts Made
in 2019–2021 by Fiscal Year

Sum of Converted Amount in USD	Column Labels			
Row Labels	**FY2019**	**FY2020**	**FY2021**	**Grand Total**
Burkina Faso	508,895	376,708	520,308	2,890,557
Dominican Republic	866,242	235,106	152,317	6,567,949
Ethiopia	69,357	55,604	104,499	834,822
Ghana	925,348	411,816	1,102,606	10,889,281
Guatemala	18,858	19,331	13,545	200,351
India				101,037
Liberia	501,083	210,462	358,451	2,395,877
Peru	327,770	321,985	139,413	1,355,280
Rwanda	864,545	956,307	988,559	4,855,633
Sierra Leone	169,347	93,828	76,351	548,476
Uganda	210,373	130,175	1,004,868	1,345,416
Grand Total	**4,461,819**	**2,811,324**	**4,460,917**	**31,984,679**

Source: Edify Data Base

Some qualifications about the school loans are worthwhile to mention here:

- Some schools do not take loans either because they don't want to, the amount is too small to meet their needs, or they don't meet the criteria required by the lending partners.
- Some schools take loans more than once.
- The repeated loans could be for the same or different purposes.
- A proprietor can take two loans for two separate projects: classroom expansion and computer labs or two incremental loans for the same project (e.g., classroom expansion).

Gender Composition

The gender composition of the school proprietors varies from country to country, with the highest ratio of women clients being in Guatemala (88 percent), followed by the Dominican Republic (84 percent), and the lowest in Burkina Faso. Globally, women proprietors constitute about 57 percent on average. The country breakdown is shown in Table 3 below.

Table 3: Gender Breakdown of Proprietors

Country	Men	Women
Ghana	61 percent	39 percent
Dominican Republic	7 percent	93 percent
Rwanda	74 percent	26 percent
Burkina Faso	91 percent	9 percent
Liberia	61 percent	39 percent
Peru	69 percent	31 percent
Guatemala	34 percent	66 percent
Ethiopia	70 percent	30 percent
Northeast India	90 percent	10 percent
Uganda	68 percent	32 percent

Source: Edify Data Base

Sustainability

Edify believes empowering low-fee independent schools to increase access and provide quality education by expanding enrollment through improving the quality of education and the number of school buildings and related facilities. But these steps are not sufficient; long-term continuity intrinsically intertwines with financial sustainability.

LFIS often operate for decades, and the only way they can continue to educate disadvantaged children is by ensuring the schools stay organizationally and financially sustainable. Organizational strength, ownership, and operating surpluses are key factors of sustainability. Buildings alone will not suffice.

The degree and duration (life) of sustainability invariably link to the ownership and source of funding for building the schools and for covering the operational costs incurred to run them. This is portrayed in Edify's sustainable school hierarchy triangle below.

Figure 1: Sustainable School Hierarchy

Sustainable School Hierarchy

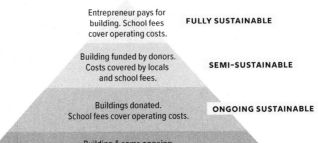

Entrepreneur pays for building. School fees cover operating costs. — **FULLY SUSTAINABLE**

Building funded by donors. Costs covered by locals and school fees. — **SEMI-SUSTAINABLE**

Buildings donated. School fees cover operating costs. — **ONGOING SUSTAINABLE**

Building & some ongoing expenses donated. Other expenses paid by parents. — **PARTIALLY UNSUSTAINABLE**

Building & ongoing expenses are donated. — **TOTALLY UNSUSTAINABLE**

edify.org

Figure 1 shows the different levels of sustainability of schools varying with the way they are built and financed. Each of these categories is briefly described as follows:

- Fully sustainable schools are privately owned and run with a surplus. The school owners pay for the building facilities with their own savings or borrowed capital. In such schools, all operational costs are financed with internally generated incomes, including school fees and other income generating activities undertaken by the schools concerned. No donations or subsidies are received ever.

- Ongoing, sustainable schools resource all funds, materials, and labor needed locally, but some or all of these are donated by locals. All ongoing operating costs are covered by school fees.
- Ongoing, sustainable schools have buildings fully funded by foreign donations, but all operational costs are covered by school fees.
- Ongoing, sustainable with community subsidies schools use foreign donor grants to construct buildings, and then operational expenses are covered partly through local contributions and partly through school fees.
- Partially sustainable, locally subsidized schools are schools where buildings and some ongoing expenses are paid for by foreign donated money and other expenses are covered by parents.
- Unsustainable except for government subsidies schools have no source of income other than the national government paying all operating expenses.
- Unsustainable schools have buildings and operations fully funded by foreign donations. Schools that are fully built and operated with donations and turned into community ownership are vulnerable to cease operations if donor support stops.

Edify supports schools that are built and funded by local entre-preneurs who charge school fees to cover their operational costs in an effort to achieve and maintain full sustainability. In pursuing this, Edify strives to help LFIS maintain sustainability as follows: income generation, business management skills, leadership skills, better learning environments, improved learning outcomes, and education technology.

Although many of the LFIS are driven more by social mission than profit-making, they should be run in such a way that they generate income to cover their costs. This is how they will provide educational services on a sustainable basis and serve as a free-enterprise solution to the global education crisis.

Income Generation

Whether for-profit or not-for-profit, LFIS are small-scaled social enterprises run to generate income through the provision of valued educational services for which they charge reasonable fees. As such, school fees (tuition and registration) constitute the main source of LFIS revenues. The other sources of income are non-fee related, such as commission from the sale of books, uniforms, etc., or the rental of school buildings for activities such as church and community meetings.

School Fees

The level of LFIS revenues from school fees directly correlate with the size of school enrollment. The more students a school attracts, then the higher fee incomes it mobilizes. What does Edify do to help LFIS increase their fee-based revenues?

Edify helps them increase their physical capacity to enroll more students than they currently do. Edify's loan capital enables them to build new classrooms for accommodating more students and thereby increase their fee incomes. Also, improved quality of education and increased rate of academic achievement positively impact the levels of enrollment and income. Edify's support boosts both.

School fees charged also affect the school's income. Many LFIS do not fix their school fees on the basis of full cost consideration. Often fees are based on the information the proprietors have about the fees charged by other schools; sometimes they leave out several costs and expenses that are actually incurred. This may be partly because the entrepreneurs are socially oriented and partly because they do not have the business skills to make a financial analysis. Edify encourages and trains LFIS proprietors in basic business skills, including profit-loss analysis (see below), to help them establish fee rates that are commensurate with delivery expenses. That is, they are taught to charge based on the service they provide, not based on what the nearby schools charge.

Fee-based revenues also depend on the effectiveness of fee collection and cost management. Many proprietors of low-fee independent schools lack proper and consistent systems and practices for collecting, recording, and managing school fees and expenses. In many instances, school fees seem to be collected and managed haphazardly. Some collect fees at the start of each quarter/term. Others do so on a monthly basis, while others collect throughout the year—when parents can pay. Approximately 15–20 percent of the fees are often not collected during the school year.

Similarly, all school expenses do not seem to be made on the basis of budget allocations. For example, a proprietor might buy a bus but not anticipate fuel, driver, and maintenance costs. If the bus breaks down and there are no funds to repair it, the bus will be unused and fail to generate income. Diverting school funds for personal use is another bad practice. Regarding this, one Edify financial training partner advises school entrepreneurs, "Don't embezzle from yourself." Schools run much better when the outfitter pays themself a predetermined monthly salary and doesn't use school funds for family birthdays, Christmas, etc.

Edify has provided training on QuickBooks accounting software to many schools that had a reasonably competent bookkeeper. This typically causes the collection to go from 85 percent to 95 percent. Given all this flows to the bottom line, this provides more money for improving and expanding the school.

Non-Tuition Fee-Based Incomes

These incomes relate to those revenues generated through other activities undertaken by low-fee independent schools to diversify their sources of income. Some of these include incomes generated through the use of computer labs as income centers, school buses, and canteens serving snacks and soft drinks.

Education Technology and Computer Labs. Edify gives loans to low-fee independent schools for educational purposes. As long as loans have to be repaid, computer labs become cost centers. However, some low-fee independent schools turn these into income centers by keeping them open for their own students who want extra practice on weekends and after school for a fee. This practice not only meets a much-needed service in the community but also maximizes the use of the computer labs, and it enables proprietors to earn more income and children to learn more. The incomes generated in this way pay the loans for computer equipment and contribute to sustainability.

School Buses. The buses/vans bought by using Edify loans do not transport school children free of charge. Fees are paid and, like the computer labs, generate income that contributes to loan repayment and overall school revenues.

Cafeterias (Canteens). These are school kitchens that supply hot meals to students. Many low-fee independent schools invest in developing and improving their canteens to make money by selling food to students as well as teachers in their schools. This enables proprietors not only to ensure children get nutritious and regular lunches but also generate extra income. Some low-fee independent schools use Edify's loan capital for developing school canteens.

Bookshops. Students buy their school materials, including books, exercise books, pencils, pens, school bags, snacks, and uniforms from other places. Many low-fee independent schools offer goods needed by students and generate income. Edify's loan capital can be also used for bookshops.

Exposure to New Income Ideas/Initiatives

Edify improves learning environments by providing loans to schools to improve lighting, ventilation, handwashing stations, separate boys' and girls' bathrooms, walls around the school to safeguard children, etc. Edify also improves leadership by group trainings on how to recruit, retain, and motivate teachers better, how to develop a mission statement, strategic plan, and educational technology plan to increase enrollment and pedagogies, and how to provide children with employable skills.

In addition to encouraging, equipping, and funding some of the above diversified list of income sources needed to boost the sustainability of LFIS, Edify endeavors to expose proprietors to new ideas and options they can possibly apply to generate more income. Some examples are given below.

HLC Approach. The HLC (Hippocampus Learning Centers) was established in 2003 by Umesh Malhotra to address the problem of education among poor children in India and has a simple solution: increase access to services and programs that improve the learning of children in rural India.[17] This is achieved through the establishment of education centers in villages at which two education programs are offered: a kindergarten program for children ages 3–6 and an after-school program for children in classes 1–7. However, HLC finds that establishing centers and providing services are together not enough to increase access. In order to truly serve the rural population of India, HLC provides these services at very affordable prices.

The fees collected go toward the costs of running the centers and the salaries of teachers. HLC's goal is to make each village center self-sufficient. The fee varies by program. A kindergarten student pays about US \$32–\$48 per year, depending on their level. A student at the after-school primary education programs pays US \$19. Although Edify does not intervene in the determination of school fees and school hours (this is entirely done by the proprietors of low-fee independent schools), sharing the HLC experience sheds light on the different tools that schools can apply to increase their revenues.

Teach a Man to Fish Approach. This UK-based NGO was established in 2006. Using the slogan "Education that pays for itself," Teach a Man to Fish works with schools across the globe to create new sources of income consisting of enterprises to build their ability to generate revenues and operate on a sustainable basis. It also works to empower young people by providing a better quality (academic) and more relevant (technical skills) education.

The list of enterprises run by the schools includes vegetable farming, beekeeping, livestock, poultry, brickmaking, and carpentry. While they generate income to the schools, the enterprises are also used for training the students in skills that make them employable. Furthermore, as their income increases, the schools lower the fees paid by students.[18]

Edify recognizes the invaluable experience of Teach a Man to Fish and its partners in Africa and Latin America. Edify shares the lesson it has drawn with low-fee independent schools and encourages them to find ways of adapting whatever lessons they find feasible in their respective contexts. Doing this will likely increase their revenues and make education even cheaper (proprietors might lower their fees as a result of increased income) and more effective as the students will have opportunities to participate in the school enterprises in practical terms: learning by doing. In the case of farming enterprises (e.g., vegetable gardening) students learn how to use fertilizer and better seeds that result in better production. Getting involved in carpentry work could increase interest in math, engineering, and science subjects.

Aravind Eye Clinic Approach. The Aravind Eye Clinic was founded by Dr. G. Venkatasuwamy in 1976 with an 11-bed hospital in Madurai, India, with the aim of eliminating needless blindness. Since its inception, the clinic has handled more than 34 million outpatient visits and performed more than 4.3 million surgeries. About 60% of these are subsidized or provided free to the poor using incomes from paying clients. The clinic charges the rich and gives free or subsidized services to the needy. The high-quality, fast service has allowed Aravind Eye Clinic to pay market rates to surgeons, thereby generating significant cash flow to fund free, subsidized surgery for poor people.[19]

Edify believes that many LFIS could benefit from the Aravind Eye Clinic approach. Most of the LFIS supported by Edify serve children living in poverty, including orphans. Some of these children are offered scholarships (sponsorships) by the proprietors. While this is good practice, it reduces the financial sustainability of schools. Following the Aravind Eye Clinic approach, schools could mix middle-class and poor children to be sustainable.

Sunrise School in Rwanda is a good example. The school was founded by Bishop John Rucyahana in 2001 with financial assistance from American donors. Although it started as a school for educating genocide and HIV/AIDS orphans, the high quality of education and standard of learning conditions attracted students from wealthy parents. After only a few years of operation, the Sunrise senior secondary school scored highest on the national exams of all senior secondary schools, including elite schools charging $10,000 per year. The fees paid by more affluent students have been used to subsidize the expenses incurred by the school to educate the orphans.[20]

Blended Learning Approach. This learning approach combines traditional classroom instruction and e-learning and is becoming increasingly important.[21] If in the future a low-fee independent schools can conduct blended learning well, the school can educate twice as many children with nearly the same facilities. One group of students can be in classrooms from 7:30 a.m.–11:30 a.m. Another group would be in class from 12:30 p.m.–4:30 p.m. When not in class, students would work on eTablets for three to four hours per day. This would dramatically increase school cash flow. This extra income could pay for the eTablets. The extra income would pay the monthly installment payment on the loan for the eTablets.

If a school has sufficient land, it could set up chairs and long tables covered by an awning and have students work on their eTablets at school. This would allow the school to have half as many eTablets as students because half would only use them when not in a classroom.

Blended learning saves time and money and also enhances learning as "children learn best when they are exposed to different methods and approaches to instruction."[22] The greatest advantage of blended learning is that it enables differentiated learning, allowing children to learn the basics at their own pace. It also teaches them technology skills and how to become a lifelong learner.

Summary

Children are at the heart of Edify's educational program, and the program seeks to make every decision on what is best for the children. Edify strives to create conditions for out-of-school children to be in school by helping LFIS to expand and those in school to receive quality education by helping them improve existing facilities.

Given their limited resources and lack of access to capital, many low-fee independent schools in developing countries find building new schools/classrooms and buying land challenging. Despite the great demand, they are constrained from enrolling more children because of physical (spatial) limitations. Moreover, it can be difficult to improve the physical learning environment by improving (maintaining, renovating) the quality of existing facilities in regard to toilets, clean water, lighting, ventilation, science and computer labs, and school transportation. Yet despite the various problems they face, student scores in LFIS are higher than those in government schools.

By providing loan capital through partnerships with reputable local lending institutions, Edify enables LFIS to expand and improve buildings and other facilities such as science and computer laboratories and school transportation to create more access to education for impoverished children. Moreover, Edify's loan capital also enables LFIS to enhance learning achievement through the improvement of the physical environment and non-physical learning culture through teachers' training. Increased learning achievement means increased pass rates, which means an increased reputation followed by increased enrollment and increased access.

Edify's loan capital enables LFIS to be profitable and achieve sustainability by:

- Increasing scale (access) by building/expanding classrooms and improving the physical learning environment and non-physical learning culture and quality of education, which means increased enrollment resulting in increased fee incomes.
- Diversifying their source of revenue through financing "new" income-generating activities and exposing them to new innovations.
- Improving their financial health resulting from increased collection and utilization of school fees and effective budgeting and accounting systems, improved school management, and strategic planning.
- Reducing their vulnerability to government harassment, costly bureaucratic procedures, and possible closures.

The improvements in the third and fourth bullet points emanate from the various skills gained by proprietors and teachers following the training and related monitoring and coaching activities by Edify in partnership with lending and training partners.

The ultimate purpose of Edify's contribution to sustainability is to see that LFIS reach a stage whereby:

- Managerial and governance practices are professional and result in improved student learning environments and outcomes, genuine caring for children, school financial sustainability, and social justice through education that gives children an opportunity to work their way out of poverty
- Compliance with government requirements
- Impact assessment tools that are applied by the schools themselves in achieving continuous improvement.
- A Christ-centered culture and practice is in place to ensure continued discipleship work.

4

CHRIST-CENTERED TRAINING

In addition to providing loan capital for improving and expanding educational facilities, Edify provides training services for building human capacity by equipping proprietors, leaders, and teachers to acquire the right skills and attitudes needed to operate a school effectively and sustainably and to deliver quality and transformational education to the students. This chapter will present the justification for and explanation of types of Christ-centered training services provided; who is trained and why; how the trainings are implemented; and who the trainers are.

Business Transformation Training

Because of their educational and professional background, most of the proprietors of the LFIS have limited business and financial skills for running their schools as effective and profitable social businesses in compliance with government policies and regulations. Keeping good financial health through proper budgeting, financial planning, and accounting systems is, therefore, rendered difficult. Moreover, record keeping is generally poor and done manually with very few implementing computerized accounting. Another common problem relates to the lack of separate business and personal income and expenses. School leaders often comingle the school with their personal finances. Poor financial management weakens the school's financial sustainability.

Although they operate as social businesspeople, many entrepreneurs of LFIS are unfamiliar with or have limited knowledge of key local and national policies that affect them. These include school registration laws and procedures, auditing, business laws, tax laws, insurance/pension laws, and labor laws. Poor knowledge of these laws usually put LFIS in vulnerable situations that sometimes cause closures.

To address this problem and strengthen sustainability, Edify facilitates business and financial skills training workshops for school proprietors usually in partnership with the lending partners. In Rwanda and Ghana, the training is designed and facilitated by Edify business transformation officers. The plan is to do the same in all countries. Here is a brief discussion of some of the topics covered.

Fee Collection and Enrollment Management. This training is designed to enable school leaders improve on the fee collection rate and enrollment numbers as school revenues are determined by the number of students enrolled and the effectiveness of fee collection. The participants are trained on how to develop and practice effective enrollment management and fee collection policies and skills to ensure they collect fees on time and in full. The purpose is to enable schools to develop.

QuickBooks Training. Edify provides the QuickBooks accounting software and facilitates skills training to school accounts officers on how to use it in order to build their capacity to keep financial records of business transactions digitally. More specifically, participants are trained on how to create students list, bill students, receipt of fees, expense records, checking and cash accounts, and accounts receivable and accounts payable ledgers. The training enables them to issue invoices to students, generate financial reports (profit and loss account and balance sheet), prepare budgets, and do variance analysis as well as monthly bank reconciliations.

Accounting, Budgeting and Taxation. This relates to introducing participants to accounting, budgeting and taxation concepts, principles, and techniques. They are trained not only to recognize the importance having proper accounting and record keeping, accounting policies, and school budgets, but also to develop and practice them. They are also trained to understand the tax laws applicable to the operations of LFIS and comply with them.

Government Requirements and Internal Controls. Proprietors, leaders, and accounts officers are trained on government regulatory requirements to ensure compliance. They are also trained on developing and maintaining effective internal controls. Compliance is key as it helps schools from being harassed by bureaucratic officials and even from being closed down.

On the other hand, the training activities related to business and regulatory requirements contribute to the reduction of the schools' vulnerability and ensure that LFIS do not fall prey to government harassment, bureaucratic traps, costly penalties/briberies, or closures.

Moreover, Edify encourages LFIS to create their own associations to create opportunities for mutual learning, information sharing, attaining unity of purpose, and strengthening their ability to influence policies in their favor through advocacy and lobbying.

Education Transformation Training

Not only do most LFIS schools have limited business skills, but they also have limited management, leadership, and marketing experience. Yet they lead an average of twenty-five teachers and support staff and relate to parents and other official establishments and networks. This causes deficiencies in staff recruitment, retention, compensation, appraisal, incentives, and development (mentoring and supervision) as well as communication and promotion. The combined effects can be low morale and high turnover, which declines productivity, increases disruptions, and increases costs and, hence, sustainability problems.

Most LFIS need to develop clear vision, mission, and strategy to be able to run effective schools that are capable of offering state-of-the art education to children. They also need effective governance and leadership that is committed to creating conducive learning and teaching environments aimed at achieving high levels of academic excellence and employability. To be inviting both physically and socially LFIS will need to create an environment of trust, integrity, accountability, transparency, safety, productivity, professionalism, and stability. Making all this happen requires new governance, leadership, management, teaching, learning, communication, and relationship skills (both internal and external). Let's look at some of the training activities Edify offers and facilities to achieve these goals.

Leadership Empowerment Accelerated Programs. LEAP identifies real-time needs of partner schools and creates the appropriate platforms to provide solutions to demand- and data-driven issues. These include human resource management, child protection and safeguarding, financial management and practices, technology integration and e-learning, devotionals at home and during e-learning, teacher professionalism and licensure, and teacher motivation. The purpose is to equip and support school leaders with the right knowledge, attitudes, and skills to appreciate, implement, and adhere to existing and new government requirements and other educational policies and practices.

Conditions for Learning. This training seeks to provide the requisite knowledge, attitudes, and skills to school leaders in the areas of building a culture of learning, health, wellness, WASH, facilities and safety, teacher recruitment, induction, and professional development.

Participants are also exposed to information on child protection and safeguarding to enable them to develop and enforce protection policy in their schools. The overall objective is to help proprietors and leaders appreciate the importance of improving school governance, environment for learners and teachers, learning outcomes, Christ-centeredness, communication, peer learning, and networking.

Early Childhood Development and Classroom Management. This training is designed with the aim to help participants develop and improve early childhood development programs. Included in the training are creating an inviting learning environment, nutrition, relationships, curriculum and resources making, assessment of learning, family and community engagement, and classroom management. The training is intended to help school proprietors and leaders understand the importance of having an integrated early childhood program, identify developmental learning stages appropriate for young children, design appropriate interventions for children who are developmentally delayed, demonstrate the necessity of creating an intentionally inviting school culture, and developing classroom management skills to improve learner-behavior management.

Strategic Planning and Execution. This training seeks to facilitate the process of creating/using school vision, mission, core values, school culture, and the DNA of the school to identify their current state and their desired destination. Based on their school-specific SWOT/PESTLE analysis results, participants are guided to set goals, objectives, strategies, activities, and financial plans/budgets. Participants are encouraged to communicate their plans for alignment and buy in before the final execution and periodic reviews. The overall objective is to provide the trainees with the requisite knowledge, attitude, and skills to develop and implement a three- to five-year strategic plan and succession plan for their schools. This will help them be intentional about working toward achieving their shared mission and vision statements, create a framework to guide decision making, create avenues for fundraising and networking, be abreast with strategic planning tools such as SWOT and PESTLE, determine school priorities and allocate resources to opportunities, establish/strengthen partnerships, analyze critical issues and identify options to address them, improve financial planning and projections, ensure sustainability and accountability, and become transgenerational.

Two other initiatives run as part of the school leadership and management training mainly done in Ghana include Teacher Professional Development Training that aims to raise the level of teacher professionalism and the Education Leadership Institute, which is an annual conference that brings school leaders to discuss, learn, and cross-fertilize ideas on current educational trends.

The school leadership and management training activities aimed at improving school governance, learning/teaching environment, and quality of education are designed, planned, facilitated, and monitored by Edify education specialists in consultation with the school owners and leaders. The education specialists also do follow ups and coaching through pre- and post-training school visits as well as online communications.

Education Technology Training

Let us immediately point out that Chapter Five offers a more detailed description on the EdTech program. One of the pillars of Edify's program is education technology aimed at enhancing learning outcomes and employability. Not only does Edify provide loans through its local lending partners to school proprietors, but it also helps them with the installation and maintenance of their computer labs by training IT teachers through its education technology team. This way, IT teachers are equipped to run the computer labs profitably and to effectively teach the students in computer skills and enhance their utilization as education tools. To facilitate EdTech training effectively, Edify deploys skilled education technology integration officers (ETIOs) who consult with and support schools in effectively integrating technology with learning. Edify's goal in supporting the use of education technology is to enhance student learning and to increase employable skills. Edify believes that when schools effectively integrate technology with learning, the students will grow both academically and spiritually as they gain access to learning resources and learn to use them well.

The ETIOs also help school leaders strategically plan for their use of technology within their schools and consult with them on how to access the devices that they will need. Connecting schools to micro-finance partners and technology vendors helps the schools to afford the technology and to reliably access devices for schools. They identify opportunities for schools to connect with training to improve their efforts and actively engage the schools with learning opportunities. The EdTech team prepares and delivers trainings, while following up to help schools put what they've learned into practice.

Moreover, the ETIOS assist schools to develop employable skills by providing opportunities for students to engage in technology-related learning activities that they would not otherwise receive within local curriculums. The need for coding skills is recognized around the world and the EdTech team provides ways for students to engage in learning coding and robotics skills to prepare for the future workplaces they will encounter. They also supervise a coding competition in which students in Ghana, for example, spend months developing their projects in teams, using a coding language called Scratch, and then compete against other schools in their regions with the best projects being recognized at a national level.

The ETIOs also help to develop and implement projects that impact student learning with technology in schools. For example, Edify developed a customized learning device that we called SMILE to enable students to access education resources without requiring the use of the internet and to improve their critical thinking skills. In the years since the EdTech team implemented this project, schools have been able to connect their students with free educational resources, including opportunities to engage with Scripture through the schools' technology devices.

Character Formation Training

Christ-centered education (CCE) is the core of Edify's program and is devoted to the development of character rooted in the values and principles of the Lord Jesus Christ. This is about promoting holistic (undivided between secular and sacred) education aimed at developing Christ-centered character among proprietors, teachers, and students to generate God-fearing future leaders. It is the foundation of all Edify does. All the products and services provided by Edify are rooted in this one core product. Thus, the presentation is rather more comprehensive than the other training products.

Education and Character Formation in History: A Prelude

Where there is education there is some type of character formation, whether intended or not. As a form of transferring skills and knowledge from one generation to another, first in informal and then in formal ways, education has existed since the placement of Adam and Eve in the garden of Eden with the provision of God's instructions. God educated Adam and Eve about His creation, their responsibilities, and rights on earth, and how they should relate with Him, one another, and the environment. In its non-formal ways, education is as ancient as human existence itself, as is character formation. Formal education and character development have coexisted from ancient Greek, Roman, Confucian, Taoist, Aztec, Egyptian, and Babylonian times until the twenty-first century and will continue to do so in actively preparing the youth of one generation to hand off knowledge to the next generation.

The term "character education" is simply the current term for what is a millennia-old issue. It has lived under various names and still does in different parts of the world—for example, values education, moral education, civic education, social-emotional learning, citizenship education, positive youth development. No society can survive if it does not deliberately foster the development of civic character in each subsequent generation of youth.[1]

A Christ-Centered Education and Character Formation: Edify Model

Like all educationists, Edify believes effective character education can be achieved only when it integrates values. The value-based character education movement is a positive step forward in the education of future citizens. However, values are inextricably rooted in paradigms/worldviews.

What is a paradigm? A paradigm "stands for the entire constellation of beliefs, values, techniques shared by members of a given community for analyzing and interpreting problems and for reaching conclusions (solutions)."[2] It becomes a discipline, an outlook, an ideology, or a philosophy applied and promoted by like-minded people. It also becomes a target that opponents criticize and undermine. We interpret our world and develop our values, attitudes, perceptions, and behavior through paradigms. In the words of Covey:

The word paradigm comes from the Greek. It was originally a scientific term, and is more commonly used today to mean a model, theory, perception, assumption, or frame of reference.

In the more general sense, it is the way we 'see' the world—
not in terms of our visual sense of sight, but in terms of
perceiving, understanding, interpreting. . . . It is a theory, an
explanation, or model of something else.[3]

In their book, *The Transforming Vision*, Wolterstorff and College
talk about worldviews:

Our worldview determines our values. It helps us interpret
the world around us. It sorts out what is important from what
is not, what is of highest value from what is least. A world
view provides a model of the world which guides its adherents
in the world. It stipulates how the world ought to be, and it
thus advises how its adherents ought to conduct themselves
in the world. In a sense, each world view comes equipped
with an eschatology, a vision of the future, which guides and
directs life.[4]

In other words, worldviews shape our values, which then form our
character and then our culture. We are, to a greater extent, what
our worldviews make us, and our worldviews are what we make
them and what has been imparted to us. We are taught, we think,
and we act according to our worldviews. Worldviews are makers or
breakers of character.

The point is while there is a general unity in the move to apply
values-based character education as a remedy to the general moral
decline, there is disunity in terms of the content of values emanat-
ing from the differences in the worldviews of various programs. The
worldview-value dialectical combination determines the effectiveness and outcomes of the character education programs since each

program seeks to form character traits in line with the worldview in which it's rooted.

Edify espouses a Christ-centered worldview through which it analyzes and addresses human potential and problems. Unlike the general character education in public and secular private schools, Edify's character education program is deeply grounded in biblical values and principles.

What is a Christ-centered worldview? A Christ-centered worldview (also called Biblical worldview) refers to the set of ideas and beliefs rooted in the Bible through which followers of Jesus Christ interpret and interact with the world. Unlike the secular worldview, which puts nature and man at its center, God is the center in a Christian worldview. Answers to life's core issues related to where we have come from, why we are here, what is wrong with the world, and how it can be fixed are sought in the beliefs about God, creation, humanity, moral order, and purpose.

The Christ-centered worldview recognizes God's supremacy as the Creator and Sustainer of all things by His will and as deserving to receive all the glory and honor from humankind, whose purpose is to live in love, care, respect, and harmony with one another, God, and the environment under His ordinances.

- "You are worthy, O Lord, to receive glory and honor and power; for You created all things, and by Your will they exist and were created" (Revelation 4:11).
- "The earth is the LORD's, and all its fullness, the world and those who dwell therein. For He has founded it upon the seas, and established it upon the waters" (Psalm 24:1–2).

- "God created man in His own image. . . . Male and female He created them, . . . and said to them 'Be fruitful and multiply; fill the earth and subdue it.' . . . Then the LORD God took the man and put him in the garden of Eden to tend and keep it" (Genesis 1:27; 2:15).
- "Seek first the kingdom of God and His righteousness, and all these things shall be added to you" (Matthew 6:33).

The core values and beliefs of the Christ-centered worldview draw from the Bible because "All Scripture is given by inspiration of God, and is profitable for doctrine, for reproof, for correction, for instruction in righteousness, that the man of God may be complete, thoroughly equipped for every good work" (2 Timothy 3:16–17).

In contrast to the secular worldview that is rooted in human reason, the Christ-centered worldview is rooted in the acknowledgement that man is a creation of God with limited and temporal capabilities for knowing and accepting the lordship of Jesus Christ through, by, and for whom all things have been made. Without having faith in Him, following His principles, and embracing the fear of God as the beginning of wisdom and the source of all good things and virtues, humankind is bound to fall short of knowing what is right or wrong.

Humankind can be good and can do good things, i.e., can have constructive thoughts and actions, because a human being is the bearer of God's image. Secular character education has made—and is likely—to make additional, positive contributions to the formation of better people. At the same time, humankind has limited powers and secular character education, depending on the values within which it is promoted, and it can also develop citizens with destructive characters and actions.

There are many historical examples. To cite two: the character education that was taught during the period of fascism in Germany and Italy and the character education that was taught in the socialist countries during the communist era of the Soviet Union. The systems disappeared and so did the lack of values with them. Many followers of Jesus believe secular character education produces a temporal character that changes with time and context and lacks universality.

Those followers further believe authentic character and constructive human citizenship formation are possible only when humankind embraces core beliefs about truth and life that are deeply rooted in God's values and is transformed by them inside out. Character education rooted in Christ-centered values produces internally transformed people and character that is timeless and universal. It does not change because human systems change. It is the same yesterday, today, tomorrow, and it is everywhere.

The hope is that such character will say no to requesting or paying bribes attendant with corruption. Such a person should believe God will hold them accountable for all their acts, which will cause them to forgo earthly gain in hopes of heavenly reward. Not all products of education that emphasizes the values of Jesus will be honest, but if many are, these people could overcome the corruption that oppresses the poor in developing countries.

This is the kind of worldview Edify adheres to and its character education is developed and taught according to these core beliefs. Hence, this creates the need to invest in a Christ-centered education

(CCE) to enhance authentic character education, which will lead to authentic character development.

Benefits and Attributes of CCE

So far, we presented the history and definitions and the differences of character education in general and CCE. We also provided brief descriptions of two worldviews: secular and Christian. Like all other education service providers, Edify recognizes the critical role character education plays in providing effective education. However, while the character education given in non-Christian schools advocates secular "values education," Edify promotes character education grounded in Christ-centered values and principles. For this reason, Edify believes its character education is more authentic, profound, and long-lasting, whereas the secular character education is more superficial in nature. Edify hopes children develop a personal relationship with Jesus Christ that will last a lifetime and guide their character every day.

This section presents a brief description of some of the short-term and long-term benefits that constitute the rationale for Edify's promotion of CCE through the low-fee independent Christian schools it supports.

CCE is likely to present the ultimate role model for ultimate character. Albert Schweitzer once said, "Example is not the main thing in influencing other people. It's the only thing." Also Paul gives some advice about modeling after Christ:

- "Therefore be imitators of God as dear children. And walk in love, as Christ also has loved us and given Himself for us, an

offering and a sacrifice to God for a sweet-smelling aroma"
(Ephesians 5:1).

- "Imitate me as I imitate Christ, just as I also imitate Christ"
(1 Corinthians 11:1).

Edify believes CCE presents the ultimate role model, Jesus Christ, for the ultimate character. Role models play an important role in both informal and formal education and more so in character education. Children usually learn better and remember better when things are explained to them through visual media, stories, and role models:

> Role model education can be seen as effective because it bridges the gap between the ideal and reality. Education becomes experiential, as students learn a little about their teachers' lives, and how they embody the values they are trying to pass on and explore.
>
> The gap between theory and practice is bridged as ideological concepts become realities before the eyes of the students. Once they have truly understood an idea because they have seen it firsthand through a teacher's expression of it in the way they conduct themselves, they are only then in a true position to judge its validity to their life, and then make the relevant lifestyle decision.[5]

Role models can be contemporary or historical figures. They can be family members, teachers, friends, politicians, scientists, religious leaders, or film stars. Among the contemporary ones, such as teachers and parents, youth choose role models through personal observations and experience. They also hear about past role models through stories and books, which bring them to knowing, connecting, and identifying with their chosen role models. They also attach different preferences of role models, one of which relates to social nearness. With reference to teachers, for example, Bucher says, "Children, when faced with worthy models at this proximity, will latch on to them and their ideals, and fully consider them as role models."[6] Thus, Edify seeks to train teachers to be good role models.

Data on preferred models collected from 1150 pupils between the ages of 10–18 from Austria and Germany, for instance, showed that "those personalities of social nearness to the participants had the greatest 'model effect' for them. Mother, fathers, and relatives were mentioned with the greatest frequency. After that came religious models, and only then mass media personalities such as movie and television stars, and sports figures."[7]

Role models, both past and present, are picked by youth on the basis of their attractive character, actions, and ideas that they want to imitate and emulate. Youth want to be like them, think like them, and act like them.[8] So Edify trains teachers to follow Jesus as their model to be good role models for students.

Following the exhortation of Paul to imitate Jesus, billions of people throughout the globe have been, are, and will be imitating Him through generations in the past and generations to come. Throughout history, He has been the role model for the ultimate character and people have striven to grow into His likeness. Jesus is the ultimate embodiment of the ultimate character the world desperately seeks, and learning from His life and teachings is an integral part of authentic character education.

Why is it important to imitate Jesus? What is there to imitate for the world? Without purporting to be exhaustive, Jesus not only taught but lived up to the following key character traits: love, righteousness, forgiveness, reconciliation, humility, mercy, selflessness, justice, impartiality, integrity, honesty, accountability, dependability, peace, joy, vulnerability, and servanthood.

Although it may mention Him as a historical religious figure, secular character education does not present Jesus as a role model. The inspiring life and teaching of Jesus can be taught and presented as a role model in a manner that is alive and powerful only through authentic character education rooted in CCE. He is the standard by which we measure ourselves. Although He lived and taught approximately two thousand years ago, billions of people have been impacted, are being impacted, and desire to be impacted by the life, work, and personality of Jesus.

Klaus Issler, for example, states, "The more I examine his life and teachings, the more I come to respect and appreciate who Jesus is, how he lived his human life, and his self-giving compassion and generosity in what he accomplished for us. Jesus is my hero, someone worthy to imitate."[9]

Although many have concerns or are even offended by the term "Christianity" because of acts or attitudes by a small percentage of Jesus' followers, a reasonable person will find it hard to criticize Jesus, who stood for love, selflessness, humility, deliverance, peace, valuing both genders, and caring for the sick, disabled, and outcasts. The world would be a very different place if everyone lived by these principles.

In the same vein, it is likely that students who learn about the teachings of Jesus will take Him as the epitome of the ultimate character and imitate Him as their hero. Imitating Jesus is the ultimate outcome of CCE for any individual, school, community, and nation. This is one critical reason why Edify promotes character formation rooted in CCE.

CCE is likely to be the basis for authentic character development (ACD). Plato is known to have said, "Education makes good men and good women act nobly." The notion that education makes better people is a widely held belief. As a working definition, an ACD is a character formation rooted in Christ-centered values, principles, and teachings as written in Scriptures, not only to instill knowledge of human values but also to create opportunities for inner change. Students are not only taught these virtues and principles in classrooms in the form of stories and theories but also are given opportunities to practice and behave accordingly. They do this to internalize and develop the character traits learned while at school without waiting until they are in the marketplace as accomplished citizens.

Edify believes learning academic and vocational subjects in the best way possible and applying them to benefit others and oneself in an honest and loving manner to serve society and enhance their personal development. However, while they are significant milestones in people's lives, these skills, on their own, will not make better people. Those who learn history, politics, and democratic principles tend to respect others, including their cultures, values, and opinions. Such social skills enable them to be accommodative, tolerant, and live in relative harmony with others. These are significant milestones in human lives. As Plato said, students may grow into a situation whereby they might act nobly. They might also become relatively better people, as Jackson asserted.

The character education currently promoted by the secular educationists has been stripped of its religious content and relegated to human psychological and sociological perspectives within which what is morally "right" and "wrong" is prescribed and taught. It is also more focused on changing things by rules, rewards, and punishments, and it is context-bound with varied agendas.

Secular character education generates human values and knowledge, which are important components of character. However, human values and knowledge on their own do not constitute or produce better character and better people as "knowing right from wrong is more than a simple process of being aware of specific social rules, and doing the right thing is not a simple matter of putting those rules into practice. . . . Being a good person . . . is more than a matter of understanding what is morally right."[10]

Although values are seen as one of the foundations for character, "character is different from values in that values are orientations or dispositions whereas character involves action or activation of knowledge and values." Secular character education is basically about a legalistic code of ethics and does not evoke nor create opportunities for inner change or transformation.

Secular character education dismisses the importance of CCE, i.e., the place of God, in our character development and rather relies on human willpower to change people's character for the better. But willpower on its own is far from being sufficient to develop the desired character. As Klaus Issler points out:

> Perhaps because willpower works in a simple sphere—such as deciding to open a door, or getting to a certain destination—we've assumed willpower also works on a grander scale in

changing our character. That is a mistake. Willpower alone was never meant to carry the weight of right living—it is too puny to defeat the various temptations we face and to change the sinful habits and compulsions we've developed over a lifetime.[11]

Willpower too often wilts in the face of temptation offering pleasure or personal gain. Top business schoolteachers saw some of their graduates fail miserably in industry ethics and or Wall Street. Character education is about developing better character and better character is about making better people. However, every character education rooted in a secular worldview doesn't necessarily lead to the generation of ACD. Edify believes holistic education can happen only through CCE.

ACD is the embodiment of Jesus' values, principles, and practices in an individual who is holistically (heart and mind) transformed inside out and thinks and acts accordingly. A person with an authentic character outflows with love and all other traits as naturally as apple trees produce apples. Klaus Issler asserts that deep character formation or inner heart wholeness comes when "we attend to the core of our self—the heart—and cooperate with God's good work within" and not through "rule keeping and external behavioral conformity."[12]

Edify believes individuals cannot be whole without undergoing a Christ-centered spiritual transformation. Whole person (or transformational) development requires deep economic, social, political, and spiritual changes. Brown and Moffett recognize the relevance of developing the whole child by asserting educators should be "making an enduring commitment to ensuring that the total child (including his or her civic, emotional, physical, and spiritual needs) is at the heart of the school renewal process."[13]

A Christ-centered spiritual transformation is the "mother" of all transformations, which comes as a result of knowing and accepting that Jesus is the way, the life, and the truth and that the fear of God is the beginning of wisdom. It may be impossible to be transformed holistically without such core beliefs and submission, which then make the development of authentic character impossible. As Theodore Roosevelt said, "To educate a man in mind and not in morals is to educate a menace to society."[14]

Edify believes developing authentic character among students that they continue to practice and enhance during their adult life in the marketplace comes from receiving CCE in schools. As Proverbs says, "Train up a child in the way he should go, and when he is old he will not depart from it" (Proverbs 22:6). Edify also recognizes that character formation is not a quick fix. It is a long process and goes beyond school life and can be realized only by the faithful application of the values and principles of Jesus and empowerment of the Holy Spirit. Edify seeks to facilitate character development that will overcome the selfish human nature on a long-term basis.

Through CCE, students are:

- Equipped with the knowledge of Jesus' virtues, practices, and principles with the likelihood that they emulate Him as an example
- Exposed to the various virtues and graces presented in Scriptures as constituting an authentic character
- Able to transform inside out and evolve a Christlike character following the knowledge and acceptance of Jesus as the source

of truth and life and that authentic character comes from deep inside-out transformation. Such a person outflows with love, joy, peace, humility, faithfulness, gentleness, self-control, compassion, patience, kindness, goodness, care, honesty, accountability, integrity, stewardship, responsibility, respect, justice, diligence, etc.[15]

In a nutshell, CCE is strengthening and deepening the Christ-centered faith and practice among school-going youth. In more common terms, it is students being taught the values and principles of Jesus and helped to deepen and practice their Christian faith as a result of which they become God-fearing leaders who seek to build flourishing Godly nations.

CCE is likely to enhance academic performance. When they are internally transformed and follow the example and principles of Jesus, students learn as unto the Lord, teachers teach as unto the Lord, administrators manage as unto the Lord, and parents look after their children as unto the Lord. As a result, they begin to discharge their responsibilities not only as an obligation but also as a vocation. This means all the stakeholders get united in making education fun, enjoyable, and "natural," and they give it their all. The necessary energy, resources (time, money, knowledge, etc.), creativity, and support are mobilized to achieve high academic scores and overall excellence. Teachers, students, and administrators begin to be punctual, avoid absenteeism, and maximize their time use. The highest possible class and school discipline is maintained, school violence ceases, and safety is secured. Mutual respect abounds and enthusiasm is generated.

As CCE is also based on the true recognition of the great place of children in God's world and strives to treat them the way Jesus treats them, it is learner-focused and allows for maximum freedom, participation, interaction, critical thinking, and innovation among students. "Test all things; hold fast what is good. Abstain from every form of evil" (1 Thessalonians 5:21–22). Testing and rebuking all things are as important Christ-centered principles as are convincing and exhorting with all long-suffering and teaching (2 Timothy 4:2). In this instance, CCE also meets another education goal formulated by Martin Luther King Jr.: "The function of education is to teach one to think intensively and to think critically: Intelligence plus character—that is the goal of education."[16]

CCE is likely to enhance peace. Jesus said, "Peace I leave with you, My peace I give to you; not as the world gives do I give to you. Let not your heart be troubled, neither let it be afraid" (John 14:27). CCE teaches students that Jesus is the source, maker, keeper, and giver of true peace, and following His example will prepare them to be peace lovers, peace builders, and peacekeepers both in and outside schools and when they're adults.

Moreover, very often conflicts and fights arise because people, tribes, and nations are not willing to forgive one another and instead resort to retaliation instead of forgiveness and reconciliation. "Forgive us our debts, as we forgive our debtors" (Matthew 6:12) was what Jesus taught His disciples to pray. Jesus taught empathy, to love our neighbors as ourselves. CCE teaches forgiving and loving one another and resolving differences amicably. It teaches mutual understanding, tolerance, and respect in the way Jesus demonstrated. We are to love peace, not the sword. Further, "Blessed are the peacemakers, for they shall be called sons of God" (Matthew 5:9).

Those who follow and apply Christ-centered principles choose to love and forgive, which are the basis for peacemaking and peace-keeping. Moreover, this is also likely to stop disenfranchised youth from joining terrorist groups and participating in terrorist activities. Prayer is another tool students are encouraged to apply to prevent conflicts and preserve peace. Learning and embracing these principles at a school age is likely to enhance peace in schools and in societies later.

CCE is likely to enhance the capacity to fight corruption.

> Corruption, which has always existed, is today an obstacle to effective good governance. In many parts of the world corruption in the form of public misconduct has led to illegal and morally crooked practices such as bribery, misallocation of resources and the misuse of power and influence for personal or corporate gain at the expense of the wider society. The disturbing trend of corruption has devastating consequences for the wellbeing of the society.[17]

Although it is most rampant in Africa and tends to be seen as an African problem, corruption is global. It is part of the fallen nature of man and is unfortunately practiced in all societies, regardless of their levels of development. Corruption might express itself in different ways in different civilizations and cultures, but it is always the same in substance.

Much has been said about many of the African leaders who turned their respective countries into their own money-making machines while millions died from famine. And that is true. The exposure of the British members of Parliament cheating the nation by claiming unlawful expenses and the bankers and housing companies in Europe and America that cheated their people and the whole world are recent examples that also prove corruption is universal. According to the 2019 report of Transparency International, approximately 66 percent of the 180 countries in the index scored below 50 with an average of 43 on a scale of 0 (highly corrupt) to 100 (highly clean).[18]

The common causes of corruption are dishonesty, lack of transparency, lack of accountability, selfishness, and greed. It is the drive for self-enrichment and disregard for the interest of others that cause people, particularly those in power and influence, to commit such unjust and often cruel acts against their fellow human beings to whom they are meant to be trusted servants and examples of good character.

CCE teaches honesty, transparency, loyalty, accountability, responsibility, sharing, and generosity in the way Jesus taught during His time. His called Christians uphold these values and fight corruption in all possible ways. Teaching these Christ-centered character traits can stop students from lying, stealing, cheating (e.g., during exams or otherwise), bullying others for personal gain, etc. Deeply transformed people are likely to avoid practicing corruption, to expose and condemn corruption, and to establish laws and take actions to curb corruption. They will do it for their God, their people, their countries, and the world.

Moreover, the love for money and greed is another source of corruption. People idolize money and treat it as the major source of happiness and power. They worship it as their master and go to extremes, including corruption and unlawful gain, to get and accumulate wealth. It can become destructive to their lives and the lives of others. CCE teaches the love of money is the source of all evil and it is not good to accumulate but to share. This is likely to be the guiding principle of people who have been through CCE.

CCE is likely to enhance justice. "He has shown you, O man, what is good; and what does the Lord require of you, but to do justly, to love mercy, and to walk humbly with your God" (Micah 6:8). Justice, mercy, and humility are intertwined. Learning about loving and showing mercy to our neighbor and the inseparable relationship between loving one's neighbor and loving God are likely to cause students to act justly toward others.

Acting justly here means loving all with the love of God without discrimination by gender, age, creed, race, or social status, empowering the powerless, freeing those in bondage, sharing with the disadvantaged (social groups, regions, and countries), and serving one another. The sense of humility also means students will learn to see others as better than themselves by serving and not lording authority over them. Students learning about practicing fairness, denouncing injustices and oppression, and upholding servant leadership attitudes are likely to practice the same in their adulthood and thereby enhance justice.

CCE is likely to enhance health. Alcohol and drug abuse and immoral media images and films have caused many youth not to perform as they should in school as well as suffer physically and mentally. Several have lost their lives because of substance abuse or ended up in prison.

Early sex and promiscuity, early pregnancy and abortions, and widespread substance abuse have deteriorated health conditions among teenage girls throughout the world. "750,000 girls get pregnant every year in our country. Teenage pregnancy has become a carcass. It is really eating us up," says the director of TUCCE in Ghana.[19]

CCE teaches about the dangers of such practices and the benefits of abstinence until marriage. These are likely to enable students to keep away from personally destructive practices, such as substance abuse, sexual misbehavior, and violence, which often involve bodily harm. In his study, William Jeynes establishes that religious commitment and religious education have significant statistical effects on school safety, moral behavior, and substance (alcohol and drugs) abuse.[20] In other words, CCE is likely to help students embrace the principles of avoiding destructive behavior that is not in line with Christ-centered principles and live healthier lives as young people and develop habits they carry into their adult years.

CCE is likely to enhance environmental care. God has clearly placed humans in a position of responsibility over creation. Genesis 2:15 says, "The LORD God took the man and put him in the garden of Eden to tend keep of it." We recognize all created things belong to God and we are accountable to Him as stewards of creation. God commissions us to rule over creation in a way that sustains, protects, and enhances His works so all creation may fulfill the purposes God intended for it. We must manage the environment, not simply for our own benefit but for God's glory.[21]

CCE teaches students in classrooms about the creation being given to humankind to use as resources. Mankind has to act responsibly and be a good steward. In other words, the instruction He gave to Adam and Eve is the same instruction that applies to the present generation. Children are taught to see and respect the environment as God's and to use it and tend it for His glory. This is likely to create environmentally aware friendly people when they join society as producers, policy makers, and administrators, thereby creating a responsible stewardship.

CCE is likely to enhance productivity and prosperity.

- "Then God blessed the seventh day and sanctified it, because in it He rested from all His work which God had created and made" (Genesis 2:3).
- "Whether you eat or drink, or whatever you do, do all to the glory of God" (1 Corinthians 10:31).
- "Whatever you do work at it with all your heart, as working for the Lord, not for human masters, since you know that you will receive an inheritance" (Colossians 3:23–24, NIV).

CCE teaches that God worked to create the universe and mandated humankind to work. Therefore, work is to be taken seriously and for the glory of God. Not only that, it also must be executed with excellence. As in all areas of life, ultimate accountability is not to our immediate human employers but to God who will reward us.

Viewing one's work as God-ordained and doing it both for men and God, and primarily for God, is likely to create a work ethic that can increase diligence, enjoyment, enthusiasm, and productivity. This does not mean people have to work without resting, nor is this meant to be motivated by a desire to be rich. He set the model of working and resting that must be followed. It is also written, "Do not wear yourself out to get rich" (Proverbs 23:4, NIV).

Work and rest go hand in hand and reinforce each other. Working without resting decreases efficiency and productivity and vice versa. A decline in productivity means a decline in wealth and prosperity. However, productivity (performance) on its own doesn't generate prosperity. More is needed. As Peter writes, "Giving all diligence, add to your faith virtue, to virtue knowledge, to knowledge self-control, to self-control perseverance, to perseverance godliness, to godliness brotherly kindness, and to brotherly kindness love. For if these things are yours and abound, you will be neither barren nor unfruitful in the knowledge of our Lord Jesus Christ" (2 Peter 1:5–8).

CCE is likely to enhance family relationships. Families are the main source of character education for their children. They are the closest physically and emotionally and, therefore, they have the highest level of influence. Parents and children are in a relationship of mutual influence. Broken homes and dysfunctional homes do not offer a healthy environment for children. In such homes, alcohol and drug abuse by parents, sexual and physical abuse of children, and parental conflicts often compounded by poverty create an environment that negatively affects the well-being and development of children. A study undertaken by the Institute of Education at the University of London finds, "When compared with their peers from more advantaged backgrounds, children from poorer background, whether from intact or non-intact families generally do less well across a number of measures, such as health and educational attainment."[22]

CCE teaches the Christ-centered principles of effective and healthy families in which marriage is seen as instituted by God and not to be broken and family relationships are valued and lived as gifts from God.

- "A man shall leave his father and mother and be joined to his wife, and the two shall become one flesh" (Matthew 19:5).
- "Children are a gift from the LORD; they are a reward from him" (Psalm 127:3, NLT).
- "Children, obey your parents in the Lord, for this is right. 'Honor your father and mother,' which is the first commandment with promise: 'that it may be well with you and you may live long on the earth'" (Ephesians 6:1–3).

CCE also involves parental participation and dialogue on education and character pertaining to children on a one-on-one basis or collectively. On the other hand, children openly share with their parents what they have learned at school, including their challenges. This is likely to enhance mutual understanding and strengthen relationships between children and parents as well as between parents.

Most importantly, when the children form their own families later in life, their understanding of the requirements of a healthy family within a Christ-centered worldview, the avoidance of self-destructive habits such as alcohol and drug abuse, in addition to a better family economy and all other Christ-centered character traits they have embraced, CCE is bound to enhance family cohesion.

In short, Edify promotes CCE framed in the biblical worldview to enhance ACD because it is the only way to develop authentic character. This is the best way of achieving the goal of education: developing better people through greater academic excellence and authentic character. The presentation made a case for the critical role that authentic character plays in achieving academic excellence and overall success in life. As Luis Sena says, "Education is a redemptive activity if it develops the potential God has put in every human being and imparts a biblical worldview and fights ignorance with knowledge about the glory of God and uses the gospel to explain the world and our purpose in life."[23]

Herein lies one of the reasons for Edify's choice to promote CCE rooted in the joy of serving others: it presents Jesus as the ultimate example of ultimate character and offers opportunities for students to grow in His likeness.

How Edify Promotes CCE

In the section immediately above, we presented the types of training activities facilitated by Edify among its partner schools with a focus on CCE. We also presented the rationale for Edify's investment in CCE. In the presentation that follows, we will discuss the essentials and related intentions of CCE by referring to some of the major training activities that directly relate to the promotion of CCE aimed at bringing about ACD. This is followed by a description of the mode of implementation.

Training Teachers. The overall strategy of the CCE training program consists of four objectives:

- To enhance the understanding of, commitment to, and depth of proprietors' spiritual transformation to enable them to embrace CCE as part of their vision and curriculum and commit resources for equipping their teachers with the required skills and giving them permission and support to facilitate CCE in the classroom.
- To bring about spiritual transformation among teachers and impart technical skills needed for: 1) integrating a Christ-centered worldview into academic teaching, 2) Christ-centered

developing lesson planning, 3) applying Christ-centered student-centered teaching, and 4) enhancing Christ-centered relationship building.

- To bring about spiritual transformation and impart a Christ-centered worldview and biblical knowledge among students to create conducive environments for ACD in the classroom.
- To create opportunities for students to strengthen their newly acquired Christ-centered character further by forming youth fellowships to undertake Bible studies, prayers, worship, and outreach activities both within and outside their schools.

The ultimate goal of Edify is to help LFIS create access to and improve the quality of education among children living in poverty to produce transformed future wealth generators, job creators, and nation builders guided by a Christ-centered worldview.

To achieve this, Edify provides loans to school proprietors to build classrooms and computer labs as presented in the previous chapter. Building more classrooms allows for more children to have access to education. As shown in the previous chapter, the furniture, the equipment, the ventilation, the lighting, the size of the classroom, and the availability of technology are also important components of the learning environment. All these are important and improve learning outcomes.

What is even more important is what happens in that classroom. And what happens in the classroom is determined by what the teachers do and how they do things. The proprietor builds the classroom, creates the learning space for students, mobilizes the students, and employs the teachers to educate them. But even with the most rigorous supervision and rules, the proprietor is not able to directly determine what happens in the classroom. Only the teacher does that.

Being at the front line, the teacher is the interface and the key link, the deliverer of all goods and services offered by the school to the children. Through them all knowledge is diffused, and minds and hearts are molded, academic achievements are made, and student well-being is maintained. The teacher is the school, and the school is the teacher. They are the role model to students. As Jon Saphier et al. assert:

> Of all the things that are essential to high performing schools, nothing is more important than the teacher and what that person knows, believes and can do. A teacher skill makes a difference in student performance, not only in achievement scores, but also in students' sense of fulfillment in school and their feelings of well-being.[24]

For this reason, teachers are the immediate primary target of Edify's training in the promotion of CCE in LFIS. Edify believes this will deliver quality academic and character education just as the provision of loans to the proprietors enables them to build classrooms and computer labs to create more conducive learning environments. In other words, Edify's training focuses on equipping the teachers with the knowledge and tools they need to facilitate CCE among students.

Edify also recognizes the training of teachers will be futile without the proprietors' recognition of the relevance of and commitment to CCE in the realization of their long-term vision. Therefore, in addition to the business and leadership training they are offered, proprietors are also trained in CCE both separately and together with the teachers. The full recognition and ownership of CCE by proprietors generates the support and authority needed by teachers to facilitate CCE effectively.

Worldviews. Edify believes the broader knowledge bases the teachers have, the better the quality and depth of learning they bring to the classroom. Edify also recognizes the quality and paradigm of education is determined by the worldview within which it is delivered. As part of its CCE program, therefore, Edify seeks to train proprietors and teachers on the history and content of the prevailing worldviews/paradigms in comparative ways. Proprietors and teachers are taught on the advantages of a Christ-centered worldview over a secular worldview in terms of providing holistic (undivided into secular and sacred) education and facilitating holistic transformational development.

In this regard, the training challenges the conventional perception that sees academic and spiritual education as opposites and dismisses any effort to intermingle the two. On the contrary, proprietors and teachers are taught to value the two sides as mutually intertwined and appreciate the various benefits of CCE, including its contribution to the achievement of academic excellence (improved learning outcomes) and employability. They are taught to embrace CCE as an asset, not as a liability.

Vision and Mission Development. In most cases, LFIs do not have written vision and mission statements and business plans to guide their programs. The few that have them are often poorly articulated and fall short of providing clear direction. Edify offers training in visioning and strategic planning techniques to enable the proprietors to develop vision and mission statements and business plans that clearly set out their long-term and short-term objectives and activities. This includes the recognition of the role of CCE in achieving academic and character excellence and the need to offer CCE as part of their curriculum with full commitment and resource allocation.

With a clear and well-articulated vision and mission for undertaking CCE and the needed resource allocation, the proprietors are likely to create an environment that is physically, academically, and spiritually conducive to teach the Christ-centered worldview and the principles of Jesus. Also, both teachers and students are enabled to deepen or experience spiritual transformation, the mother of authentic character development in their respective schools. The proprietors' understanding of and commitment to the CCE concept and practice is paramount since they own and control the schools. They open and close the door, and Edify works only with those who are voluntarily willing to open their doors.

Perception of Teachers' Role. Teaching is generally seen as one of the lowest-paid jobs in our world today. In many developing countries, it is often seen as a "last resort" job. Both society and the teachers seem to have a low perception and appreciation of teaching. This is particularly so in LFIS where teachers do not always have proper training and are paid even lower salaries.

In the training workshops supported by Edify, teachers in LFIS are taught to appreciate and embrace their role beyond the conventional perception. They are trained to see themselves as engaging in the business of developing God-fearing, future professionals in the form of engineers, scientists, mathematicians, historians, economists, entrepreneurs, teachers, and so on by imparting academic, vocational, relationship, and behavioral skills.

Christ-centered teaching not only trains people in physical skills but also transforms them through the knowledge of Christ. Just as manufacturers produce goods, teachers produce people. No business is more important than making people, and there is no business without people. Teachers make the people who make not only people but also make goods. They educate educators who educate others and produce the goods and services needed for life. The engineers who make cars, airplanes, tractors, and rockets are taught by teachers.

Moreover, the role of teachers, including Christian ones, is very often confined to teaching a specific subject in a specific field and to making sure the students learn well and achieve good academic scores. While this forms an important part of their role, teachers are also taught to view their role as wider than that. They are also taught to see themselves as shepherds and leaders shaping the minds and hearts of young students by instilling in them basic character traits that become critical for their success and the success of the nations they will lead.

Christian teachers produce Christian students who become Christian leaders, engineers, doctors, entrepreneurs, teachers, and other professionals, who continue as disciples in their places of work, having been equipped with God's wisdom, knowledge, and truth. They become witnesses of Christ in both word and deed. They are trained to teach children with love, respect, care, and attention, and to value them as highly as Jesus did. More importantly, since the children learn more from what they see than from what they hear, teachers are trained how to "walk the talk" and set a good example.

They are, therefore, trained and encouraged to view teaching as a gift from God, as a vocation, as a mission, as an act of worship, and that it is God-ordained and must be treated and pursued as unto the Lord in response to the Great Commission of making disciples of all the nations, teaching them to observe all that Jesus commanded (Matthew 28:19–20). The overall message is to teach as unto the Lord.

In this regard, the training is intended to help teachers realize and appreciate the academic, economic, social, and spiritual significance of their role as teachers and to dismiss the conventional perception. Loving, owning, and identifying teaching with Jesus, the Master Teacher, boosts their morale and commitment and brings joy and empowerment to the classroom in favor of authentic character development rooted in CCE.

Biblical Integration. The CCE facilitated by Edify seeks to train and encourage teachers to receive teaching as a mission and bring biblical knowledge to the classroom in its most natural form. This, however, does not mean Christian teachers should stop teaching academic subjects and give evangelical sermons in the classroom. On the contrary, Christian teachers are trained to do both with excellence. They are encouraged to teach mathematics, physics, chemistry, biology, history, English, arts, business, and other topics with academic vigor, discipline, and standards to enhance the students' understanding and knowledge of the topics studied.

At the same time, teachers are trained to go beyond the secular way of delivering their teaching and skillfully and deliberately plan to provide biblical perspectives in all the subjects they teach: "To recognize their role as a calling with the purpose of preparing students for works of service."[25] Seeing academic subjects from a biblical worldview and demonstrating to the students how these reveal the character and nature of God, creation, humankind, moral order, and purpose is tantamount to biblical integration. This will broaden the content and basis of learning. Taught from a biblical perspective, mathematics and science become clearer and more interesting and exciting. Biblical integration enables the students to think biblically and critically, and it serves as a powerful way of knowing that God is truth and the source of all knowledge. The students' perspective and understanding, therefore, widen, enabling them to excel in their academic performance and character development.

But this is easier said than done. For Christian teachers to effectively facilitate biblical integration into the academic subjects they teach, they not only need to be deliberate and intentional but also equipped with biblical wisdom, knowledge, and understanding. Christian teachers can give to others only what they have. Little or no biblical knowledge and understanding means poor or no biblical integration.

They are therefore trained on how to integrate Christ-centered worldviews in the various academic subjects they teach by identifying principles, truths, and Bible verses, and they are provided with guidance and the tools to do so. They are also encouraged to study the Bible to deepen their own knowledge and spiritual transformation as part of the CCE program.

Effective integration of a Christ-centered worldview requires more than tools and biblical knowledge. It also requires intentionality and planning. The teachers have to be deliberate about biblical integration and plan to do it.

To achieve this, teachers are not only trained to develop daily lesson plans but also encouraged to be intentional and prepared to do biblical integration. They are trained and encouraged to prepare biblical verses and stories as part of their lesson plans that are appropriate to the themes they teach in the class. In other words, the daily lesson plans are expected to show how the Christ-centered worldview will be reflected in the subjects they teach.

For example, when children are taught math in grade one, they are shown only how to write the number one. They are also taught there is only one God and there is no one apart Him. They are taught in the beginning God created one man and one woman.

In teaching subtraction, the story of how Gideon defeated the Midianites in Judges 7 could be told. Gideon had at first 32,000 fighters, then 10,000, and finally only 300. The principle that victory comes from God, no matter the number of soldiers involved, is then drawn and shared with the students as they also learn subtraction.[26]

In teaching science, both the creation account in Genesis 1 and Psalm 139:13 could be referenced: "For you created my innermost being; you knit me together in my mother's womb" (NIV). The purpose is that while children are taught about secular theory of evolution, they are also taught what the Bible teaches: God created the universe and we have been created in His image and designed to multiply and fill the earth.

Managing Discipline. "Discipline is not punishment and should never be confused as such. It is order, training, relational, and life-changing if it is understood as discipleship."[27] Conventionally, most people, including Christian educators, identify discipline with punishment, which often occurs when established school rules are not followed. Children who comply are rewarded, and those who disobey are punished. This is a mechanistic view of managing discipline by externally imposed means and has nothing to do with organically induced inner change. Hence, it's bound to be superficial and temporal as anyone could choose to play by the rules to avoid punishment and get the promised rewards. This kind of discipline doesn't go beyond the classroom and the school.

Authentic discipline is about discipling, teaching, and molding children, and it relates to inner change and how they behave inside and outside the classroom. And this occurs when children are taught, related to, and discipled within the framework of a Christ-centered worldview that is rooted in love and mutual respect with no biases related to power, wealth, gender, race, or age.

Teachers are trained to recognize the role of discipline as an all-time ingredient in excellence and how to manage it in the classroom on the basis of biblical instructions. They are taught to embrace discipline as self-control and as a form of discipleship, using any discipline issues as opportunities for learning and not for just punishing. Focusing on the negative behavior embarrasses and discourages the children, and focusing on the positive behavior teaches acceptable behavior and helps children become Godly individuals. They are taught to handle the effort of enhancing self-control in such a way, so it doesn't turn into making people docile and negatively submissive. When they address discipline problems, they are encouraged to identify causes and use dialogue as a means of restoring discipline. In this way, children keep discipline, not because of the fear of teachers, authorities, and rules, but because of their own conviction as a result of the heart change they have undergone. As teachers practice this mode of disciplining students, they inculcate a culture that goes beyond the school premises with long-term impact on society at large.

Another tool teachers are trained to develop and use in keeping class discipline is lesson planning. With good lesson planning, lessons or practices flow steadily and students are kept busy in the classroom and will have little or no chance of making noises while a class is in session. This helps the students to concentrate, listen, and learn better. On the contrary, poor lesson planning creates gaps and pauses that allow students to talk to their classmates and lose concentration.

Participating in Faith Activities at School. In addition to the knowledge transfer through biblical integration, teachers are also trained in how to do evangelism among children and how to form student clubs to facilitate CCE by actively participating in faith activities that take place outside the classroom. These include:

- Running regular teachers' prayer and devotions.
- Having regular teachers' fellowships/retreats.
- Praying for students generally and individually as necessary.
- Participating in student devotions and fellowships as necessary.
- Helping students form discipleship clubs through which they undertake Bible studies.
- Participating in students' outreach planning and implementation within and outside school.
- Giving support and feedback to students when they undertake Christ-centered activities.

Living the Faith. As William O'Brien said, "The success of an intervention depends on the interior condition of the intervenor." Biblical integration in the classroom and participating in school-based, Christ-centered activities are necessary components of CCE, but they are not sufficient. Students don't learn only from the theoretical and experiential knowledge that teachers deliver through lectures, supervision, and assessments. They also learn from the teachers' overall character and attitudes and their practical engagement in school-based, faith activities. How the teachers present themselves and how they are as teachers and as human beings are other important sources of CCE. As stated by Donavan Graham, "Christian educating and teaching redemptively require us to create an atmosphere of grace in which our students can breathe the life-giving air of the gospel. We must engage in the educational process in a way that demonstrates *living* the gospel, not just *talking* about it."[28] In this regard, being is teaching in itself. "Imitate me, just as I also imitate Christ," said Paul (1 Corinthians 11:1).

In most instances, learning by imitation tends to be more powerful than the knowledge imputed orally or in writing. The students hear their teachers saying, and they see them doing. The former is abstract and the latter visual. Learning by imitation, that is, internalizing what they see and observe, tends to be more powerful than learning by hearing. Particularly so when the saying and doing contradict each other, in other words, when the teachers fail to "walk the talk."

It is easier to lecture than to present oneself as a good example. The Christian teacher prepares their lesson and controls what is offered to students. In normal conditions, it would be right to assume that they have learned what has been delivered. On the contrary, the Christian teacher can neither guarantee nor guess what aspects of their character have been imitated by the students. This forms the unspoken form of teaching and is often determined by the interior condition of the teacher.

The being aspect of the Christian teacher demands that they display Godly character at all times. They are expected to live the faith and present themself as "salt and light" among the students so what they see and learn is in line with the principles of Jesus. Most critical is that the students should be able to witness and experience Christian teachers who are deeply Christ-centered and driven by the greatest commandment: love.

To achieve this and enhance CCE effectively, teachers are trained to display qualities that inspire, encourage, free, and empower children to make them feel they are respected, valued, and contributing members of the school system. Some of the qualities that teachers are trained and encouraged to practice include the following:

- *Giving attention.* Students need to feel their teachers pay attention to what they think, say, do, and feel. They need to be noticed. They need to feel cared for. When they are sad, they need to be counseled. When they are sick, they need to be visited, and when they succeed, they need to be celebrated. When they need help with their work, they need to be assisted. When they receive their teachers' attention, students find joy in learning, and they will perform better and attention to others.
- *Every child is special.* Students have different talents, gifts, challenges, and temperaments. While caring for and paying attention to the general student body as a whole is key to student-centered learning, teachers need to recognize every child is special and has special needs and needs special attention and care. Teachers learn that distinguishing the different conditions and levels of learning among students

and adapting teaching approaches and working with them accordingly will bring the best out of students.

- *Appreciation.* Students thrive when anything they do or say, small as well as big things, is appreciated by their teachers. Telling a child, "Yes, you can," speaks greatly in how that child sees themselves. They feel uplifted. As they grow in a culture of being valued and appreciated, they will recognize and appreciate and uplift others.

- *Forgiving.* Like anyone else, students make mistakes and do wrong things that might cause disappointment and anger among teachers. In such instances, teachers should do two things: express bold love by firmly and constructively confronting the problems and by forgiving students for any wrongdoing. Forgiveness releases while non-forgiveness binds. The students feel loved when they are forgiven. By exercising forgiveness, teachers create the culture of bold love accompanied by logic in the minds of students, which they will apply in the next generation as a form of conflict resolution.

- *Integrity.* This is "walking the talk," i.e., keeping promises. Students feel loved when teachers are honest with them and keep their promises. This includes keeping time in class and giving feedback. This makes them feel respected and loved.

- *Giving the best.* This is about the efforts, including lesson planning and preparation, teachers make to deliver quality education. When students see their teachers want what's best for them, they feel worthy and loved. They then share what they have experienced with others. Students who see hardworking and diligent teachers are likely to become like them.

- *Conflict resolution.* This is the time to address any relationship and behavioral issues among students in the classroom through constructive discussion and mutual understanding— not through unexplained, physical, or other forms of punishment.
- *Non-threatening environment.* This is about releasing and freeing students by creating a non-threatening learning environment. Students thrive, learn, and perform better when they feel confident about thinking freely, taking initiatives, expressing curiosity, daring to make mistakes without being threatened, and knowing their teachers are approachable and friendly. Teaching in a non-threatening environment is a powerful means of enhancing critical thinking.

Discipleship clubs/student fellowships. To strengthen their faith and spiritual transformation, students are also encouraged and supported to form Bible fellowship/discipleship clubs in their schools and undertake Christlike activities. Such activities help the students to increase their biblical knowledge, worship, and prayer culture and to undertake outreach activities both within and outside their schools. With the help of trained teachers, students establish and run effective, student-led discipleship clubs. They are also equipped to do outreach activities, sharing the love of Christ in word and deed, among students within their schools (peer evangelism), people in the communities, students in other schools, and their respective families. Connections are also made with Christian youth organizations such as Campus Crusade, CEF, Scripture Union, Awana, etc. Moreover, they are encouraged to actively participate in their churches and other Christian youth groups.

Moreover, youth leadership training camps are organized one or two times a year for three to five days whereby student leaders are trained in biblical skills, leadership skills, networking skills, and evangelism. Many give their lives to Christ at these events.

Distribution of Christian Literature. In addition to the actual training activities, Edify also facilitates the distribution of Bibles and other relevant Christian learning materials in schools to strengthen the CCE program. Christian literature is in short supply, particularly in Muslim countries, as both students and schools cannot afford to meet the demand.

How Edify Implements Its CCE Program

This section describes the way Edify facilitates the implementation of its CCE program in relation to the roles of training partners and Christian transformation and training officers deployed by Edify.

Partnership with training partners. In consistence with its principle of avoiding duplications, and ensuring good stewardship, Edify implements its CCE program in partnership with like-minded local and international Christian training organizations. Edify believes this is also good practice in strengthening local capacities and maximizing resources.

In the Dominican Republic, Edify partners with AMO and APRENDI.[29] In Peru the partnership is with Desarrollo Cristiano Del Peru (Christian Development of Peru).[30] In Guatemala we partner with John Maxwell Foundation. In Ghana we partner with Awana and Biblica.[31] In Burkina Faso we partner with AEAD and ACSI.[32] In Liberia, the partnership is with Awana and CLA.[33] In Sierra Leone we partner with Awana and ADI.[34] In Ethiopia we partner with ISTM, EVASUE, and MALD.[35] In India the partners include CSI and DAI.[36]

The trainers provide the literature and facilitators needed for the actual training and for the post-training implementation. The training of proprietors and teachers takes place mainly in venues outside the schools that are modest in terms of costs. These could be low-cost hotels, community halls, church halls, or school halls. On-site training also happens within the schools themselves. Although schools are expected to contribute to the cost of training, Edify covers most of the expenses incurred (food, facilitation fees, training materials, facilities, travel expenses, etc.).

The Role of Christian Training and Transformation Officers (CTTOs). In each program country, Edify employs one or more (depending on size) CTTOs who plan, organize, coordinate, implement, monitor, and report on the training activities funded and supported by it. They develop annual training plans by working hand in hand with school owners. This is the first and most important role of the CTTOs.

The other important role of the CTTOs relates to finding like-minded, local Christian training organizations to undertake the training activities. They then organize visits to schools for the training organizations to have an exposure to the environment and needs and potential of the proprietors.

In the early years of the training program, the common practice followed by the CTTOs in conducting training activities went as follows: prior to each training event, the CTTOs would send out invitations to proprietors to select and send trainees to attend; find suitable and reasonably priced training venues; and organize training materials and handouts in collaboration with the training organizations.

Over the years, this approach has not always been effective as some of the candidates were selected on an ad hoc basis and failed to demonstrate compatibility with the content and purpose of the training in regard to passion, qualification, and commitment. The basis the proprietors used for identifying potential trainees was inadequate as there was little or unclear communication regarding content, relevance, and purpose.

To rectify the past, the CTTOs are currently encouraged to actively engage the proprietors in terms of designing the specific trainings and to discuss the training outline with them prior to inviting them to ensure they understand the training. Many schools do this through School Transformation Committees (STCs), which are composed of stakeholder representatives under the leadership of school proprietors. In most schools where there are STCs, the membership consists of the proprietor, school leaders, teachers, finance personnel, students, and in some cases even parents. The purpose is to shift the responsibility of transformation (CCE) from the school owner to a wider circle of stakeholders to ensure that the goal of transformation is owned and implemented by all concerned—so it is not treated as the responsibility of the school owner alone. The STCs recruit trainees and plan, coordinate, and evaluate training activities within the schools and ensure that transformation is facilitated as a whole school business. This process also ensures the trainings are demand-driven and not supply-driven. The proprietors then are enabled not only to select the right trainees but also to send them with defined expectations.

During the training, the CTTOs make sure logistics are satisfactory, the needs of both the trainees and trainers are met, and participants are punctual at all times so as to maintain a high level of attendance, participation, and learning. They also must prepare evaluation forms and ensure workshops are properly evaluated by the participants before they are concluded. Another important task the CTTOs do in conjunction with the training organizations relates to the facilitation of developing action plans. The participants draw up actions plans that they are expected to discuss with their school leaderships and implement on their return to their respective schools.

During the post-training stage, the CTTOs visit schools together with the facilitators of the training organizations or on their own to follow up on whether or not the trained leaders and teachers have been applying the newly acquired tools and skills, to strengthen them if they have, and help them start if they have not done so. This is an important role because during this stage the CTTOs perform their mentoring, coaching, praying, and encouraging roles, which involves dialogue, probing, informing, interacting, listening, empathy, and mutual learning and growing. The CTTOs document their lessons, including transformation stories, and share with the wider Edify community. The CTTOs also help with the facilitation of the formation and effective functioning of discipleship clubs in the schools and organize youth leadership training camps in partnership with training partners and trained teachers.

Moreover, not only do they ensure that relevant training materials and Christian literature such as the Bible are distributed in schools for use by teachers and students, but they also monitor that they are effectively utilized.

They do all this to ensure the trainees are not only receiving knowledge and skills but also translating what they have learned into practice and thereby enhancing a Christ-centered education in the schools as they are trained.

In short, the CTTOs encourage and support schools to:

- Expose students to the Word of God. In this case, the CTTOs encourage schools to develop a culture of practicing devotion with a comprehensive roster for worship, Bible teaching, and praying on the one hand, and establishing and operating effective discipleship clubs on the other. These activities are facilitated by trained teachers with the aim to be run by the students themselves in the long run. To ensure these are effectively undertaken, the CTTOs ask follow-up questions such as: Are worship topics listed on your roster? Does the roster show the names of trained teachers participating? Can you name the students who have been trained to lead worship? What memory verse was assigned the previous week? Does the school have a discipleship club? If so, what is the membership like and how frequently does it meet per month? Is there evidence of the meeting?
- Encourage Christlike behavior to mold future leaders who do justice, love mercy, and walk humbly with God. In this case, the CTTOs encourage schools to engage students in outreach activities whereby the children go out and do community service both in word (sharing the gospel in other schools and neighborhoods) and deed (participating in community activities, such as cleaning, visiting/helping orphanages, making donations to the poor, etc.) The follow-up questions

asked by the CTTOs in this regard include: Does the school show there is a list of Christlike behaviors to encourage in children? Does the school formally recognize students for Christlike behavior? How often does the school recognize Christlike behavior? Does the school engage students in community service? How often do students engage in community service?

Summary

This chapter attempted to present the nature of training supported by Edify as one of the core pillars of its program by referring to business and leadership training, technology training, and Christ-centered training. The discussion covered the rationale and modalities, the social targets, and the implementers of the various trainings in varying degrees.

Unsurprisingly, more emphasis has been given to the inter-relationship between education and character development both in historical and contemporary contexts. Whether in its formal or non-formal nature, education has had the undeniable goal of making better people, which has been identified with character formation.

But education is value-based, and this makes a difference in the nature of the character being developed. Until the Enlightenment in the seventeenth and eighteenth centuries and the rise of Marxism and Darwinism in the nineteenth century, people believed morality and character formation went hand in hand and practiced accordingly.

Postmodernism brought separation between the secular and the sacred, creating two worldviews: Christ-centered and human-centered. Although there is a general recognition that character education should be value-based, there is disagreement regarding whose value should be the basis. Character education given in schools today is therefore rooted in either secular or Christ-centered values.

Edify espouses a Christ-centered education (CCE) rooted in a Christ-centered worldview because this paradigm puts God at the center and is instructed by biblical principles, norms, truths, and core beliefs. Whereas character education that is rooted in secular worldview relies on human reason, rules, and standards and refers to external character traits, CCE seeks to bring about holistic, inside-out heart change that results from faith in Christ Jesus and a commitment to live transformed lives under God's ordinances. CCE produces authentic character development that is deep and lasting, timeless, and universal with Jesus as the ultimate role model.

Teachers constitute the prime vehicle for effective facilitation of CCE in the schools as they hold the keys to what happens in the classroom. The quality and impact of CCE on character formation among students is therefore critically dependent on the knowledge, skills, and commitment of teachers. The more spiritually transformed and committed they are to implementing CCE, the more effectively they will be able to diffuse transformation that brings authentic character development. This is a necessary condition, but it is not sufficient. They can do this only if CCE is part of the vision and mission of the school proprietors to which they are committed. Hence, this explains the focus of CCE training on equipping proprietors and teachers.

When proprietors are committed to CCE and teachers are properly equipped with the skills, aids, and tools to do biblical integration and bring a Christ-centered worldview to the classroom, form and participate in student spiritual activities in and outside schools, and relate with and teach students with care, attention, appreciation, love, and forgiveness, a fertile ground for the promotion of authentic character development is created. This way, LFIS are enabled to produce transformed future leaders who will do justice, love mercy, and walk humbly with God and build flourishing Godly nations as unto the Lord.

5

TECHNOLOGY AND EDUCATION

In this chapter, the discussion will focus on the role of using information and communications technology (ICT) to support learning in general as well as Edify's support to boost the ability of low-fee independent schools to create an environment that is conducive to enhanced teaching and learning. The aim is delivering quality education, building lifelong educational skills, and producing greater employability of students.

The chapter is divided into two parts. The first part provides an introductory overview of the general global scenario of education technologies. The second part deals with education technology in low-fee independent schools and the related role of Edify.

Global Perspective: An Overview

"The combination of education and technology has been considered the main key to human progress. Education feeds technology, which in turn forms the basis for education."[1] We view this comment as relevant to preparing students for employment in the twenty-first-century knowledge economy.

According to UNESCO:

> Education and technology can and should co-evolve in
> mutually supportive ways. While people tend to think of
> education as perpetually lagging behind technology, there
> are numerous instances in which education has prompted
> technical innovation. . . . Education can also dictate hardware
> design choices. . . . Many in the education community are
> working to ensure that changes in technology push pedagogy
> forward and conversely that innovations in pedagogy
> influence technology.[2]

Following the ICT revolution during the last two decades, the
world has seen a phenomenal transformation in education technology both in variety and complexity. Today, it is estimated that
more than two billion people have access to the internet and five
billion have mobile phones. ICTs are "a diverse set of technological tools and resources used to communicate, and to create,
disseminate, store, and manage information and consist of computers, the internet, broadcasting technologies (radio and television)
and telephony."[3]

More importantly, large numbers of young people in both
developed and developing countries and among poor and rich
social groups are in possession of mobile devices. The number is
even larger in developing countries. "Mobile phone technology in
developing countries now accounts for four out of every five connections worldwide. In a recent report by the GSMA into m-learn-
ing, more than half of all young people surveyed in Ghana, India,
Uganda, and Morocco who had accessed the internet, had done
so on a mobile device."[4] Although they were originally marketed

mainly as communication and entertainment devices, mobile technologies have come to play a significant role in economies and society at large.[5]

Charles Kenny, a senior fellow at the Centre for Global Development, suggests: "This [mobile] technology wasn't developed as a development tool yet has become one of the greatest vehicles for change. Young people are natural adopters of new technologies and certainly the potential for technology and digital media to be a force for innovation, education and change is just beginning to be realized."[6]

According to Jhuree, the nations of the world have recognized the pivotal role that ICT plays in enhancing education through the improvement of teaching and learning:

> It is no longer a question of if technology should be integrated in the school setting, but a question of when and how to integrate technology so that it benefits all the parties concerned—students, teachers, administrators, parents and the community. Countries that fail to recognize and act according to the trends in new content and new methodologies in education and training may find it very hard to compete in the global economy.[7]

In a concerted effort to achieve the Education for All (EFA) and MDG goals, multilateral and bilateral donors, national governments, NGOs, and the private sector as well as educational and research establishments have invested not only in using available mobile technologies but also in constantly innovating newer and better devices for facilitating technology-enhanced learning.

During the early 2010s, for example, the focus was on deploying low-cost laptops. While that is still important, emphasis now seems to have shifted to the use of tablets or simple e-book readers and e-tablets and Smartphones in developing and developed countries.[8]

UNESCO defines mobile devices as consisting of "any portable, connected technology, such as basic mobile phone, e-readers, smartphones and tablet computers, as well as embedded technologies like smartcard readers."[9]

In pushing this global effort forward, UNESCO has been implementing several pilot projects that have attempted to use mobile learning technologies in partnership with prominent technology leaders, such as Nokia, Microsoft, and other international and national players, and these are increasingly being scaled and replicated. The increasingly growing application of ICT devices in education seems to have changed the landscape of learning both inside and outside schools. UNESCO predicts the next ten to fifteen years will see an even greater transformation in the mobile learning movement. Some of the technological advances that will impact mobile learning in the future include the following:[10]

- Technology will be more accessible, affordable, and functional.
- Devices will be able to collect, synthesize, and analyze massive amounts of data.
- New types of data will be available.
- Language barriers will be broken down.
- Screen size limitation will disappear.
- Energy sources and power capacity will improve.

The internet is currently expensive, but some mobile phone and internet providers are starting to give discount rates or even free air plus internet time for schools and education content. Forward-looking governments will encourage carriers to provide internet connectivity.

One important factor that will contribute to the ever-increasing development and use of ICT devices is the rise in corporate and government investment in education and e-learning technology.

Groupe Speciale Mobile Association, for example, estimates that expenditures for mobile learning will rise from US $3.4 billion in 2011 to US $70 billion in 2020.[11] By 2030, global expenditure in education in developing markets will fuel a massive expansion as technology drives unprecedented re-skilling and up-skilling in developed economies.[12]

Equipping schools and universities and keeping them up to date with ICT equipment and building the necessary infrastructures is an expensive business.[13] The huge volume of capital and the advanced nature of technology involved in developing ICTs for education in schools means that developing countries, particularly low-income countries, will find running the race financially and technically difficult. This is likely to widen the already existing digital divide.

Hulegaard says, "The main population that lies on this side of the [digital] divide are the poor."[14] The main reasons for the digital divide, which is defined by Molinari as "the gap between individuals and communities that have access to information technologies and those that don't," include: lack of access due to affordability, lack of knowledge on how to use the technology, and lack of knowledge of the benefits of the technology.[15]

In the context of the "information economy," the absence of access to computers threatens to leave the vast majority of Africans behind. Without training to use the internet to conduct business and engage in lifelong learning, Africans are likely to be left behind by the economic and digital divide. World statistics of internet users for the first quarter of 2020 showed that only 11.5 percent of Africans used the internet compared to over 50 percent in Asia.[16] Africans without computer skills will be relegated to menial jobs and be the labor force for advanced economies that capitalize on the knowledge economy. This problem is likely to be exacerbated in the future given the rapid population growth in Africa unless drastic measures, such as the digital economic initiative for Africa (DE4A) launched in support of the African Union "Digital Transformation Strategy for Africa" with the $25 billion support of the World Bank, are taken and effectively implemented to counteract the trend.[17] The problem will be further exacerbated as robotics and other technologies reduce the need for menial labor.

If children in African schools and other emerging regions are not taught to use technology, there will be massive unemployment coupled with rapidly growing populations. This could be a breeding ground for civil unrest and terrorist groups.

Why Edify Invests in Education Technology

Like UNESCO and other promoters of global education, including donors and national governments, Edify believes ICT can constitute a pivotal tool in the enhancement of education through improved teaching and learning. Edify has, therefore, plans to grow its investment in ICT at schools in the years to come.

As in all cases, Edify's investment in ICT is demand-driven because LFIS ask for them as part of their strategic plan to provide quality education, and parents value ICT as a necessary educational tool for their children. Chris Crane recalls during his visit in Ghana how a parent-teacher association (PTA) member in a remote village told him the PTA had accessed parents the equivalent of $10 for each child enrolled to equip a computer lab for their children to learn computer skills. The parent said, "It is a computer world. If we don't make a computer lab available, our children will be left behind."[18]

Below are some of the reasons why Edify helps LFIS set up computer labs and promote education technology.

Education technology could enhance quality learning. One of the obvious key factors that determines the quality of education is the availability and quality of learning materials, including books. The more access students have to books, especially culturally relevant books, the more frequently they read, which results in improvements in literacy and overall learning enhancement.

In developing countries in general, and Africa in particular, education suffers partly because the availability and quality of books are inadequate. Particularly in rural areas, books are in short supply and in poor quality. In most cases, if there are books—and often there are not—they are out of date and not contextually relevant.

Many developing countries are "book poor." Children who cannot read forty words per minute by age nine risk being behind peers for their lifetimes. Thus, without books many will be left behind. The good news, however, is that developing countries are "mobile rich." Internet connectivity is widely available, however, often expensive. But costs are likely to decline greatly going forward.

Access to learning materials is no longer dependent only on the availability of printed books and libraries. A lightweight, handheld reading device can contain 20,000 books—many free—and other educational reading materials. Books published more than seventy-five years ago, including many dossiers, are available from various online sources for free since the copyrights have expired.

As books, local textbooks, and storybooks are increasingly being digitized by publishers and distributors, future learning materials are likely to be more available via ICTs than libraries and printed forms. Amazon, for example, claims to sell more Kindle books than printed books. Although digital books often have to be scrutinized and adapted to contextual conditions and standards, more varieties of inexpensive or free books are also increasingly becoming available on the internet.[19]

Students will increasingly have easier access to internet devices than to libraries and books. The likelihood is they will increasingly download materials (educational or others) and read on their mobile phones or internet cafés or school computer labs rather than in libraries. In this regard, handheld devices, such as Amazon's Kindle and other inexpensive e-tablets, have constituted the latest technology for books in digital form to be viewed and read by users. According to David Risher, the cofounder and President of Worldreader:

> The need is urgent. The world is in the midst of a global learning crisis. 53 percent of children in low- and middle-income countries cannot read and understand a simple story by the end of primary school. The Covid-19 pandemic has worsened educational inequalities worldwide. As the leading

digital reading specialist, Worldreader works with partners to address this crisis by bringing digital books to millions of children and youth.[20]

Mr. Risher further elaborates:

At a very basic level, having an e-reader is equivalent to having a set of books at hand. This represents an enormous improvement over the status quo, where access to books is extremely limited: Botswana, a country the geographic size of France, has fewer than 10 bookstores, and the village library of Kade with a population of 17,000 inhabitants in Kwaebibirem District, Eastern Region, Ghana, is nearly empty of books. Imagine for a moment the power represented by e-readers: Students can walk around holding a library of books larger than all those in the bookstores and libraries of their country. . . . The e-reader satisfies an important core need, providing access to the books of the world at a moment's notice. And it does so in a way that's accessible to both students and teachers, strengthening the bonds between them rather than disrupting their relationship.[21]

The use of e-readers can support and encourage general reading and literacy skills. In Kenya and Ghana, for example, the use of e-books showed that children spent up to 50 percent more time reading than before the introduction of e-readers and their reading fluency scores increased quickly.[22]

In addition to reading, students also use their mobile devices for texting education messages. For example, UNICEF's recent study in Zambia, South Africa, and Vietnam found that 40 percent of Vietnamese children surveyed in rural areas used the internet for educational purposes, with 34 percent sending school-related text messages. In urban areas this spiked to 62 percent and 57 percent, respectively.[23] English is the language of ICT. As they read and text using mobile devices, students improve their literacy and writing skills, thereby improving their overall English language skills, which is important for employability and lifelong learning. As most of the academic subjects are taught in English, students who improve their English are also likely to see an overall improvement in their academic performance.[24]

Edify believes education technology is also likely to motivate students to engage and take ownership of their learning experiences because technology allows for these experiences to become more exciting, interesting, stimulating, empowering, visual, interactive, and creative, thereby resulting in improving student attention, participation, and desire to learn. A Worldreader staff member in Ghana told Chris Crane the children, especially boys, find it "cool" to read from an e-reader, as compared to a printed book. Greater digital reading could improve the quality of education. Class attendance, academic performance, pass rates, and opportunities for further education are also likely to improve:

> ICTs such as videos, television and multimedia computer software that combine text, sound, and colorful, moving images can be used to provide challenging and authentic content that will engage the student in the learning process. Interactive radio likewise makes use of sound effects, songs, dramatizations, comic skits, and other performance conventions to compel the students to listen and become

involved in the lessons being delivered. More so than any other type of ICT, networked computers with internet connectivity can increase learner motivation as it combines the media richness and interactivity of other ICTs with the opportunity to connect with real people and to participate in real world events.[25]

Edify is also aware that numerous education technology efforts have failed, yet some are succeeding. Having good hardware and software only gets a school to the starting block. A good ICT strategy, coupled with diligent implementation, is very important. A proprietor who vigorously encourages full usage of education technology and commits to their teachers' ongoing professional development is crucial.

Education technology could enhance quality teaching. As in the case of students, education technology also makes the availability of information, books, and teaching materials easier, faster, and cheaper for teachers. This means teachers get more sources for broadening their general and subject knowledge and preparing their lessons from wider perspectives. It also provides opportunity for teachers to communicate with students in times of "shelter at home" when internet connectivity is available.

The use of education technology by trained teachers also helps them prepare lessons and design materials more easily. They can also keep up-to-date student and academic data, which they can access and update anytime and anywhere. Education technology also helps teachers produce more accurate and higher quality student reports. Education technology can serve as a useful tool "in handling a number of the administrative tasks both by teachers (e.g., lesson planning, preparing handouts, recording of student results, student record keeping, etc.) and administrators (computation of school performance, keeping records of employees, preparation of school budget, etc.)."[26]

Education technology could also serve as an effective medium for sharing ideas and working on projects collaboratively. As Luis Osin states, "Today, when a major effort is being invested in the transformation of the classroom, moving away from frontal, expository, didactic presentations to environments where learners are active discoverers and builders of knowledge, the computer is the tool with the potential to help in reaching these goals."[27]

In this regard, Edify connected three different low-fee independent schools (Agape School Complex, The Flobar Academy, and Leading Light Academy) in Ghana with Valley Christian School (VCS), one of the top Christian schools with successful achievement in character formation in the US, to tutor each other and complete projects together with the aim to promote mutual learning and Jesus-centered transformation using the internet.[28] This pilot project arranged regular communication between the three principals at VCS with principals in the three schools in Ghana. They also did the same for two teachers and students from each of the Ghana schools with their respective counterparts at VCS. They all connected via internet and video conferencing to interact and exchange views, information, education materials, experience, teaching, and integration skills to enhance mutual learning and professionalism as well as biblical integration. Despite internet connection problems, busy schedules, differences in time zones and school holiday cycles, etc., the principals were able to share information that the schools in Ghana found extremely helpful, such as better classroom management techniques and new ways to think about biblical integration in teaching and learning. Although the arrangement is informal and the communication rather sporadic, VCS and the three schools still continue to relate and exchange experiences.

Bringing technology into the classroom does not reduce the need for good teachers. Rather, education technology helps teachers move away from teacher-centric to learner-centric practices. In other words, education technology does not replace teachers but supplements teachers' instruction in classrooms and likely makes teaching easier and relatively more motivating to learners. Speaking of the learning devices applied by Innovation for Learning Foundation, Seth Weinberger, the founder and executive director, made the following statement:

> The school of the future is not going to look that different fifty years from now. There will still be a teacher in the classroom helping the kids learning. It is going to be a change of the tools that the teachers use. These teachers want to do good. That is why they are teaching and when they see the success and they come to me and they say this kid learned because of what we did, it is a win for technology, it is a win for that kid but, most of all you have enabled this teacher to succeed in her vision and her dreams and that is incredibly powerful.[29]

Memorizing thousands and thousands of facts, most of which will be forgotten soon after the test, is not preparing children for the future. Rather, knowing which facts should be memorized, and where to find the rest, and then understanding how to use their knowledge to analyze, synthesize, collaborate, produce, and create with the facts is crucial for the twenty-first-century economy.

Education technology could enhance life skills. Edify believes that as students access information through education technology outside and inside the classroom setting, they become more exposed and knowledgeable of local, national, and global issues. This is likely to enhance their engagement in civic affairs and processes and prepare them to become capable citizens.

Moreover, the use of education technology enables students to improve their English, share knowledge, strengthen communication, and improve coordination and team skills as well as self-responsibility, which are necessary for employability and success in the workplace. In a labor market where computer knowledge and skills are increasingly becoming ubiquitous, the acquisition of basic computer skills places students in a more competitive position.[30] ICT competence is a modern-day passport to employment.

ICT also enables youth to be better informed of global and national developments and to engage in social movements and participate in bringing about social change. Taking such responsibilities develops civic competencies among youth. CDI, a network of 800-plus schools, uses technology as a medium to fight poverty and stimulate entrepreneurship, thus creating a generation of change-makers in thirteen countries.[31] According to CDI:

> [The most important thing] is not the technology skills; it is using those skills to awaken the critical understanding, the critical consciousness that you can transform your life. . . . We were under the illusion that we were powerless to change things; that collective mind-set is dramatically changing. Empowered by internet technology, especially social media, people around the world are rejecting repressive

governments and policies and choosing a more inclusive way to live together.[32]

Education technology could enhance global competitiveness. In the increasingly globalized economy, Edify also believes that not only could computer skills enable graduates to become more competitive in the global labor market, but also help develop a vibrant ICT ecosystem in their own countries. Developing economies that are run and operated with a work force that is computer competent are likely to have higher productivity in the global information-based and knowledge-based economy and capitalize on the intellectual skills of their citizens leading to increased wealth creation.[33]

In other words, Edify not only invests in education technology because it could benefit low-fee independent schools and their graduates individually, but also because such an investment is likely to bring benefits to whole nations and communities through improved efficiency, productivity, and competitiveness. In their report, *Transformation-Ready: The Strategic Application of Information and Communication Technologies in Africa*, which was prepared for the African Development Bank, the World Bank, and the African Union, Lishan Adam et al. state, "Governments of developing countries see it [education technology] as necessary to build more knowledge-based societies not only to improve the efficiency of domestic economies but also to take advantage of economic opportunities outside their own borders."[34]

ICTs also make education institutions themselves more attractive in the market related to the peer schools. In the words of Lishan Adam et al.: "Investment in ICT is being seen by education institutions as a necessary part of establishing their competitive advantage, because it is attractive (particularly in those parts of the world where young people have near-ubiquitous access to ICT) and because it is deemed essential by governments, parents, employers and funders of higher education."[35]

Referring to the impact of changes in educational innovations, Lewins states: "In many educational systems in developing countries, the losers in the change process are those clients on the margins of the existing system. Rural children and teachers in isolated, under-resourced, and neglected schools, with many unqualified teachers and little access to information, are those least prepared for the change."[36]

Because of their geographic and economic positioning, many LFIS are the potential "losers." Edify's investment is likely to make significant contributions to enable them to build their ICT capacity and attain a competitive edge to gainfully participate in the increasingly innovative changes taking place in the education world. Digital learning devices offer social justice in the form of equal opportunity to develop the computer skills of rural children. Technology also offers access to the rapidly increasing body of open-source, world-class education content. Despite the possibility that many well-educated children, when older, might leave for cities or go overseas, some are likely to remain in their villages and introduce much economic advancement opportunities to their fellow villagers.

Edify's Support to Education Technology

The previous section provided a description of the rationale for Edify's support to education technology. Edify not only supports ICTs because of the anticipated positive impact of computer-based delivery of education on learning and quality of education but also in response to the recognition of the value of and demand for ICTs by both the proprietors of low-fee independent and parents who educate their children through these schools.

Computer Labs

Outreach. The Edify CLASS project primarily provide access for students to acquire digital literacy skills and to promote STEM learning. Students move from learning about the theoretical aspects of ICT to gaining practical technology skills through the use of the computer lab.

Students develop their keyboarding skills, learn word processing, and computer-based research skills as they use the digital resources provided. Additionally, the software supports math skill development, English language learning, and science and computer coding. However, the computer labs accomplish multiple objectives. The proprietors have used them as a marketing tool for their schools, leading to increased popularity, enrollment, attendance, and retention. By offering access to computers outside school hours, they also become an additional revenue-generator.

Since 2011, Edify has worked with its lending partners to offer the CLASS Computer Lab product in Ghana, Burkina Faso, Liberia, and Rwanda. Although the education technology program supported by Edify is still growing in terms of coverage, computer labs have been installed in thirty-six different schools in Ghana, twenty in Liberia, ten in Rwanda, and seven in Burkina Faso, bringing the total to seventy-three computer labs as of February 2020.[37] In Liberia and Burkina Faso, two computer labs totaling sixty-two terminals running on solar generated energy were installed for two all-girls schools.

Composition and Structure. What do labs consist of and how are they structured? The computer labs deployed by Edify utilize a thin client model. The computer labs in all schools have a similar layout and consist of brand-new equipment and offer educational resources that students can use to learn digital skills, access educational resources to improve learning outcomes, and help them develop employable skills in the course of usage.

Using thin clients, the maintenance is minimized, and the longevity is maximized. Thin clients are low-cost, low-power, low-maintenance devices that provide the basic input/output functionality (keyboard, monitor, and mouse) and offload the processing to a central server. This design minimizes the maintenance required because if the server is functioning, then all the thin clients will be functioning as well. An additional benefit is that if the server is upgraded, the rest of the terminals benefit from that upgrade. Typically, a single server can run fifteen to twenty thin-client terminals and can take up to twenty terminals of thin clients. The lab therefore can be increased in such multiples to meet a class size. Because each terminal is not running a full computer, each terminal draws less power, which translates into a lower operating cost.

In the school context where computer labs have been deployed, a terminal, consisting of the thin-client device, a monitor, keyboard, and a mouse, is a more effective solution instead of laptops because two to three students commonly share a terminal and benefit from a larger screen size. Additionally, the hardware parts of the device, the keyboard and mouse, are more easily and economically replaced than a built-in keyboard and trackpad found in a laptop.

Acquisition and installation. The labs belong to the schools and are owned by individual proprietors. Edify provides the required loan through the implementing partners and technical assistance before, during, and after installation.

As a starting point, Edify conducted an exploratory study that entailed talking to proprietors, assessing their perspectives, and observing the types of technology they already had as well as talking to local suppliers and education officials. The early exploration indicated a widespread demand, and the computer labs solution suited the Ghanaian context since they were affordable and durable.

The next move is for the lending partner, Sinapi Aba Trust (SAT), to embrace this as a feasible SME product and design and promote it among school proprietors through flyers, site visits, training events, and one-on-one talks. During the process, Edify educational technology staff hold discussions with the proprietors to give them a proper understanding and appreciation of the costs and benefits of labs. This ensures the labs are demand-driven and have a full buy-in by the proprietors before they take the loan.

After a decision by the proprietors to invest in labs, they submit their loan applications to a Ghanaian microfinance lending institution (SAT). In appraising the loan applications, SAT applies two criteria: 1) the schools must demonstrate a good financial health expressed in a good financial record with a rate of sustainability to support its ability to repay the loan, and 2) the schools must show the availability of a secure separate room (space) for installing the labs and their commitment to provide the required administrative support. Upon fulfillment of these criteria, the loan is approved.

However, the loan is not given directly to the proprietors in cash. Following the tripartite agreements between the proprietors, lending partners, and Edify, the loan capital is used by the Edify technical support team for all the purchases and installation of the education technology with the involvement of all parties.

All the components of the labs are bought locally for various reasons:

- Edify believes in using locally available resources as part of its development philosophy. In this regard, using local suppliers and resources, even in the case of imported supplies, is more appropriate in terms of scalability, maintenance, and sustainability.
- Importing goods, such as computer hardware, often involves bureaucratic red tape, corruption, and costly delivery delays and frustrations.
- When shipping and importing expenses are considered, local prices may approximate prices in the United States.
- Delivery time is shortened, and a local vendor supports the purchase with warrantees.

Moreover, proprietors are encouraged to buy new computers and not used (secondhand) ones for two main reasons: 1) compared with new computers, used ones may be much cheaper per unit but far more expensive to run as maintenance costs are high due to frequent breakages that cause operational interruptions, pricy and scarce spare parts, high cost of technicians to do the repair, and a relatively shorter life, and 2) computer labs equipped with used computers are less attractive to parents and students and will not help low-fee independent schools to increase enrollment. Due to the high cost and little impact on the growth of enrollment of second-hand computers, proprietors will be unable to generate income sufficient to cover their expenses, let alone make profit. Calculations are made by Edify technical staff and presented to proprietors to help them make comparisons and choose the right option.

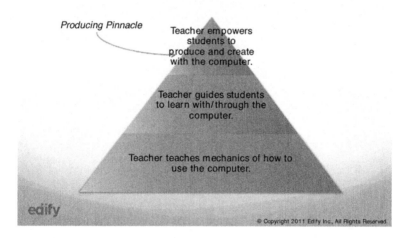

Computer Lab Hierarchy

Producing Pinnacle

Teacher empowers students to produce and create with the computer.

Teacher guides students to learn with/through the computer.

Teacher teaches mechanics of how to use the computer.

edify

This hierarchy represents the Teachers EdTech implementation process and explains the role of the computer lab in training teachers and how teachers impart computer skills among the students.

This explanation gives teachers the right understanding that integrating technology into the classroom is a growth process and sequential. And it all begins with them. Teachers are made to understand the tool (different parts of the computer system) and how aids the teaching and learning process. Teachers then guide students to learn with and through the computers. If this process is implemented effectively, students' scores not only increase but students are also empowered to find ways to use the computers effectively by themselves.

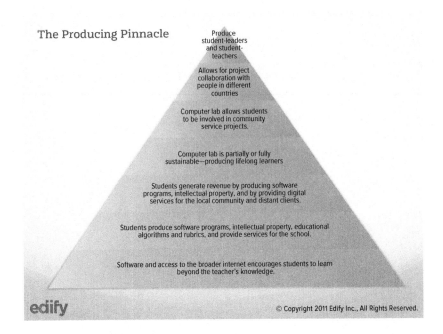

The Producing Pinnacle

Produce student-leaders and student-teachers

Allows for project collaboration with people in different countries

Computer lab allows students to be involved in community service projects.

Computer lab is partially or fully sustainable—producing lifelong learners

Students generate revenue by producing software programs, intellectual property, and by providing digital services for the local community and distant clients.

Students produce software programs, intellectual property, educational algorithms and rubrics, and provide services for the school.

Software and access to the broader internet encourages students to learn beyond the teacher's knowledge.

edify

Producing and collaborating is the fourth item in the EdTech Implementation plan for schools. With *access* being the first, followed by *integration, learning outcomes, producing, and collaboration.*

The producing pinnacle is a breakdown of the different growth stages students go through after using their technology devices for a certain period of time and have attained the fourth tier.

These two hierarchies guide our internal decision-making processes related to teachers' training support, proprietors' EdTech monitoring activities, students' EdTech activities, and the overall use of EdTech in schools that have acquired them. Using the pyramids, we not only are able to deal with the issues of accessibility but also make informed decisions on what content to create to maximize learning outcomes.

SMILE and SMILE-pi. The SMILE (Stanford University Mobile Inquiry-Based Learning Environment) software is an inquiry-based educational portal that champions 100-percent student participation in class and builds an interactive teaching and learning environment. The purpose of SMILE is to promote inquiring minds through explorative learning and the development of critical thinking skills and problem-solving activities. SMILE enables students to generate, share, and evaluate multimedia-rich inquiries. Students have the opportunity to ask all kinds of instructional-based questions, and as they do that, they begin to naturally form ideas from all aspects and develop a proactive learning attitude. The SMILE software creates a highly interactive learning environment that promotes higher order learning opportunities (e.g., creation of inquiries, presentation of questions, analysis of peer-generated questions, evaluation of individual students, and overall class performance); engage students in inquiry-based learning sessions at a global scale; and generate transparent, real-time learning analytics.

SMILE benefits. SMILE offers several benefits to students:

- Highly interactive learning environment
- Enhance learners to analyze and evaluate their own work
- Increased critical thinking and logical reasoning skills
- Problem solving skills development
- Generate, share, and discuss subject-based enquiries at the same level
- Can be used anytime for both personal and interactive level
- Peer-to-peer review and evaluation

Occasionally, SMILE is used interchangeably to refer either to the SMILE software or the SMILE-*pi* hardware device. The SMILE-*pi* is built upon the very popular smartphone-sized computer called the Raspberry Pi. The cost is about US $200, and it comes fully loaded with software and educational content. It is a low-power device that operates like a Wi-Fi router and can connect to fifteen to twenty wireless devices or a computer lab through its built-in ethernet connection. Connecting to the SMILE-*pi* means the device connects to a web server on the device that offers a learning portal loaded with educational software, which supports learning outcomes such as critical thinking, math skills, science skills, and exploratory and creativity skills.

Edify Early Grade Reading Project (EEGRP)

The Edify Early Grade Reading Project (EEGRP) provides Amazon Kindles for teachers and students to promote literacy programs in schools. EEGRP has shown the ability to improve reading and comprehension skills in early grades and above after a two-year pilot program in Ghana. The e-readers increase the reading comprehension skills of pupils by 66 percent and decoding of words by 26 percent using the Early Grade Reading Assessment (EGRA) tool among partner schools.

The EEGRP project is currently running in two operational countries: Ghana and Liberia. A total of 800 devices have been deployed to 37 Edify partner schools. The e-readers are deployed with 112 books onboard, made up of both local curriculum textbooks and storybooks suitable for both lower and upper primary students. The device has an in-built *Oxford English Dictionary* for finding the meaning of new words, and the battery life spans 14 days when fully charged.

EEGRP benefits. The EEGRP offers many benefits to schools:

- Increased access to books (both local and foreign textbooks) to solve the issue of lack of reading of reading materials, which is a common issue in Africa, and to bridge the poverty gap between the rich and the less privileged in the classroom
- Increased enthusiasm for reading since books on e-readers are easy to understand, have localized content, and offer convenience in reading
- Increased resources for teachers for lesson preparation and student engagement
- Increased familiarity with technological devices

Edify Innovation Through Computational Thinking (EICT)

The EICT project aims to equip students in Edify partner schools with computer thinking skills by teaching coding. While not every child dreams of becoming a computer programmer, acquiring computer and problem-solving skills, logical thinking, and developing question-asking skills for real-life situations are twenty-first-century skills every child should have. The program started in Ghana with three schools with 100 iPads personally donated by the former Apple VP of education. The donor's charge was to have the app included on the iPads teach the children how to code. It worked far beyond our expectations!

Students have access to Swift Playgrounds, an app that provides puzzle-like programming activities that help students understand both basic and advanced coding concepts. Students also have access to other built-in coding activities that help them develop their problem-solving skills through evidence-based programming using drones and Sphero robots.

The program has grown from the initial three schools to now five schools, with students graduating from using Swift Playgrounds to building apps using the Python programming language, learning how to program the Arduino open-source microcontroller, and using that to create security systems, and even a smart dustbin! Using the Scratch programming software, students have programmed math programs, created games, and even built digital aquariums!

Training. Essential to adoption and integration of any new technology is strong initial training and ongoing professional development. Education technology will only succeed if the proprietor, head teacher/principal, and ICT teacher are trained and then implement what they've learned.

Edify's training plan contains three complementary aspects:

1. *Initial Training*: Time is spent with the stakeholders in the school: the proprietor, the head teacher, and the education technology teacher. The features of the new technology are presented, and participants are trained for its use. The team that represents the program management team are given hands-on training on EdTech program management, ongoing teacher engagement and support, and sustainability activities and practices to ensure the longevity of the intervention. The entire teaching staff are given practical training sessions on the technical, integration, and usage to drive adoption and successful implementation of the technology-based program.

2. *Ongoing Training*: *EdTech Summits for Teachers.* As the technology becomes a fixture in the school, more knowledge is gained

about the use and implementation as well as new ideas for further integration. Edify provides a training track for education technology teachers and others to move from adoption to mastery of technical subjects, which includes a way to validate knowledge and participants to be recognized. These include literacy (creative writing and reading skills), digital literacy, math, and science summits.

3. *Annual Training Conferences: Edify Educational Technology Conference.* This is an annual conference by the technology transformation department to showcase to Edify partner schools the importance of acquiring and integrating technology in teaching and learning. Also, it presents a platform to discuss current educational technology trends to encourage students to produce and collaborate through the use of technology. Also, industry players are invited to share in-depth knowledge on trendy topics in the educational technology field. These annual conferences have been undertaken in four countries in Africa and are open for any participation through virtual means.

All these efforts are geared toward leveling the educational playing field to ensure every child in an Edify partner school has access to practical, project-based learning driven by technology. Although we are far from implementing education technology in every school, we are making strong progress. This could be through e-readers to improve reading and literacy skills, the computer lab to improve digital literacy, and the SMILE-*pi* program to improve critical thinking skills of students through asking high-order, critical thinking questions.

The conference ends with an award ceremony to recognize and encourage outstanding schools, school proprietors, teachers, and students who have made good use of the technology and exemplified exceptional tech integration skills in the course of the academic year.

Technical Support. For the continued and fully integrated use of technology in a school, the hardware and software must work to their fullest capacity at all times. Edify's Accelerating Support System is an innovative way to reduce the cost of technical support while ensuring maximum up-time of equipment and software. The Accelerating Support System works as follows:

- *Self-Serve.* The ICT Teacher at an Edify Program School location will first try to solve the issue using past experience and knowledge up to and including accessing an Edify-provided knowledge base that contains solutions to common problems.
- *Short-Code/WhatsApp Support.* If the problem is unable to be solved by local troubleshooting, a support request text should then be placed via the short code (only available in Ghana) or via WhatsApp message to an Edify technician. The technician will respond by text or phone by the end of the next business day. The Edify technician will then proceed to work with the ICT teacher via phone, text message, or email to solve the problem.
- *Telephone Support.* If the problem is unable to be solved by local troubleshooting, a phone call or SMS text message should then be made to an Edify technician. The technician will respond by SMS or phone by the end of the next business day. The Edify technician will then proceed to work with the ICT teacher via phone, text message, or email to solve the problem.

- *Remote Access by Edify's Education Technology Officer.*
  The ITC teacher places the school's computer lab under
  the control remotely of the education technology officer
  who troubleshoots.
- *On-Site Visit.* If the problem cannot be resolved remotely, the
  Edify technician decides an on-site visit is required to solve
  the problem, and they will schedule an on-site service call
  with the Edify program school representative.

A Note on EdTech and COVID-19

- The COVID-19 pandemic exposed two important things:
  the lagging of the education sector behind other sectors in
  terms of applying the new technology of doing business and
  the emergence of EdTech as an inevitable and vital tool for
  future learning of both elementary/high school and university
  levels.[38] Thus, governments, international organizations,
  donors, private businesses, and schools are beginning to
  recognize education technology and e-learning as important
  ways forward and starting to make efforts to improve
  and expand internet access and capacity to accommodate
  online learning.
- During the pandemic, Edify's partner schools, which
  developed their EdTech capacity, have generally been able
  to respond better to students' needs by resorting to blended
  learning using internet services. This consisted of providing
  online and offline lessons simultaneously. In the case of
  Ghana, for example, about 70 percent of the schools with
  computer labs were able to provide online learning and
  continue serving their students.[39] In Latin American countries

(Peru, Guatemala, and the Dominican Republic) where internet infrastructure and access are relatively better than in Africa, over 70 percent provided online lessons. Although several schools had computer labs in Rwanda, they were not able to offer online learning because the teachers had no skills on available online learning platforms, children had no devices at home that could enable this online learning possible, and most of the teachers were laid off.

- In August 2020, Edify undertook a survey interviewing school owners and leaders operating 308 different schools and looked into their responses to the COVID-19 pandemic. The survey found that about 75 percent of the Edify-supported 308 client schools were able to continue providing education support to students despite the closure of schools due to the pandemic, and 96 percent of the 49 core schools, the high-performing cohort among Edify schools, did so.[40]

- Different devices and platforms were used in different countries depending on the availability of human and technical (computers, laptops, tablets, smartphones, etc.) capacity as well as access to and quality of internet infrastructure. Google classroom and WhatsApp were the most commonly used platform across the 11 countries that Edify serves. Of the 308 Edify-supported schools surveyed, about 67 percent used WhatsApp.[41]

- It was relatively more difficult for schools in rural areas to make good use of the established computer labs, platforms, and devices because of a lack of internet access, connectivity, and access. Other obstacles hindering e-learning from becoming effective included a lack of computer skills and devices among teachers, students, and parents.

- The schools with EdTech have also become more popular and sought after among parents and students with the likelihood of increasing enrollment and income. As a result, all types of schools, including those which were not so keen before, have become relatively more interested in investing in online capacity development than classroom construction, which was the case prior to the COVID-19 pandemic. This was a huge mindset shift among LFIS owners and leaders toward appreciating the critical role of internet technology as a tool for education.

Summary

This chapter provided a brief account of why mobile education technology has become a vital tool in the enhancement of teaching and learning in our world today. It discussed the rationale and nature of Edify's education technology program.

During the last twenty years, particularly in the twenty-first century, the world has been investing huge volumes of capital in promoting technology-enhanced education as a means of achieving the EFA and MDG goals.[42]

Education technology integration needs major investment in infrastructures, networks, capacity, and training. This involves complex technology and developing countries are likely to find running the race difficult. In a globalized and competitive world, a clear digital divide exists between developed and developing countries, and the gap is likely to widen.

In Edify's experience, schools run by entrepreneurs are likely to implement education technology better than government schools. Computers at public schools are often not repaired in a timely manner. Some public school teachers older than forty years old want no part of computer labs as they fear being embarrassed by students who will quickly surpass them in their abilities to use computers. Some public school teachers in Ghana, when asked about using computers, say, "BCC," which means "born before computers." In other words, their generation did not use computers and they do not plan to use computers. Some say, "Do not worry me with technology." Some are not interested in the new learner-centric models but rather the older, "sage on the stage" rote learning system of teaching.

Edify believes education technology enhances quality learning, quality teaching, inclusion, life skills, and global competitiveness and, as part of its effort to lessen the digital divide, is investing in low-fee independents schools to provide education to deserving poor children in developing countries. However, Edify does not invest in education technologies just because they have been proved by research or because they have become popular. Edify invests only if it has established that ICTs are demand-driven, are successfully piloted, meet local requirements (policy, technical, cultural, etc.) in the countries where it operates, and the school entrepreneur is willing to make significant effort to implement the technology well.

Edify also recognizes that education technology is not a panacea on its own, nor is it a substitute to teacher-led learning. It only plays a powerful supplementary role in making education more learner-centered, creative, innovative, critical, and empowering. To be successful, education technology will have to always be administered by teachers who are not only pedagogically competent and student-friendly but also who have the skills to teach about education technology as objects and how to use them as learning tools.

Edify recognizes the paramount role played by teachers in the effective implementation of education technology. Edify runs a constellation of support programs to ensure that teachers:

- Have a buy-in, competence, commitment, and motivation to operate the education technology that is put before them.
- Know and love student-centered learning approaches. Education technology is participatory, interactive, and learner-centered, and it is bound to be effective only if instruction is given by teachers capable of applying a pedagogical approach that is empowering, enjoyable, and free from the "teach to pass exams" philosophy to prepare students for lifelong learning.
- Are retained to operate over a longer span of time. Frequent changes of teachers not only increase costs but also cause disruptions and lapses. In this regard, Edify trains and encourages proprietors to invest in teacher training and compensation to keep them satisfied and motivated to perform better.

During the pandemic when many schools were closed down, the significance of having a well-developed education technology was made evident. The schools that had developed their education technology were able to continue delivering education online while those who hadn't failed to do so. There is now a general acceptance among school owners that education technology has become a necessary part of successful learning in the future, and they are willing to invest in improving and expanding their online learning capacity. This includes providing laptops to teachers. Edify will work toward enabling them to realize this goal.

6

THE INTEGRATED
PROGRAM MODEL

In the early years of Edify, the program was credit-driven. It was more about giving loans to school proprietors through partnership with local microfinance institutions for improving and expanding physical educational facilities, including ICT, with the agreement they would allocate at least three hours per week to conduct Christian education in their respective schools. The microfinance institutions (MFIs) selected the schools that committed to do this according to their lending criteria after which they received training services offered by Edify. In other words, the recruitment of schools was first done by the MFIs. Over time, a Christ-centered transformation was placed as the core business around which every activity revolved, and the process of recruiting schools changed. It was difficult to fully establish the level of schools' commitment to Christian education. Instead of relying on the MFIs, Edify resorted to reaching out to schools directly and training them in preparation to join the program, which included taking loans. A shift was made from the application of credit-first-and-training-second approach to a training-first-and-credit-second approach. Both approaches were experimental and allowed for geographical variations as every country undertook activities related to their respective contexts with little or no interaction with the other. Nor was there any systematic effort made to integrate and standardize the program.

This is no longer the case. With the formulation of the Integrated Program Model (IPM) in 1998, activities are in the process of being implemented, managed, operationalized, and measured in more strategic and effective ways. The purpose of the IPM is to harmonize Christian transformation, student learning, school sustainability, and operational program management to improve the quality and quantity of program outcomes as well as the quality of data generated and thereby ensure program effectiveness through which Edify's mission is realized at a country's level. To ensure strategic and effective program implementation, the IPM classifies Edify's partner schools and related interventions in a cluster of programs, of which three of them are applied in sequence (client, core, and champion) and two of them, pilot and connect, are simultaneous with the sequential ones.

The sequential programs are:

Client Program. This program is the point of entry to schools for the long-term relationship with Edify's process for school development. The schools selected to participate in this program are Christ-centered schools whose proprietors are followers of Jesus Christ, they serve at least fifty students who come from families in the lower and lower-middle economic segments, and they are willing to work in a cluster of ten to twenty other schools in their respective areas. Edify seeks to help these client schools make sure they adopt and apply a Christ-centered approach to education as their organizational mission and identity, improve in all the school transformation domains, and actively participate in collective learning for about three years. After fulfilling about 90 percent of program requirements, they move to the next level: the core program stage.

Core Program. This program is the second step in Edify's process. Approximately 10 percent of the client schools are eligible to be in the core program. The requirements include a minimum of twelve-months-participation in the client program and five years in the education business, a student population of at least a hundred, provision of both primary and high school education, and at least 50 percent of the teachers believe in Christ. Edify's interventions in core schools relate to investing more intensively in the areas of developing kingdom culture inside and outside schools, building systems, processes, and structures to ensure transformational and sustainable improvements, and in building capacity and commitment to support other schools. At this stage partner schools are expected to demonstrate deeper commitment to CCE by all school stakeholders, build sustainable school systems, and collaborate with other schools by joining local networks. The core schools are assessed every year, and after three years of focused and intensive transformative support aimed at making them become model schools, at least 60 percent of the core schools meet 80-percent program compliance and move on to the champion stage.

Champion Program. This is the third step of Edify's process. The schools that participate in the champion stage consist of schools that have completed the core program with excellent results, have served more than ten years in the provision of a Christ-centered education, display a good financial sustainability record, own their own buildings (where applicable), have potential to reproduce their model, are willing to invest resources to get accredited, and invest in educational innovations. In these schools, Edify focuses on helping them to effectively integrate the functions of academics, discipleship, and sustainability as well as model a transformational community and emerge as coaches in others. After thirty-six months of intervention, about 90 percent of the champion schools are expected to have systematized and innovated most of the school transformation domains, initiated or completed an external accreditation, and exercised a leadership role in their respective regional and national school networks. They are also expected to comply with about 80 percent of program requirements.

The simultaneous program types are:

Creative (Pilot) Program. This program of the IPM system is meant to be implemented simultaneously with the client, core, champion, or connect programs. With the creative program Edify works with a single or a group of schools for a period of two years, introducing them to tested (proven) and innovative tools for improving and expanding a Christ-centered education with the aim to integrate these in their systems and design mechanisms for scaling up the use of these tools. The creative (pilot) program ends when participating schools achieve 90-percent compliance to program requirements, which includes having functional capacity to complete satisfactorily the testing cycle of the innovation proposed to be tested with this program. Some of the factors that may indicate the potential replicability of the creative program are schools that have succeeded in accomplishing the program's objectives and have demonstrated financial capacity to acquire the innovation being tested.

Connect Program. This program may be started simultaneously with the client, core, or champion programs. The ideal sequence is to start it as early as possible in the process of school development.

The connect program allows any number of Christ-centered schools not necessarily associated with Edify's programs to participate. Partner schools are integrated into Edify's learning clusters, which are schools willing to pay an annual membership fee to improve a Christ-centered education and individual Christians (educators, professionals, entrepreneurs, pastors, etc.) who are interested in promoting a Christ-centered education as part of a wider movement. About 80 percent of Edify partner schools participating at this stage are expected to have been integrated into local and national associations of Christ-centered school owners, contributed to the creation of the CCE knowledge and resource bank, and are associated with local Christian organizations and churches to expand and sustain their CCE mission. This takes place on an ongoing basis and compliance to program requirements will be reviewed every two years. The connect program aims at accomplishing the highest level of sustainability of Edify's impact in a region or a country.

Impact Assessment

Edify places high importance in impact assessment and invests in establishing and practicing appropriate frameworks, indicators, and tools for making sure its program brings impactful changes on the schools and students they serve.

To achieve this, Edify has formed a team of impact assessment specialists serving at global, regional, and national (field) levels. The international team develops policy frameworks, indicators, and tools for effective impact assessment, and provides training, supervision, and coaching to the impact assessment officers (IAOs) operating in the field.

With the guidance and technical support they receive from the international team, the IAOs design and implement contextualized monitoring and evaluation programs in consultation with the global team and the country directors. Some of the specific tasks they undertake include the following:

- Design the systems and strategies for monitoring and evaluation. This relates to reviewing and suggesting ways to develop or improve the framework (Outcomes Map) that guides field operations, contributing to the development of indicators to track progress, and supporting the design of the assessment tools (for baseline, performance, and impacts assessments, etc.) to measure progress of work on the indicators.
- Facilitate a learning process throughout program implementation. This relates to enhancing staff's capacity on M&E processes, helping the field team in gathering transformation stories, supporting program staff to conduct training assessments, and coordinating data collection activities.
- Ensure that the lessons learned contribute to improvement. This relates to helping their team and local partners to interpret the assessment results, comparing assessments from different years to show the level of improvement, reviewing the database, and sharing relevant information for the country's program planning, supporting program planning processes, annual work plans, activity planning, and managing reporting processes, especially for special projects.

Although no direct impact assessment training is provided to school proprietors and leaders, the monitoring and evaluation exercises undertaken by IAOs and subsequent analyses help them to see their weaknesses and strengths and thereby improve overall effectiveness. Some of them also participate in the direct assessment of other schools and draw a great deal of useful lessons to apply in improving their programs. In other words, the IAOs contribute to the facilitation of mutual learning and generation of knowledge in the significance impact assessment, which is often neglected by the majority of LFIS.

The Outcomes Map

The evolution of the Outcomes Map is another milestone in Edify's program. As an approach to program assessment, the Outcomes Map is a roadmap that gives a description of the causal path by which each of Edify's activities contribute to achieving Edify's mission. Edify's theory of change outlines the expected results that connect the activities to the mission. There are three levels of results: impact, outcome, and output. In designing the Outcomes Map, the impact level results were the first to be identified. These include the three key realms (academics, discipleship, and sustainability) that underpin the realization of Edify's mission. This was followed by the definition of the outcome level results, which are the changes that need to occur for the impact level results to happen. Then the output level results were also outlined to clearly state the specific action steps that schools need to take to facilitate expected changes. These output level results are the basis for Edify's interventions in the field. For example, an input of a training in financial systems is expected to lead to an output of better school fee collection policies. This will lead to an expected outcome of the school having improved financial health, which will contribute to a desired impact, and the school becoming more sustainable. A school becoming more sustainable means one of the three key components of the Edify mission has been accomplished in the school.

In the area of assessment, the focus so far has been on output and outcome level results indicators. At the level of impact, Edify's system is still in the development of the right method to complete the full circle of program effectiveness. Training follow-ups target the outputs whereas the annual school assessments give feedback on how the schools are performing on both the output and outcome level results. The assessment results from the latter become the basis for targeted support for schools at different stages in their developments.

The Outcomes Map includes five output and five outcome level results reflecting the three key realms of school transformation: academics, discipleship, and sustainability. They include:

Impact Level Results	Outcome Level Results	Output Level Results	Realms
Edify partner schools more accessible	Edify improves relationship with partner schools.	Edify improves introductory interactions with new schools	Calculated directly from the database (Schools don't work on this)
		Edify improves interventions (loans and training) given to existing schools	
	Access to quality education for children	Schools have ways to maintain or improve enrollment	Academics
		Improved relationship between school and their direct stakeholders	
Edify partner schools more sustainable	Improved financial health	Fee collection processes in place and functioning in Edify partner schools	Sustainability
		Schools have their own budgeting and accounting systems in place and functioning	
	School management and strategic planning	Schools improve their leadership	
		Schools have functional school transformation committees	
	Compliance with government requirements	Schools have valid registrations and approvals from the necessary government institutions	
		Schools fulfill statutory payments (taxes and Social Security)	
Edify partner schools improve a Christ-centered education	Students in Edify partner schools embody Christlike values	Schools increase exposure to the Word of God	Discipleship
		Schools encourage Christlike behaviors	
	Improved environment in Edify partner schools	Schools improve learning environment	Academics
		Schools improve environments for teachers	
	Improved student learning outcomes	Schools show evidence of improved learning	
		Schools improve the use of education technology	

The assessment was linked to the core program. It started the 2013–2014 academic year in the Dominican Republic, the 2014–2015 academic year in Ghana, and the 2016 academic year in Rwanda. The assessment is carried out annually and focuses primarily on schools in the core program. A set of comparable schools that served as control were also surveyed at the beginning and the end of the core program. In recent times, the latter has been replaced with a random school assessment that focuses on schools that have not been in the core program before.

The core program is a three-year intensive transformative program that serves 10 percent of Edify partner schools that are committed to Edify's goals and hungry to learn. These schools receive training and are followed up with regularly to help them become model Christ-centered schools. Every year, schools in the core program are assessed to show their growth in each of the indicators. School report cards are shared with the surveyed schools that help them keep track of their progress. After the three-year period, the core program schools exit from the core program based on their annual performance on the indicators as well as other factors. New schools are then incorporated into the core program.

Edify uses this data not only to show the holistic development of involved schools but also to evaluate which of the Edify-offered programs and activities lead to the most positive outcomes. Using the Outcomes Map, Edify is able to evaluate the impact effectiveness of its operations and also improve its programs to better serve schools and achieve its mission. The development of a simple but effective impact-assessment method is a priority objective for Edify.

Most Significant Change

Most significant change (MSC) is another methodology Edify adopts in assessing the impact its program makes. As a technique, MSC was developed by Rick Davies in the 1990s as part of his PhD research in Bangladesh. It is a participatory form of monitoring and evaluation and "involves the collection and selection of stories of change, produced by program or project stakeholders. MSC can be used in projects and programs where it is not possible to precisely predict desired changes beforehand and is therefore difficult to set pre-defined indicators of change."[1]

As such, MSC is a qualitative methodology and doesn't generate quantitative data. It is applied for undertaking qualitative impact assessment of aspects of change that are difficult to quantify. Although its implementation may vary depending on the context and type of intervention, the five steps that are normally followed include:

- Defining domains of change.
- Deciding how and when to collect stories.
- Collecting significant change stories.
- Selecting the most significant stories.
- Verifying the stories.

Change is observed and experienced differently by different participants and ranks and the MSC process facilitates the gathering of data from all stakeholders involved and capturing and reflecting the different perspectives. These are then discussed, analyzed, and ranked in a participatory way. So far, this approach has been applied only in a few countries. The future plan is to apply MSC in more countries to do both qualitative and quantitative measurements of transformational impact happening in Edify partner schools.

The 2021–23 Strategic Plan

After celebrating its ten-year service anniversary, Edify developed a three-year strategic plan covering the period of 2021–2023. The strategy is based on three organizational themes: focused, healthy, and simple. The preamble of the strategic plan reads:

> In a nutshell, "Focused" indicates the concentration on the essence of Edify's mission: Christ-centered education. "Healthy" describes the people's attributes and the culture required to fulfill the mission, build Kingdom of God relationships, and nurture all the people associated with God within Edify's community. "Simple" communicates the intention to design and implement all organizational processes in a way that balances effective stewardship and excellence in sustainable mission impact.

The three-year strategic plan comprises goals and objectives articulated by each of the three functional divisions: field operations, development and edification, and philanthropy and central services. In the case of field operations, the goals and objectives are formulated with the aim to effectively implement the IPM in a focused, healthy, and simple manner.

Focused. The goal is to improve the quality of discipleship and learning outcomes. The main objectives include building, growing, improving, and strengthening core schools, champion schools, and connecting networks when contexts allow.

Healthy. The goal is to strengthen school owners' networks and associations. The main objectives include identifying and forming in-country networks and associations, developing learning communities, promoting corporate prayer meetings, and fostering spiritual support when contexts allow.

Simple. The goal is to narrow training and educational technology offerings. The main objectives include information gathering and standardization of training event themes, narrowing of training events offered by Edify, increasing online training, rolling of diplomas on Christian transformation and academic quality, and measuring the quality of training events when contexts allow.

7

VOICES FROM THE FIELD

As shown in the table below, Edify has given out 5,735 loans to schools in the 11 countries in which it has been operating, and it has trained 26,467 teachers and 27,062 school leaders in 10,785 schools, impacting almost 7.8 million students between 2010 and September 2021.

Table 4: Cumulative Impact as of
September 30, 2021 (Edify's Fiscal Year)

Country	Starting Year	Number of Loans	Teachers Trained	School Leaders Trained	Schools Impacted Loans & Training	Students Impacted
Dominican Republic	2010	1,725	8,776	2,986	1,393	949,849
Ghana	2010	1,438	3,681	2,714	1,116	1,391,056
Rwanda	2011	315	2,600	2,475	806	646,578
Burkina Faso	2013	294	932	1,093	310	297,439
Liberia	2013	717	1,413	2,111	822	568,964
Peru	2014	353	2,826	6,771	1,720	1,786,520
Guatemala	2014	52	1,923	1,084	535	214,088
Ethiopia	2015	43	1,142	719	240	144,834

Northeast India	2016	11	1,111	222	109	90,556
Sierra Leone	2017	98	744	855	325	183,016
Uganda	2019	707	1,319	6,032	3,409	1,346,389
Total		**5,753**	**26,467**	**27,062**	**10,785**	**7,743,412**

Source: Edify Data Base

In this chapter, we will present the views on LFIS and Edify's program from a field perspective. The purpose is to create space for the school proprietors, the main partners of Edify, to share their thoughts and thereby strengthen the depth and authenticity of knowledge generated and documented in this book.

The voices expressed come from eleven individual school proprietors, one from each of the countries where Edify serves. We will hear what the school proprietors say about their schools before and after their partnership with Edify in their own words.

Lule (Uganda)

Lule founded Busega Preparatory School in 1989 when he retired from his profession as a teacher. About 80 percent of the people living in the Busega community are market vendors and earn less than two dollars a day. Incomes are not only low but also irregular as there are days when many don't make any money. Recognizing that most of the people living in the community were low-income earners, Lule wanted to create access for disadvantaged children by charging affordable fees and offering quality education, thereby helping his community.

The school started with ten students in 1989 and currently has a student population of eight hundred. It employs thirty-six teachers and eight support staff. Of these, forty are Christians, while three teachers and one support staff are Muslim who adhere to the Christian culture of the school.

Lule joined the Edify program in Uganda in 2019 following a vision-casting workshop he attended on invitation by Edify. In his own words, "I liked the vision and mission of Edify, and I immediately registered my school as a partner."

Following the partnership, Lule and some of his school leaders and teachers have benefited from the products and services offered by Edify. This included participating in business and accounting skills training, servant leadership, Christian education facilitation skills training, education technology, etc. According to Lule, the newly acquired skills have helped them improve their fee collection, accounting, and Christian education systems and practices. They have also been inspired to embrace the concept of education technology and to set up a computer lab as soon as financial conditions are favorable.

Lule also received a COVID-19 relief loan from Edify, which he used to meet the requirements set by the government for reopening schools. Lule says, "I used the 10 million shillings loan we received from Edify to put all the standard operating procedures, such as washing facilities, temperature guns, and COVID-19 screening forms in place, in order to reopen and to pay salaries for my teachers so they could travel from their villages and resume teaching."

To strengthen the school's effort to promote a Christ-centered education, school transformation committees (STCs) and discipleship clubs (DCs) were established. This allocates time for student fellowship and teacher fellowship. The STC comprises the proprietor, director, school accountant, two teachers, two student leaders, and a parent representative. The committee plans all Christian activities, including the development of the fellowship roster for the term, outreaches, and Bible studies. The parent representative helps to sensitize other parents about the Christian culture. Parents, even those who are not Christian, often attend devotions and join in Christian activities at the school. Devotions are led by both students and teachers on a rotational basis. The school also undertakes Christian outreach activities outside the school in which both teachers and students participate in cleaning the marketplace, sharing the gospel, and praying with people.

According to Lule:

> The most significant change in our school is the formation of a STC. Before we partnered with Edify, all Christian activities were on the shoulder of the liturgy teacher, and they were not well-coordinated. After the training on STCs and DCs by Edify, we conducted an in-school training as a result of which the concepts were understood and embraced by all, leading to the formation of the two structures. The STC now runs all the Christian activities in the school. I have seen a great improvement in our weekly devotions for both staff and students as they are better organized and more effective. We thank Edify for always encouraging us and walking a journey of transformation alongside our school.

Esther Bernuy (Peru)

Esther comes from a family with long history of evangelical faith as her father was a devoted missionary and a church planter. She has a training in business administration, high school education, and preschool education. After passing through many phases of bureaucratic challenges that were overcome through prayers and God's intervention, Esther established her school, La Luz de Jesus, in 2004, with the mission to help teens at risk in her community, believing that "the best age to impact is in early childhood."

The school is located in San Hilarion Alto, Lima, which is inhabited by low-income people, many of whom live in poverty. About half of the population are teenagers and children. Esther says:

> I saw many of them in poverty, some no longer going to school, some who got drugged with *terokal* (a very cheap and easy-to-buy industrial glue used by shoemakers but whose aroma generates addiction). When I read in the Bible about the healing of the demoniac Gadarene, I understood that Christ left him clothed and in his right mind. Then I realized His ministry was not only to heal the soul but also the body with clothing and dignity. Jesus' ministry was complete.

The school started as a kindergarten with 8 students in 2004 and now has an enrollment of 250 students and employs 5 multi-grade teachers. Esther has also opened an early stimulation center and supported the management of a second school until 2019. An elementary school was added in 2020. Esther says, "This has kept us operational because at the kindergarten a good percentage of students have stopped studying. Many schools have closed at this time, but the Lord has taken care of us."

The partnership with Edify began in 2017. Since then the school has benefited from Edify's loans and training services. The loans from a local lending partner were used for improving and expanding educational facilities—two loans were for construction and another two for improving classrooms. Some of the main trainings the school benefited from include Christian transformation, governance compliance, education, sustainability (management, finance, and accounting), and education technology skills.

Esther says:

> Edify supported us a lot with loans to raise the school and with professional advice in accounting and the operational administration of the school. Especially during the pandemic, I have felt the great support of Edify because all school proprietors were disoriented and did not know what to do at the beginning of the pandemic. There was not a WhatsApp group where we could share information about our situation and encourage one another. Edify provided us with this help and encouraged us in the middle of the difficult situation we had to go through. The pandemic has allowed me to experience Edify's close spiritual care again, with the prayer chains, devotionals, the monthly prayers, etc.

In regard to a Christ-centered education in the school, Ester plans to introduce a formal discipleship program and do more than what is currently the case. Currently, the school runs a course on religion and Esther uses her science and technology classes to introduce children to God. In her words:

> I teach science and technology throughout elementary school. I take advantage of those topics to invite them to meditate. For example, I tell them: "Look, the organization of the cell is so beautiful." They reply that it looks like a city. "Well-organized, huh? Do you think that was done by chance? No,

a higher intelligence created it and that intelligence is God. Never forget it. Although others tell them otherwise, you see that nothing is random here. Everything has an order." And we end the class with a prayer.

Esther also encourages teachers "to seek the school subjects that allow the students to know the breadth and depth of God, and thus they can approach Him, and they can know His heart. Presenting God through science is something children will never forget."

Esther describes the spiritual impact of what she and the teachers do in the school:

The most beautiful thing is that, now, when I say, "Let's pray to say goodbye," everyone wants to participate. "I want to pray! I want to pray!" my students say. And I love that, because they are talking to God, and they have learned to pray very well. Parents have started to do it too. This month we had a prayer meeting, and a good group of parents attended.

Reflecting on Edify as a partner, Esther says:

Edify is a caring and empathetic organization that puts itself in our shoes to help us. They are very professional people who know the educational sector in depth. And if they don't know something, they look for someone to give us the information and they go out of their way to help us. I met Jason Morveli (Edify's Christian transformation and training officer) when he visited our school in 2018. Now I see him with more experience, with more information, and I am happy to see him and the Edify team growing.

Berkis Vargas Medina (Dominican Republic)

Berkis founded her school, Centro Educativo El Lirio, in 1991. Her dream was to become a pediatrician, which she was unable to pursue because the cost was too high. Instead she decided to educate children by opening a school. The school started with 15 children and now has 125 students and employs 14 teachers and non-teaching staff. It is situated in a peri-urban location inhabited by low-income people, most of whom are single mothers who earn their livelihood from informal employment such as motor scooters, street vendors, or casual work. Berkis is an active Christian and holds a leadership role in her church.

The partnership with Edify was established in 2013. Since then the school has benefited from the various products and services offered by Edify. The loans taken were used to improve and expand educational facilities, including the purchase of two properties, one of which is used as a school and the other as an office space.

Berkis and her staff have also attended various training activities organized by Edify in partnership with local training organizations, some of which include fee collection and management strategies, leadership skills, basic business and accounting skills, discipleship, biblical integration, biblical worldview, and pedagogy.

In addition to improving and expanding the educational facilities physically, Berkis has also been able to improve her financial record keeping and accounting system following the business skills she acquired through trainings. Berkis says, "Prior to the partnership, the school didn't keep proper accounting. Financial records were sporadic, inconsistent, and manual. It was difficult to do profit/loss calculations as personal and business expenses were not separate, and monitoring fee collection was difficult. Today, the school keeps a computerized and systematic accounting system."

The school has adopted the AMO program to promote CCE.[1] All their teachers have been trained in this program and other Christ-centered training skills. There is also a DC consisting of three different groups organized by age and grade that promotes Bible studies among the students on a weekly basis. The DC is led by the students themselves and receives facilitative support from the trained teachers. Everyone in the school attends daily and weekly Christian activities before going to classrooms as part of the school culture. Both teachers and students are assigned to lead devotionals on a rotational basis. The school has also been awarded several times for its services in the community. In 2017, the school was recognized as the "Micro Business of the Year."

In regard to the role of the partnership with Edify in the transformation of her school, Berkis has this to say:

> The first day somebody from Edify came to my school, I rejected the visit. I thank God they insisted and came again to explain Edify's program, and the partnership started. As a result of the partnership, my school has received loans, training, and education technology without which the achievements we have made would have been difficult. Our team has acquired so many skills for leading the business and for supporting students, parents, and the community. I have become an Edify promoter, not just in my area, but also in other areas where private schools exist. My relationship with Edify has been a real blessing.

Yadira Arriaza (Guatemala)

Colegio Cristiano Agua Viva was established in 1986 by Compassion International to educate children living in poverty in Mixco County, which is located in the outskirts of Guatemala City. When Compassion decided to close the school in 2008, Yadira's mother took it over with the aim to continue providing access to a Christ-centered education to the children who would otherwise have been out of school. When her mother passed away in 2018, Yadira, who had a degree in education and was a teacher in Agua Viva, took ownership of the school and has continued running it to this day in honor of her mother. Today the school employs 13 teaching and non-teaching staff and has an enrollment of 194 students at kindergarten, elementary, and junior high school levels.

The school is located in a peri-urban area in the outskirts of Guatemala City. The majority of the people in the community fall under low-income category and rely on petty trading and low-paid jobs in Guatemala City for their livelihoods. Violence and family disintegration are common features of the community.

The partnership with Edify was formed in 2019. Following the partnership, the school has benefited from the various products and services offered by Edify. Yarida says:

> The school has been able to develop a clear vision and mission, improve its leadership and administrative effectiveness, accountability, responsibility, and overall performance. The school has also made efforts to improve its appearance and learning environment. For example, with renewed leadership community participation, the school repaired the school's roof, which had not been done for over twenty years. This

created room for improved learning environment and increased enrollment.

The training in business management and accounting has helped the school to keep more effective and transparent income/expense recording, financial planning, and budgeting practices. Yarida transformed her financial management and record keeping from paper-based manual record to computerized spreadsheets. She also uses a budget management template provided in connection with the business training. This has improved the quality, speed, and accuracy of financial information, generated profit/loss analysis, and financial budgeting/planning.

With regard to the promotion of CCE, the school has created a system whereby a Bible class is taught once a week. This also includes a well-organized devotional practice in which every teacher is assigned to lead on a rotational basis. This allows for all students to be exposed to the Word of God on a daily basis through reading the Bible, praying, and worshiping together every morning before class. The school also provides room for alumni students to volunteer in the formation, direction, and organization of DCs.

The DCs meet every other Friday after school to study the Bible, pray, worship, share, and have fun together. These groups have helped them open up and grow spiritually and share the gospel among their peers in the school. The students in the DCs also engage students in collecting groceries for distribution among those in need in the community outside the school.

In characterizing the impact of the school's partnership with Edify, Yadira states:

Edify came in one of the most crucial times for me as a proprietor. My mom had just passed away, and I was left with a lot of responsibilities and challenges. All the improvements we have made in our school leadership, financial management, Christ-centered education, and learning environment have occurred through the support of Edify. Edify has brought me a huge relief, and it is why the school is still standing.

Tracy Kipgen (Northeast India)

Tracey established her school, Apple Buds Academy, together with her husband, Kamboi, in 2013. The school is located in Sapormeina, Kangpokpi District, Manipur, which is peri-urban and inhabited by low-income people, the majority of whom rely on casual and agricultural sources of income. The school spans from nursery to eighth grade. Apple Buds Academy started as a nursery school with 20 students. Today it serves a student population of 405 and employs 24 teaching and non-teaching staff.

Tracey became a believer in 1985. Her motivation for opening a school and going into education was to offer a quality education with spiritual guidance. The sources for the initial capital to build the school included her husband's savings. The vision of the school is to teach children the values of Christ and shape their minds and hearts to become like Him when they are adults.

The partnership with Edify was established in 2016, and the school has benefited from the various training and credit products offered. The school loan received from Edify through WSDS was used for building additional classrooms, which resulted in increased enrollment.

Tracey attended servant leadership, business management skills, and teachers training events organized by Edify in partnership with ACSI, DAI, SPTWD, and Elim Resource Center at different points in time. Her school leaders and teachers also benefitted from the same trainings.

Reflecting on the impact of the training, Tracey says:

> Edify training further strengthened my belief and motivated me to put servant leadership principles into practice. At a personal level, I and my husband now have a much better understanding of leadership after the servant leadership training. We have also learned a lot from other school leaders—from their personal sharing and informal interactions during the training. We have been able to connect with many Christian school owners as friends. The Christian training and the distribution of Treasure Hunts Bible and Reach 4 Life have provided real-life situations and prepared teenagers for future challenges. Participating in Edify's training has helped us to offer more strategic, effective CCE in our school. The children have started not only to study the Bible but also to behave in a Christlike manner, and this is appreciated by parents.

Furthermore, Tracey gives testimony on how her participation in the servant leadership training has changed her leadership style. She says:

> Before the training, I was doing everything by myself. Now I practice shared responsibility. I assign teachers certain responsibilities and give them an allowance for their work. For

example, I have assigned Ms. Vavah as assistant head mistress and in charge of the nursery section, which is further divided into three sections; Ms. Hatneo is in charge of classes 1–3, which is also divided into three sections; and Mr. Boboi is in charge of classes 4–8. Each person is in charge of a team of 5–7 teachers under them. Likewise, Sir Minlal is in charge of lesson plans (all teachers have to submit their lesson plans to him every Monday), and Sir Boilen is in charge of tuition fee collection. This has made teamwork more harmonious and collaborative and improved performance.

Tracey also says she was able to separate her personal and business accounts and put in place better financial management procedures following the business training Edify organized and invited her to attend.

In the same way, she appreciates the value of the Edify/SPTWD training events she attended. After the leadership and management and collaborative learning training facilitated by Edify in partnership with SPTWD, the school tried the concept of "home visits" in promoting school-parent relationships as practiced by other Edify partner schools. Tracey applied this concept in her school and found it helpful in building better relationships with parents and teachers.

She goes on to say:

The school self-review and assessment by the SPTWD-Adhyayan team has opened our eyes on what "good" looks like. Prior to our participation in this, we did not know what classroom observation was, but now I go to any class and observe how my teachers are teaching and provide constructive feedback. We also became more conscious of our responsibility toward our neighbors. Last year, we invited Logos children home students for dinner and fellowship. We also participate in activities that mitigate environmental pollution, such as keeping our school campus plastic waste free."

Moreover, the school has been able to promote a Christ-centered education more effectively than prior to the partnership with Edify. Below are some of the activities being undertaken following the trainings offered by Edify in partnership with the various training organizations:

- Discipleship clubs Bible studies, worship songs in chapel services once in a week
- Vacation Bible School (VBS) every year in June
- Teachers' devotions every day after school
- Bible memory verses for lower sections and Scripture tests for higher classes as part of assessment.
- Motivating students to read the Bible by acknowledging and giving small prizes to those who read the most during a given period of time

The school also engages in outreach activities, including visits to children's homes and care homes for the elderly as well as community projects such as cleaning streets. Also, students make small donations to the Bible Society of India through a missionary box kept in the school office.

Tracey says:

> Since the inception of the school, we emphasized the spiritual health of students though we didn't do it systematically and comprehensively. That changed following our partnership with Edify. Both teachers and students have been equipped to promote spiritual transformation to the extent that even non-Christian teachers have shown interest in memorizing biblical verses to teach students. Many parents have enrolled their children in ABA to get them to lead Godly lives, and some have reported responsible behavior in helping around the house and taking care of their parents. The Godly counseling from the school has brought children in building closer relationship with their parents.

Tsedale Kasahun (Ethiopia)

Tsedale cofounded Crosspoint Academy with her husband in 2014 to offer quality Christian and affordable education with health services and to help children living in poverty. Tsedale and her husband are both active contributors to the evangelical Christian movement in Ethiopia. The school is in a peri-urban area called Dukem, which is about 37 kms from the capital Addis Ababa, and it serves students from kindergarten to high school. Most of the population lives on incomes derived from agricultural activities, petty trading, and low-paid jobs.

The partnership with Edify was established in 2015. With the loans received from Edify through Berhan Bank, Tsedale built additional classrooms and expanded the physical capacity of her school. The expansion contributed to the growth of the student population from 48 when it started in 2014 to 1504 in 2020, and it currently employs 46 teaching and non-teaching staff.

Tsedale and her school leaders and teachers all benefitted from the training opportunities offered by Edify. Some of the main trainings included leadership for learning, early childhood, business and accounting skills, government regulations and requirements, biblical integration, and discipleship dynamics. According to Tsedale, the school was able to improve its organizational effectiveness, academic performance, and the quality of a Christ-centered education because of the newly acquired skills. She says:

> Before we partnered with Edify, we tried to do everything, including engaging the local church to offer Christian education to our students for the purpose of which we established the school. We didn't have a good strategy, and our practices were not effective. We were met by all forms of opposition, and the local authorities threatened to close our school if we continued with our Christian teaching. So we stopped doing that. This changed when we started getting support from Edify. We gained new skills and joined the Christian School Owners' Fellowship, which gave us courage to continue promoting Christ-centered education as we had originally intended to.

Unlike during the pre-Edify days, the school now makes the conscious effort to recruit Christian teachers who are willing to teach the values and principles of Christ. The school has formed Christian Teachers' Fellowship (CTF), which organizes daily and weekly devotionals and prayers. During these meetings, the teachers review the way Christian that activities take place within the school, draw lessons, and develop plans. The CTF is the pillar of the school's Christian transformation program.

Another crucial instrument used in the promotion of CCE is the students' discipleship club. The students meet on a weekly basis to study the Bible, pray, worship, and fellowship together. They promote peer evangelism within the school and community outreach outside the school.

Tsedale says:

> Our partnership with Edify has brought us confidence to continue pursuing Christ-centered education. We have been able to renew our motivation and courage to promote Christ-centered education in our school. It has helped us in developing partnerships with other like-minded schools and thereby sustain our vision and operations in the dire situation currently facing the education sector in our country, which is plagued by political instability and COVID-19. We can say God used Edify to give us the courage to continue working in the field of education. I cherish Edify for its strong dedication to bringing God into the life of our students.

Agartha Baffour (Ghana)

Agartha established her school, Living Foundation School, in 2005, with thirty students. She had no formal work experience. She had only a middle school education as she could not continue further due to factors beyond her control. Prior to establishing the school, she was a petty trader, selling secondhand clothes at the Kumasi Central Market in the Ashanti Region of Ghana.

Agartha's school started partnering with Edify in 2013. It runs kindergarten, primary, and junior secondary levels and has a total enrollment of 650 students with a staff strength of 38, consisting of 24 teaching staff and 14 non-teaching staff.

While a petty trader, Agartha sought to make a positive impact in the lives of the children in the community where she lived because she believed in the power of education in influencing the thinking, attitudes, and views of the youth to prepare them for a better future. She set up a Christ-centered school to provide quality and affordable education for children within the community and equip them with Godly values and principles.

The school is located in Kronom-Kwapra, which is a community situated within the Suame Municipal Assembly in the Ashanti region. Approximately 70 percent of the inhabitants are Christian, the majority of whom are engaged in small- and medium-scale enterprises. No public schools are in the community, and all the children are educated by the few private schools operating there.

In 2017, her school had the opportunity to participate in the five-day Edify Youth Leadership Training Camp in Mampongteng in the Ashanti Region, which was attended by both teachers and students of various DCs from different schools. The theme was "Equipping God's Workman" with a focus on topics such as "Practical Approach of Witnessing and Disciplining Students of Other Faith" (Muslim students), "My School—My Mission Field," "Whole School Evangelization" (one student at a time), "Community Evangelism and the Work of an Evangelist," and "Personal Evangelism."

According to Agartha and the school chaplain, the experience at the camp gave their participating students and teachers a clear insight on evangelism, and this developed an enthusiasm in them to organize evangelism activities not only in the school but also beyond the walls of their school. Thus, right after the camp, the school initiated its first evangelism undertaking where members of the DC started witnessing to their fellow students on a class-by-class basis. A revival began as a result of the zeal with which the gospel was shared.

Some of the evangelism activities include student-to-student evangelism during break periods and teacher-to-student evangelism in classrooms, during devotionals, and during free times. The in-school evangelism and discipling activity is carried out by the members and leaders of the Awana-trained DC. In 2019–2020, for example, forty-three students gave their lives to Christ. Among these was the daughter of a fetish priest as well as three Muslim students. This revival led to doubling the DC membership from forty-five members to ninety members within the term.

The DCs comprise groups of eight to ten students, which are led by students and supported by trained teachers under the supervision of the headmaster. The trained DC leaders in each group facilitate Bible studies with their group members, referencing the specific topic outlined for the week in accordance with the timetable for the term. The small group meetings enhance greater understanding of the Word and ensure effective participation by all in Bible discussions.

Since 2017, Agartha's school has also undertaken various outreach activities in its community. In January 2018, the DC members did not keep this revival to themselves but rather took the gospel to the streets of the Kronum-Kwapra community. The turnout for this evangelism event was massive as students and teachers proclaimed the simple message of Jesus' death, resurrection, and saving grace. Not only was the message preached to the community, but the school also embarked on some missionary outreaches through visits to the Edwenase Rehabilitation Centre and shared the Word of God as they made donations in cash and kind. A greater portion of the donations are provided by the proprietress on behalf of the school while students gave clothing and food supplies, which they mobilized from their parents. Twelve people gave their lives to Christ during the event. These and many more outreach activities were a great blessing to the community as they brought so much encouragement and joy to orphans, the vulnerable, and the less privileged. The students and teachers at the school were thereby able to express the love of God in word and deed.

Agartha says:

> I am satisfied and encouraged to do more by the transformation I see taking place among my students and the impact they make on their community. I believe that to be a school of influence characterized by Christ–centeredness goes beyond academic excellence and includes caring for the community, and my school is wholeheartedly committed to preparing every student to impact the world for Jesus Christ in accordance with our school motto, which is anchored in the scriptural instruction of Mark 16:15: "Go into all the world and preach the Good News to everyone" (NLT).

Fred Buyinza (Rwanda)

Fred's parents fled Rwanda and lived in Uganda as refugees where he was born, raised, and educated. He became a Christian at a young age and has been committed to making Jesus known in his community ever since. He has a degree in education and has served as a Christian teacher with Youth With a Mission (YWAM).

Fred established his school, Fruits of Hope Academy, in 2007. Currently, the school has a total enrollment of 650 students and employs 27 teaching and non-teaching staff. Fred explains he established the school because:

> Being a Christian teacher was not enough. I had a dream which I had not yet accomplished. My end in mind was to focus on Christian education among children. I was not satisfied with what schools were doing in terms of empowering and fostering Christ-centered education in their schools. To me, establishing Fruits of Hope Academy was another opportunity God had given me to impact the lives of children and bring about transformation in their lives.

He started operating the school with very limited resources of his own while believing God would provide.

In addition to building his school, Fred also engages in training and mobilizing other Christian school proprietors and teachers to form networks and support one another. The school entered into partnership with Edify in 2014 and has been receiving training and other support to boost its effort to provide sustainable access to holistic education to children in poverty. In addition to receiving the school loan, leaders and teachers were trained in Christ-centered leadership and teaching skills by Edify in partnership with different training organizations.

Within his school, Fred organizes Christian training to his teachers to help them understand their role as Christ-centered teachers and equip them to educate children holistically. The school also reaches out to parents within the community to teach them how raise their children in a Christian way. Moreover, the school holds an annual gathering (retreat) at the end of each academic year to follow up on how alumni students are doing in their secondary schools, teach the Word of God, and hear their experiences in kingdom building activities.

Regarding the role of students in missional activities, Fred says, "The students of Fruits of Hope Academy have now taken lead in all Christian activities, including fellowships, outreaches, and devotionals taking place within the school. Today, learners [students] organize community evangelism whereby they invite their parents to school and share the Word of God with them." Fred estimates at least 240 students have given their lives to Christ.

According to Fred, this was not the case before the school started working in partnership with Edify. Before Edify, the teachers and administrators were the ones taking the lead in all these activities. Following the training by Edify, they started realizing the importance of empowering learners for a long-lasting impact and sustainability of a Christ-centered education in the school.

Rev. Sammie J. Sorbah (Liberia)

Rev. Sammie J. Sorbah established United Christian Apostolic Senior High School in August 2003. He has BA degrees in sociology and theology. The school is in the rural town Soybin. Currently, the school has over 400 students enrolled and employs 20 staff members. Their partnership with Edify was established in 2017, and the school has benefited from Edify's lending, education technology, and training services. According to Rev. Sorbah, although his school was established to promote a Christ-centered education among children, it lacked the knowledge to do so properly. The Christian teaching and enrollment started improving after the training they received from Edify through Awana.

He says:

> Awana entered our school through Edify in 2018 when our school enrollment was yet awfully low at 90–150 students every semester. Edify in collaboration with Awana introduced us with the concept of DCs, the Awana games, and the community outreach program. These transformation methods, coupled with the many fabulous trainings, served as the turning point in our school growth.

Currently, the school is actively involved in the running of DCs and health clubs, using Christian literature produced by Awana and Cornerstone Leadership Academy, to mold the minds of students and grow in the knowledge of Christ. Three large DCs meet once a week to study the Bible together. These include: the Girls Academy, the Boys Academy, and the Kids Academy. Students are involved in prayer, praising God, and peer evangelism. In 2017, the students participated in the Transformation and Cornerstone Leadership competition at the Paynesville Town Hall and won third place. Approximately 125 students accepted Jesus Christ as their personal Lord and Savior.

Rev. Sorbah says:

> This in-school mission activity undertaken by the school aims to win more souls, distract our students away from peer pressure, and counsel those with social and psychological challenges. Our activities are positively transforming the lives

of some teachers who came into our school as unbelievers. They were converted through the school and now are serving God faithfully in diverse churches.

As part of the school's community outreach, Rev. Sorbah tells the following story:

In 2019, we launched our first community outreach program where a vulnerable family of Mr. John Kpah received food and non-food items from the school. This was a moment of new experience and very pitiful to see. Our visit to this vulnerable family was timely. During that hot sun, our students broke through Soybin community and walked toward an unfinished two-roomed, sub-standardly zinced, unplastered house. They were met by a very slim lady, dark in complexion, sitting with her children picking carnal to make oil for the day. Probably there was no money to buy oil for cooking. The next thing they heard from her was, "Thank you for coming. I was just about to go and buy a cup of rice for us to eat for today." They observed this had been a daily routine for the family.

We were told her husband worked as a janitor in one small school away from the community. Due to the hardship of life, he had to walk miles to and from his work place every day. Joyfully, our offer was like a dream to their family and placed a great smile on the faces of the little children who had been underfed for many days. People nearby looked as the students left in admiration of the charity they demonstrated to the family. The next day, the woman's husband came to the school to appreciate the students for their kind offer.

News about the event circulated around the community. The community outreach also helped in advancing the good image of our school. Through this experience both the school administration and students came to recognize the significance of promoting the culture of community voluntarism. We plan to do more in this area as part of our effort to disciple our community.

Emma Kargbo (Sierra Leone)

Emma is a pastor and has a BA in community studies. She established Agape Elementary and Academy in 2012 to offer both elementary and secondary education with an initial student population of 36. Today the school has an enrollment of 1005 students and employs 47 teaching and 10 non-teaching staff members.

Her main motivation for establishing the school was to provide quality education for children in poverty and teach the gospel in low-income, Muslim-dominated communities through the promotion of a Christ-centered education as part of the standard school curricula.

In 2018, the school started a partnership with Edify at a time it was in great need. Through this partnership, Emma was able to access loan capital that she used for improving and expanding educational physical facilities, including the purchase of a school bus, and she received training opportunities offered by Edify. As a result of the various skills training, the school participated in record keeping, quality of service, financial management and accounting, fee collection, human resources management, and a Christ-centered education has improved.

Prior to the partnership with Edify, the Christ-centered activities were limited to daily morning devotions and weekly staff prayer sessions. After the partnership and the training received, the school adopted a more strategic and systematic framework for promoting a Christ-centered education. A school DC and a choir were established, and the school became more intentional and systematic in promoting a Christ-centered education and evangelism.

The school has been engaged in conducting daily devotions for all students (Muslims included). Additionally, discipleship trainings, group Bible studies, and school choir performances in and outside of the school are being carried out as part of the school mission activities.

The school has a DC with a membership of thirty-five committed Christian students. The club members meet once a month to study the Bible, fellowship, and pray together. Although the discipleship club is structurally led by elected student leaders, it is supported by two trained Christian teachers who are involved in teaching and coaching the students. The students in the club spread the gospel among their fellow students within the school through one-on-one and group approaches. Through these student-led evangelism activities, fifty-two students, including Muslims, have given their lives to Christ.

Moreover, the students share the gospel among community members outside the school with the help of teachers and school leaders. They also share the gospel with their parents. The school also holds regular interaction with the parents and demonstrate God's love. As a result of all this, the Muslim-dominated community is no longer hostile to the Christian teaching undertaken by the school among all students.

Marcel Sibiri Nikiema (Burkina Faso)

Marcel established the evangelical school complex Le Flambeau in 2013 with the vision to create access to education in communities in poverty and to raise children of God without fault "who will shine as lights in the world" while living in "a crooked and perverse generation" (Philippians 2:15). Marcel never went to school and did not want the children in his community to be illiterate like he was. In other words, the illiterate Marcel opened a school so others may be literate and have a better future. After opening the school, Marcel decided to educate himself at the evening classes at his school. So far, he has been able to read and write, although he is still at basic level.

Since Marcel and his wife did not have the financial resources needed to establish the school, they sold one of their small plots of land to raise the money to build the first classroom block. The school started with Primary 1 with only 6 students and has now grown to a student population of 447 that is served by 16 teachers. In a Muslim community where finding Christian teachers is difficult, Marcel's vision is to recruit a 100-percent Christian staff. (Right now, he is at about 97 percent Christian teachers.)

The school is in a Muslim-dominated, peri-urban area where agriculture is the main source of livelihood. Initially, the Muslim members of the community were hesitant about placing their children in Le Flambeau, but not anymore. As they saw the quality of education was better, Muslim parents even took their children from the Muslim school and enrolled them in Le Flambeau.

The school entered into partnership with Edify in 2014 and has received loans and training services, which has resulted in leaders and teachers being trained in servant leadership, student-centered teaching skills, and a Christ-centered education.

At the spiritual level, Marcel has intensified the promotion of transformation activities undertaken with the school. Some of these include the running of Bible classes in each class on a weekly basis and the running of DCs through which activities such as Bible studies, worship songs, and games are facilitated by students. The DCs are also open to other children in the community.

Evangelism is one of the school's core activities. Usually, there is a film screening, followed by a call for conversion. For this particular activity, the proprietor put a strategy in place to get each student to invite a friend from the community who is not a Christian. It is an activity that until now has always borne fruit in terms of salvation as over fifty students have given their lives to Christ every single year. "This has positively impacted the way children behave both at home and outside that parents have gone to the extent of withdrawing their children from Koranic schools to enroll them at *Le Flambeau*," says the proprietor. To ensure that new converts grow in their faith, Marcel built a chapel near the school to make church attendance easier and attract more students.

THE INTERPLAY OF GOVERNMENTS AND LOW-FEE INDEPENDENT SCHOOLS IN EDUCATION

As stated by UNESCO: "Governments are ultimately responsible for progress on the global education goals. In poor and wealthy countries alike, governments are held accountable for education commitments, plans, implementation and outcomes."[1] UNESCO also states:

> All countries have ratified at least one legally binding international treaty addressing the right to education. Governments have a responsibility to respect, protect and fulfil this right. Currently, 82 percent of national constitutions contain a provision on the right to education. In just over half of countries, the right is justiciable, giving citizens the legal ability to take government to court for violations.[2]

Edify works in countries that have some of the least favorable economies in the world. In these countries, the governments sign treaties as those mentioned above, but due to the precarious state of their economy, they are not in the position to fulfill them. Moreover, while the governments of developing countries too often turn a blind eye to the shortcomings of their own public institutions, they aggravate the problem by putting unhealthy pressure on the private schools to meet policies and standards that government schools do not meet.

Edify fully recognizes the role of governments in providing education to children and works in collaboration with relevant government authorities and in line with national regulations. Edify serves to strengthen the capacity of low-fee independent Christian schools to improve and expand Christian education and thereby create access to quality education for children to complement—and not compete—with their respective national governments. In most cases national governments recognize the important role played by low-fee independent schools in educating children and provide support in various forms, including curriculum, standards, supervision, textbooks, teachers' training opportunities, and COVID-19-related assistance.

On the other hand, the regulatory policies and bureaucratic practices applied by national governments are not always conducive to the work of low-fee independent schools. On the contrary, they act as more of a hinderance than a helping force. In many instances, low-fee independent schools end up ceasing their services because of closures ordered by governments for various reasons—one of which is failure to meet government requirements, including physical and teaching standards.

Being aware of the problems faced by low-fee independent schools, Edify works to help them meet the expected requirements. It also works closely and dialogues with authorities responsible for education to enhance their understanding and appreciation of the difficult environment in which the LFIS operate, with the aim to foster favorable conditions in general and offer concrete support. This chapter will show how Edify works to make this happen with Peru as a case study. Let's start with a quick general look at how standards and requirements for private education are viewed by governments in Latin America and the Caribbean.

The Double Standard in Latin American and Caribbean Private Education

There is a clear double standard for what seems to be a minimum requirement needed for public schools and private schools. These requirements are demanded from all private schools, regardless of how low the fee or tuition is. This means both the school that has a $2,000 monthly fee and the school that has a $30 monthly fee are required to fulfill the exact same criteria. With this in mind, let's look at what's going on in Latin America and the Caribbean.

In 2018, the ISO 21001 certification was created.[3] This international standard is intended to help education providers meet the requirements that students need the world over. Basically, it sets high standards for running an educational institution. This certification is a prerequisite for both private education institutions and public sector institutions. The latter, constituting 75 percent of the market, are not required to achieve this certification.[4] Furthermore, while these standards pushing to advance education quality standards are appropriate, the schools that cater to at-risk and poor communities lack the necessary money to meet these requirements.

Parts of the ISO standards involve both the management and infrastructure of the school.[5] Here are a few of the things analyzed to obtain this certification:

- Licenses and permits from different government entities for the school grounds and procedures
- Safety regulations
- Structure regulations: minimal dimensions for classrooms as well as a minimum number of restrooms and play areas

In many cases, modifications have to be made to meet the standards, many of them being in the infrastructure. Many schools in at-risk locations simply cannot afford these.

In addition to the ISO standards, the governments also set different requirements for private school teachers. For example, teachers need a degree and should take part of trainings for a minimum of 200 hours per year. The LFIS proprietors and directors are also required to take continuous skill trainings in subjects related to administration and management. In Latin America and the Caribbean, the governments provide ongoing skill training only to the teachers and leaders of public institutions, leaving the private sector to find solutions to the training requirements with their own resources.

With the amount of scrutiny on private school teachers, it is only logical to think they are compensated more highly. Sadly, that is not the case. Some public schoolteachers make thrice the monthly salary of a schoolteacher in an LFIS. Additionally, public schoolteachers are members of powerful unions, which makes it hard for them to be removed from their positions regardless of performance or absenteeism.

As a result, the possibilities of a high salary, job stability (by being part of a strong union) and no demands of having to meet an annual training make being a part of a public institution much more attractive and remunerative than being with a private institution. This is even more acute in the case of schoolteachers who work in at-risk government schools. Often, teachers work in LFIS to get some work experience and then leave for jobs for positions in public schools.

Under these circumstances, the higher demands by governments on LFIS often discourage proprietors from continuing their efforts to provide a good education. This is especially tragic for schools in impoverished areas where there are few government schools.

How Edify Can Make a Difference: The Example of Peru

Peru is one of the countries that has aggressively tried to improve the quality in their education level. In 2010, the Peruvian government announced the deployment of new programs to raise the standards of their private schools. This resulted from Peru continuously being ranked in the bottom in tests like PISA (Programme International for School Assessment). The disastrous results obtained in subjects such as reading, math, and natural sciences were evidence of the low school performance and the shortcomings of the national education system. In response, the government decided to change the educational system and increase the requirements needed to open a school. The new regulations included:

- A certified inspection from the department of safety
- The enrollment of the institution in SUNAFIL (National Superintendency of Labor Law Enforcement)

- Registering the institution at SUNAT (National Superintendency of Taxes Management)
- A city hall operation license

These requirements[6] needed to be submitted to the Ministry of Education for inspection and verification. The government aimed for improvement in the school's infrastructure and management resulting in a better learning environment.

Regarding the infrastructure, attention was given to the following:

- The correct number of students per classroom so they can be comfortable, which also ensures the right ventilation in the room
- Appropriate lightning
- Having the sufficient number of restrooms, which should have running water and working sewers
- Interior playgrounds for the students

Regarding the management, all schools were required to:

- Be registered in the Ministry of Education and renew their enrollment accordingly
- Have an annual work plan, where they would detail the curricula for each subject
- Have continuous trainings for teachers and administrative staff

The education centers that fulfill these requirements are part of a registry issued by the Ministry of Education, which certifies them as schools and allows their students to obtain official certifications. Every private school proprietor's goal is to achieve this accreditation, as parents only consider those registered schools as valid options to enroll their children. An unlicensed school is not a real school.

All these new measures are meant to yield excellent results but taking into consideration the profile of a low-fee private school proprietor, the implementation is not easy. Let us take a closer look at the average Latin American partner school proprietor profile. After analyzing the data, we found 67 percent are women, and the average age is forty-nine years old. These women entered the world of education with a burning desire to change the world. They saw education as a way to create a more just society and provide opportunities their students would not have otherwise. Usually, we work with former schoolteachers with an entrepreneurial vision, who after years working for other institutions, decide to venture into their own operation. They are teachers at heart who love their students and don't see them as numbers or revenue, so they are very understanding when the parents have money problems and cannot meet the monthly payments. Often, they are too understanding, which leads to having a high number of students attending their classes after paying only the enrollment fee and owing many monthly installments. Their hearts outweigh their business savvy.

Thus, these proprietors make their administrative decisions led by their hearts and not necessarily with a busines objective. Under this perspective, doing the paperwork and spending time checking boxes to comply with the new guidelines set by the Ministry of Education is not something the proprietors are passionate about. Having the spotlight set on the day-to-day work with the children places the need to comply with guidelines and formalities on the backburner.

In 2016, the Ministry of Education issued yet another warning addressed to those schools that have not yet presented their documentation for official accreditation. After six years of warnings and extensions, the management of those schools figured it would be the same drill as always, and there would be yet another extension to get their paperwork in order.

But this year was different, and for the very first time, the Ministry of Education issued a list with over 8,300 schools in the entire country that would be closed if they did not present the required paperwork. Edify Peru's director managed to get a hard copy of this list, and after going over every name, she found 40 of Edify's partner schools were at risk of being closed. Immediately, Edify sprang into action. The director reached out to an assortment of professionals in her network, assembled a group of lawyers, accountants, and engineers who would help the school proprietors *pro bono*. One of the Edify Peru MFI partners offered their facilities, and after several days of intense work, working hand in hand to meet each individual school's need, the schools were able to present the paperwork necessary before the deadline. All 40 partner schools that had been blacklisted were able to renew their licenses.

While saving the forty schools from being closed was the main objective, Edify Peru aims to equip their partner schools with the tools needed for them to be sustainable and not rely on third parties. This is why, despite it being the hard way, instead of just gathering documents, each professional took the time to sit down and teach the proprietors what needed to be done, how to do it, and why it needed to be done. This management crash course was a one-time offer, so each proprietor had to take advantage of the resources offered and learn how to do it themselves or be left to fend for themselves whenever the Ministry of Education audited them or asked to renew their accreditation.

Considering the profile of the school proprietors, Edify Peru knew there was a high risk of the schools falling behind on their paperwork or getting lost in the bureaucratic procedures endangering the renewal of their accreditations. With this in mind, Edify Peru deployed two initiatives.

Continuous internal audits. Since the Peruvian government is set on improving the quality of education, each year they get more and more rigorous regarding both management procedures and the curricula that must be taught in each school. Said rigor translates into harder and more detailed surprise audits, so to stay one step ahead of the game, Edify Peru hired a new employee who formerly worked at the Ministry of Education auditing schools.

Edify works with a very simple six-step process. First, Edify reaches out to the school's proprietor to set up a meeting. The visits are scheduled around the proprietor's availability, considering that more often than not, they will be busy with school administrative work. During this call, Edify will also give the proprietor homework depending on the critical areas for the school. Those assignments are directly related to what the Ministry of Education auditors are strictest about:

- Accurate and updated cash flows
- Tax payments installments
- Complete payroll

- Having an updated minutes book
- Making sure the licenses and permits are complete and valid.

Second, once a meeting has been set, Edify will confirm the appointment a few days before, as a kind reminder to the school's proprietor. The proprietor also has many ways to contact Edify in case something comes up and they need to reschedule.

Third, Edify's representative will go to the school on the agreed time and date, which usually leads to two outcomes. If everything goes smoothly, the proprietor will welcome our representative and have their homework ready. Together, they will go over the documents and make sure everything is in order. If changes are needed, then our representative will point out the mistakes and a new meeting will be set, usually within a week, to give the documents a final seal of approval.

Fourth, sometimes things do not go as planned. About 3 percent the proprietors, for different reasons, will make someone tell our representative that they are too busy and won't be able to meet. In these cases, where the proprietor straight-out refuses to honor the meeting or pretends not to be present, the field representative will register the incident and inform Edify's director of what happened.

Fifth, if the proprietor welcomes our representative but has not completed their assignment, we ask what happened. In some cases, the proprietor will agree to their homework, only to figure out later they did not fully understand how to complete it. If this is the case, then our representative will spend the scheduled time clearing up questions and teaching the proprietor what to do. Edify works under a "see one, do one" philosophy. This means we take the time to explain how something is done, teach the steps and reasoning behind the actions, and then the proprietor has to do the task by themselves. As might be the case with many people, when a task seems too challenging or a person doesn't see the relevance in doing it, they often find a way to have someone else do it instead. If Edify Peru had not had this policy, these directors would not hesitate to use a few excuses to have others do the work for them and not learn what they need to know. If the proprietor does not complete the assignment due to lack of interest, the representative will also register this incident.

Sixth, this register will be forwarded to Edify's director, and she will personally call each proprietor to remind them that while they will continue to be invited to the trainings, the personal consultancy resources are only provided to those who complete their assignments, which offers tangible evidence of their interest. The service will be there for them when they decide they are willing to do the work. Once they get their priorities in order, they are free to call back and schedule a new appointment.

On the next page is a flow diagram of the process.

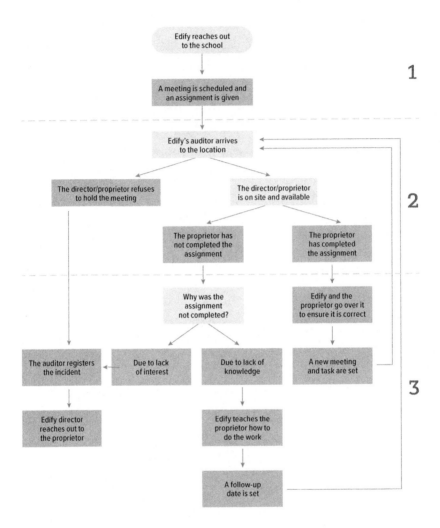

Continuous skill training certifications. Each year, hundreds of teachers are faced with the following situation: they need to fulfill two hundred hours of training, but the government won't provide workshops for them—as they do for their own teachers—and the schools they work for are low-fee schools so they cannot afford to train the teachers. A lack of training puts their jobs at risk. If a school is audited, and its teachers have not completed their continuous training requirements, then the school risks losing its accreditation. This is something they are not willing to put on the line.

Edify Peru identified this problem and worked out a solution. After meetings and negotiations with several universities, we were able to make a deal with two public universities: Universidad Nacional Federico Villareal (UNFV) and Universidad Nacional de Educación Enrique Guzman y Valle (UNE), both of whom have very strong education programs. A six-month diploma course with either of these universities usually costs US $300. Edify managed to get the program for $90 by negotiating a quantity discount guaranteeing around 500 enrollees per year.

For some schoolteachers a $90 fee might be manageable, but for others—single mothers, daughters who support their elder parents, or middle children who pay for their younger siblings' education—a $90 fee is almost out of reach. Edify wanted to make sure all teachers had the chance to take the diploma course, but it has been proven over and over again that when something comes free, people tend to dismiss it and not value it. The diploma had to cost something; it had to require some kind of sacrifice for the teachers, so it was back to the negotiation table. The final result was Edify would cover 30 percent of the program's cost, a training partner would cover another 30 percent, and each teacher would pay a $30 fee.

Other actions that Edify took to lower the program's cost include having all educational materials distributed electronically. If someone wanted a hard copy, they would have to print the materials at their own expense. One of the schools would lend their premises to hold the trainings.

The programs have a duration of six months and are divided into five academic modules. In addition, attendees have to present a final project, where they show how they are applying what they have been taught in their day-to-day classes. Along with this final project, each module has assignments, homework, and tests. To obtain a certificate, the student has to have good attendance record and a final grade of at least fourteen (out of twenty) in every module.

When Edify Peru holds a paid training event, the fee must be paid up front upon enrollment. A limited number of spots are available, and in previous trainings some people reserved a spot and then didn't show up.

The diploma course was designed to cater to proprietors, management, and teachers. Most modules are taught to the whole group, but there are two modules in which proprietors and management have different content from teachers. The main goal of these courses isn't to just check a box; Edify aims to equip each person with tools that will allow them to provide a better service.

The content of each module conforms to the subjects the Ministry of Education considers as relevant training. These include:

1. General
   a. Pedagogical procedures and relevant assessment in the learning framework
   b. Communication prowess: develop written and verba abilities
   c. The effect of family members in the student's personality

  d. Focusing on a Christ-centered education, and how this imparts to children the values of honesty, kindness, peacemaking, and loving your neighbor

2. Proprietors and management
  a. Procedures to create efficient learning assessments
  b. Monitoring learning assessment results

3. Teachers
  a. Student assessment according to the Government National Curricula .
  b. Building inclusive classrooms: how to handle diversity
  c. Fitting the curricula to embrace diversity (adjusting content to the student's reality)

All training must include a Christian component in meeting government requirements regarding teaching and assessment methodologies and annual plans The Christian module reminds the teacher that children are developing human beings in need of values that will help them become caring, hardworking, and honest citizens. Low-fee schools have many challenges, not only financial but also due to the diverse backgrounds of their students. A child who has all levels of the Maslow hierarchy of needs covered has an advantage over a child whose security and safety needs are not being met, or who is struggling to meet their social needs. A Christ-centered education reminds the teacher that they have the privilege of helping shape the personality of children, and those children need to be heard, so treating them with respect will help them learn more and learn better.

A time to reap. During the subsequent four years, Edify's partner schools continued working hard and avoided getting behind when it came to paperwork and training certifications. The 40 schools that were on the verge of closing managed to stay on top of things. Today, all 839 partner schools get help and guidance whenever the Peruvian government changes or issues new legislation, so it is not easy, but by working together we manage to comply with virtually everything asked of our partners.

We now see those years were times for sowing. They were times in which we ploughed rough lands and found the good seeds we wanted to plant. There were times in which Edify sowed the seeds and took the time to water and care for them. Remarkably, 2020 was when Edify Peru's partner schools reaped that which they had been patiently sowing for years. In January and February of that year, the world saw how COVID-19 started changing the world and the huge impact it had in Asia and Europe. Edify Peru's management decided it was time to get one step ahead in the game. They prepared for the worst while hoping for the best. COVID-19 seemed far away, but after seeing its devastation to first-world countries with strong economies and reliable health systems, we thought it best to err on the side of caution.

By the end of February 2020, the Edify Peru team had designed a contingency plan, in case worst came to worst. In March, the contingency plan was brought into action. The team created an instructional video on how to install and use apps like Zoom and WhatsApp on their desktops, laptops, or smartphones to distribute instructions to the directors and proprietors. The goal was to ensure a way to communicate with schools and make sure they understood how to use the technologies. The partner schools would not be left alone as things got hard. This video was later sent to all partner schools in Latin American and Caribbean territories

Peru's education system has two different dates for the start of school: public schools start their terms in April and private schools usually start in March. But a few schools started their classes on March 2, and by March 9 almost the whole sector had started. On March 11, Peru's president addressed the nation and said in-person classes would be suspended. On March 15, Peru was declared to be in a state of emergency,[7] and the whole country was put under strict lockdown. The storm had just begun.

The state of emergency started as a two-week affair, then it was extended for another two weeks, and two more weeks and so on. Uncertainty was on the rise; unemployment rates quickly scaled, and parents did not hesitate to show their discomfort regarding the school situation. In households where both parents work, school provides a safe place for the child to spend the day while learning and staying out of trouble. Having children taking virtual classes meant that for younger children, a parent or relative had to be at home. It also meant the child would need a reliable internet connection and a device of their own to use during school hours. From the average parent's perspective, they were simply not getting their money's worth. Why should they pay full monthly installments when the child did not use the school infrastructure? With many parents losing their jobs, having less work hours, or getting their salaries cut, it was impossible for them to continue paying.

Then with the children's best interest in mind, the government threw a curveball toward private schools, especially low-fee private schools like Edify's partners. On April 27, the minister of education announced a twelve-day window for parents to take their children out of private schools and enroll them in public schools. There would be no enrollment fee, and they wouldn't need to pay any missed installments to the previous school. To keep parents from removing their children, schools lowered their fees an average of 50 percent (in Guatemala 20 percent and in the Dominican Republic 10 percent).

The government policy resulted in around 300,000 children, from both private and public institutions, being pulled from school.[8] Numbers show two main groups: very young children whom parents thought could be taught at home and high school seniors. Regarding male high school students, families needed them to bring income from informal jobs. In the case of female students, their parents needed them at home to look after the younger siblings and do house chores. These numbers brought sadness to our hearts, as we firmly believe education is the way for children and a country to escape poverty.

With low-fee schools trying desperately to stay afloat, the government finally threw them a lifeline. The Ministry of Economy announced the "Plan Reactiva," an initiative under which the government would take from the public treasury and give loans to different industries at very low rates. Another initiative to help salvage the struggling schools was the subsidy of 35 percent of the schools' payroll. The only condition to apply for the loan or receive the subsidy was a school had to be registered and authorized by the Ministry of Education.

It took two years of hard work, but all 839 partner schools received the payroll subsidy from the government. With the help and guidance of the Edify team, 15 schools have received loans from the government, which added up to US $1.5 million. Because these loans come from the Bettina (earlier we said 839 schools received loans, but here we said 15 schools received loans government), the conditions[9] offered were very helpful: a 5-year repayment period, 1-percent yearly interest rate, and 6 months of grace period.

- The government held a public contest with several banks, including Peru's national bank, to obtain the lowest interest rate possible, given the volume of loans. As a result, the interest rate for the Reactiva program was around 1 percent.
- The maximum amount for the loan was determined according to the SUNAT, taxes, and declarations as a way to guarantee the businesses/schools wouldn't go over their paying capacity.
- The government acted as the guarantor: the amount they guaranteed depended on the loan amount.
- The schools had up to thirty-six months to pay their loans, with a grace period of up to twelve months.

Despite the financial aid and the efforts made, as of the writing of this chapter, it is estimated that around five thousand private schools won't be opening their doors again.[10] The loss of so many schools educating children living in poverty will result in some government schools being overcrowded, and many students will receive a lower quality education.

Our partners are struggling. They have been knocked down but not knocked out, and Edify's job is far from over. The plan that Edify Peru designed, which has now been adapted as a "Latin America Recovery Road Map," works on five horizons.

- Horizon 1: Resolve
  - Objective: Address immediate challenges
- Horizon 2: Resilience
  - Objective: School Status and Government Aid
- Horizon 3: Return
  - Objective: Plan to return to action and quick scaling of enrollment
- Horizon 4: Reimagination
  - Objective: Adapt to a new normal
- Horizon 5: Reform
  - Objective: Understand and comply with the new regulatory system

All these plans and actions and every single training event and counseling session have been made with the following goal in mind: the provision of loans, education technology, and a Christ-centered training to LFIS with the purpose of enabling them to promote a Christ-centered education among children living in poverty in each country where Edify has operations.

As this chapter demonstrated, Edify helps LFIs meet government regulatory requirements and comply on the one hand and not to be sidelined and treated as competitors on the other. The Peru example proves that when government values the role of LFIS in education and works with them in more collaborative ways, the educational benefits accruing to children are maximized. Therefore, Edify supports and encourages governments to collaborate with LFIS in a supportive and appreciative manner.

9

CONCLUSIONS AND RECOMMENDATIONS

In Chapter 1, we provided a brief description of the failures and subsequent global education crisis. In Chapters 2–6, we presented the history and dynamics surrounding LFIS and Edify. While Chapter 2 dealt with the history of and rationale for the emergence of LFIS and Edify, the subsequent four chapters documented and discussed the Edify model as expressed in its program. These chapters delineated how Edify's products and services consisting of loan capital, education technology, and Christ-centered training were implemented and impacted the quality and content of the education delivered by the LFIS and the stakeholders (school leaders, teachers, and students) involved.

Chapter 7 focused on the voices from the field and highlighted the views of school proprietors. In their own words, they expressed the transformative impact Edify's program had on their respective schools. Chapter 8 dealt with government regulations and attitudes toward LFIS. With Peru as a case study, it outlined the regulations and standards LFIS are expected to comply with and the difficulties many of them face in meeting these requirements. It showed how Edify works to help them achieve the required compliance.

In this final chapter, we will offer concluding thoughts and suggest the way forward. Most of the recommended pathways apply to all those involved in the promotion of education, including NGO education service providers, churches, national governments, and microfinance service providers. The recommendations proposed are in the spirit of strengthening the role and contribution of the LFIS sector in the provision of access and quality education among children living in poverty and marginalized areas.

LFIS Awareness

Most people and organizations, including education officials, have little or no knowledge of the existence and role of LFIS. During his trip to Nigeria, one of the authors, Chris Crane, along with Kola Ayiedogbon, a former bank CEO, visited an LFIS operating in a slum. After the visit, Mr. Ayiedogbon said,

> I had no idea such slums existed in Nigeria. They are right outside my environment. I traveled to work every day on these streets and never realized these slums were just on the other side of the streets. Today, for the first time, I went into the Makoko slum and saw how people live and educate themselves. It took an American who has never stepped foot in Nigeria to point out to me what has been happening in my country. This is the education revolution for Nigeria.

Many believe people living in poverty don't care about their children's education. They also assume children in poverty go to public school. The truth, however, is much more varied: many people living in poverty *do* care about the quality of their children's education and are committed to investing whatever savings they have to send their children to schools where quality education is offered.

Chris wrote this report from a trip to Ghana:

> I visited a school in a Liberian refugee camp, west of Kasosa, Ghana. The school had a very nice building for a school educating poor children. The school had been charging no fees because a wealthy Liberian had supported it. However, the Liberian was now directing his finances toward Liberia itself. The managers of the school told me they would likely close the school because they saw no way to cover the expenses of the teachers and other school expenses. I informed the school managers that there was another school in Liberia camp that charged approximately $7 per month. The school was financially sustainable. The managers could not believe the poor parents in the area could afford to pay $7 every month for their children's schooling. But they were. The nearby school had 530 children and was financially sustainable.

Prior to his trip to Ethiopia to undertake a feasibility study with Chris, Makonen visited a contracted education research team at the Department of International Economic Development, University of Oxford. To his question about the role of the private education sector in Ethiopia, the team answered it was so insignificant that they had not included it as part of their study. During the feasibility study in Addis, Makonen and Chris visited a USAID education official who echoed the view of the DFID research team, saying due to the country's communist background, the LFIS type of schools did not exist. She concluded by saying she would be surprised if we found any.

267

Contrary to the two views mentioned above, we were told by the minister of education himself that over 40 percent of the students in Addis went to private (high- and low-fee alike) schools. This was quite unusual as many governments often do not have proper records of the existence and number of LFIS in their countries. In the Ethiopian case, the government took initiative to gather such schools and facilitate the formation of a private schools association. In our discussion with the leadership of the association in Addis, we learned the association had 300 schools already registered as members in the capital alone within less than a year of its formation, and a lot more had not joined the association yet and were still unregistered.

Moreover, the limited knowledge that people have about LFIS is often biased. As LFIS charge fees regardless of whether they are for-profit or non-profit, they tend to be identified as "profit maximizers" that are driven by bottom line objectives only. They are also often equated with the regular private schools that are for rich children in prime places with prime buildings. Still more is the notion: "If private schools do exist for the poor, then they must be of poor quality."[1]

These are unqualified prejudices that give a wrong portrayal of LFIS. LFIS are primarily for the people in poverty, of the people in poverty, and by the people living in poverty doing social business to offer quality education to those who can't go to public schools because they do not exist, the schools are dysfunctional, or they can't afford private schools. Generally speaking, many of them offer better quality education than the materially better equipped and served government schools.

These stories communicate one message: the public's awareness of the existence, nature, and role of LFIS is limited and, where present, often based on misinformation. This general ignorance must be addressed through the dissemination of proper information and knowledge. As a solution, we recommend:

- Conferences should be held on national, regional, and global levels dialoguing and discussing issues surrounding LFIS.
- Learning institutions should be spurred to consider this as a potential field of academic research.
- A popular journal of LFIS should be published on a quarterly basis. This could be done as an online project.

Recognition of the Role of LFIS

Various studies show LFIS have contributed and are contributing toward education among children living in poverty in multifaceted ways. These include helping meet the demand. Several governments in developing countries have failed to cope with the demand for education. They find creating adequate space and providing quality education in an enabling learning environment either challenging or impossible. In the case of Africa, the absorptive capacity is further constrained by two major factors: lack of trained teachers and inadequate funding. According to UNESCO, approximately 69 million primary and secondary teachers are needed to achieve universal primary and secondary education by 2030. Although the total global number of teachers is said to have increased by 50 percent between 2000–2019, the supply of teachers remains acute in Sub-Saharan Africa where 70 percent and 90 percent of countries face shortages at primary and secondary levels, respectively.[2]

Moreover, while the global level minimum teachers' qualification requirements stand at 81 percent of primary and 78 percent of secondary teachers, Africa has the lowest regions at 65 percent and 51 percent, respectively.[3]

Globally, 81 percent of primary and 78 percent of secondary teachers had the minimum required qualifications, according to the most recent available data with substantial variations between regions. Central Asia had the highest proportion of teachers with the minimum qualifications at 98 percent of primary and 97 percent of secondary teachers. The region with the lowest proportions of teachers with minimum qualifications is Sub-Saharan Africa where just 65 percent of primary and 51 percent secondary teachers were trained.

As a result, tens of millions of children are still out of school because they have no access to school in the first place or they have dropped out because of poor education systems and practices. The overall absorptive capacity is limited, and the supply deficit is huge. It is estimated that 49 percent of the 57 million children who are currently out of school "will probably never set a foot in a classroom."[4]

The LFIS came into existence to fill the gaps in public education by creating additional access to education. In many of the poor areas of the developing countries, more children go to such schools than government schools, partly because governments do not have enough resources to educate all the children in their countries and partly because the quality of education in public schools is generally poor. Moreover, government schools have inherited systems that make embracing pedagogies that will significantly increase education difficult. Entrenched institutions such as teachers' unions can sway elections and disrupt education.

Reducing the gender gap for education. The traditional approach of student recruitment puts girls, particularly those in rural and marginalized areas, at a disadvantage, which results in less girls enrolling or staying in schools. Some of the traditional reasons for the gender disparity are girls are compelled to spend more time on domestic chores than on their studies, parents prefer paying for their sons than their daughters when they face financial challenges, and parents fear sending their daughters to schools where undiscipline and insecurity are rampant. Early marriages and pregnancy are other factors that keep young girls out of school.

LFIS are cognizant of these widespread problems and offer a favorable environment for female students. Contrary to the traditional approach, LFIS offer a more favorable environment for education of female students because they:

- Are generally located within communities and are in walking distance.
- Practice strict discipline and supervision of student movements during school hours.
- Have better policies to control bullying.
- Make sure a proper teacher's attention is given to students.
- Maintain general security.
- Practice high moral standards that contribute to the reduction of behavioral problems in schools.

These practices also mean that girls do not drop out at the same frequency as they do in public schools because of pregnancy and performance problems. In Christian LFIS, children are also taught to view both men and women as equal bearers of God's image and there is no male or female, for all are one in Christ. In other words, parents feel safer sending their daughters to such schools than government ones. For these and other reasons, LFIS are appreciated by parents of all faiths as all parents attach a high value to the safety of their children.

Many studies have also shown that LFIS often offer better quality education. These are some of the factors that have enabled LFIS to deliver quality education and achieve higher academic performance and pass rates:

- Unlike in public schools, teachers in LFIS face the risk of being fired when they are absent from work without approved reasons.
- Most teachers in LFIS see teaching as a vocation and discharge their responsibilities accordingly.
- Smaller class sizes allow students to get adequate attention from their teachers. Unlike teachers in public schools who deal with large numbers, teachers in LFIS have an opportunity to establish one-on-one relationships with their students and attend to their different needs and also have time to give them personalized mentoring and support.
- A non-threatening and loving environment as well as respect for children in many LFIS encourages students to generate and critique arguments in a constructive manner. Assured by the absence of punishments and reprisals for their critical views, students learn how to engage in constructive dialogue, debate, and argument and thereby develop their critical thinking skills. They are, for example, encouraged to critique

secular ideas and views from a Christ-centered viewpoint.
They are also encouraged to question social, economic, and
political injustices, including corruption, which they see and
hear about in their communities and countries.

- An active participation of parents in their children's education
and school matters. Teachers do everything possible in
ensuring parents are updated on a day-to-day basis by asking
them to read their children's reports, helping them complete
class assignments, attending PTA meetings, reading school
publications, and giving suggestions to improve school
practices. The interest shown and the active support given by
their parents inspire and help children to work harder and
perform better.

In most LFIS, therefore, the quality of education students receive is
often better, academic scores are higher, more students pass exams,
retention is higher, and more students move from lower to higher
grades and beyond.

Creating jobs. LFIS employ an average of fifteen to twenty-five
employees (teachers and support staff). This contributes to national employment, thereby increasing the number of income-earning
people in the economy. School construction by LFIS also means
builders get jobs, and the purchase of building and other materials
enhance backward and forward connections. All these economic
transactions related to LFIS expansion raise the level of income and
effective demand (purchasing power) in the economy.

Improving quality. LFIS are increasingly becoming popular
among parents as a better option for giving their children a quality
education. As a result, they are growing in number. According to

research by the Centre for Development and Enterprise (CDE) in South Africa, LFIS there grew by 44 percent while the government schools fell by 9 percent over a period ten years as the reputations of LFIS spread and demands for their services increased.[5]

Viewed globally, the private sector seems to be growing faster than the government sector. Another paper by CDE states:

> Between 1991 and 2003, private school enrollment grew far more quickly than public school enrollment worldwide. For example, the average growth in private primary education has been 58 percent, compared with a 10 percent growth in the public primary school sector. Interestingly, private primary education grew in Africa, by 113 percent, as opposed to 52 percent for public education. This is a faster growth rate than the Arab states, where private education increased by 109 percent, and South-East Asia where the growth was 76 percent. In developing countries most of this expansion has been in private schools for the poor, which make schooling accessible for disadvantaged communities and marginalized groups.[6]

All in all, the role of LFIS in complementing the public effort in educating the poor, the marginalized—particularly girls—and achieving the MDGs has been phenomenal.

Answering criticism. Unfortunately, although there have been some positive developments in certain circles, the world has generally tended to sideline, remain silent about, or even deny the role played by the LFIS. David Archer, head of program development at ActionAid, for example, argues, "To suggest somehow that supporting low-cost private schools would boost school attendance flies in the face of the evidence. . . . It is ironic at a time when girls are a priority in primary education, as this kind of initiative will almost certainly discourage girl attendance. The big gains in the end come when school is free."[7] Kevin Watkins, a senior fellow at the Brookings Institution (a Washington-based think tank), expresses a similar skepticism at the notion of charging poor people school fees. He says, "If we are talking about poverty reduction, the idea that poor people should be paying for education is absurd."[8]

The truth of the matter is, however, a "free education" doesn't exist. According to the UN, in Sub-Saharan Africa school fees consume nearly a quarter of a poor family's income, covering not only tuition, but also indirect fees such as membership of parent-teacher associations, community contributions, textbooks, and uniforms.

Education in government schools costs money, and the costs are increasingly growing. Parents pay various hidden and open fees and are finding educating their children increasingly becoming expensive. More so as the quality of education they are paying for is constantly deteriorating. Kenya, where primary school attendance surged following the abolition of school fees, is a good example. *The Economist* issued on February 22, 2014, describes the scenario in Kenya as follows:

> There can scarcely be two words in Kenya that cause more resentment than "school fees." It is now more than ten years since charges for state primary schools in east Africa's biggest economy were abolished by law. Yet it is an open secret that education is not truly free. In fact, fees are rising. Dorcas Mutoku, a policeman's wife whose two sons attend a public primary school in the capital, Nairobi, has found that levies

have simply been renamed. She has to find the equivalent of $35 for a one-off "signing-on" fee and pay almost as much again for admission fees. End-of-term exams, uniforms and books cost at least another $10 per child."[9]

In fact, the Kenyan National Parent's Association accused the education minister and his top civil servant for failing to implement the law and brought a lawsuit saying that the government is guilty of "extraordinary doublespeak." The parents hold that the "illicit fees are not being spent on better books and facilities but are merely padding the incomes of school administrators."[10]

In many instances, the expenses parents incur in LFIS are not hugely different from those in government schools and can even sometimes be lower. In Kenya, research by the Brookings Institute found the fees for two-thirds of children in Kenyan private schools are lower than in the supposedly free state system."[11] And even where they are slightly more expensive, the parents and students often get better value for their money in LFIS. Mwangi Kimenyi, a Kenyan economist at the Brookings Institute, explains: "Donors and governments have broadened access to school at the cost of creating a dysfunctional public-education system where millions of children are attending school but not learning."[12]

Some of the reasons relate to the high rate of teachers' absenteeism and competencies. A 2013 World Bank Report found Kenyan teachers were absent almost half the time. And pupils in Kenya's state schools received on average little more than two-and-a-half hours of instruction a day. Another study found that only one-third of public sector teachers scored at least 80 percent when tested on the curriculum they are meant to teach."[13]

We agree with Pauline Dixon that:

> Despite the evidence there are still some with international aid organizations, governments and academia who do not acknowledge the success and potentialities of low-cost private schooling in developing countries. The failure to acknowledge such developments and admit their significance in relation to government schools is a sort of denial. Many are in denial about what is happening in schooling throughout a large part of the developing world.[14]

Sidelining or being silent about the role of LFIS is tantamount to denial and an unfortunate historical error. It does not do justice to education and is an insult to the proprietors who have responded to the plight of neglected, low-income communities by filling the supply gap created by public failure, the students who receive their education in these schools, and the parents who sacrifice their little savings to educate their children.

Since it started its first loan guarantee program aimed at helping private education in Ghana in 2005 and then in many other Sub-Saharan African countries, the International Finance Corporation (the private arm of the World Bank) has begun attributing some level of recognition to the contribution made by the LFIS sector. DFID and USAID have done the same during the last five or so years. Furthermore, some national governments have started realizing and appreciating the complementary role of LFIS. These are long overdue positive changes and should be celebrated. However, they are a drop in the ocean, and the general global recognition and appreciation of LFIS has remained very limited and has generated very little or no support.

It is time for the international community to take good stock of the role that has been played, is being played, and will be played by LFIS in educating the poor who would otherwise have been left behind, and then provide the full recognition and support the sector deserves. It is time for the world to recognize LFIS as part of the solution to the global education crisis and not as part of the problem.

Mobilizing funding for LFIS. The quality of education and the academic performance are both determined by the learning environment. In terms of physical factors, the size and quality of school buildings and classrooms, furniture, aides, ventilation and lighting, and toilet facilities all influence the degree of learning and teaching. Although they have done much with all the limitations surrounding them, LFIS have so much need in making sure they have a full-fledged, physical learning environment that meets all standards to satisfy the learning and teaching needs of students and teachers, respectively.

The other very important physical factor relates to the building of computer labs and state-of-the-art learning technology and devices suitable for all ages—both for educational and employment purposes. Computer skills also contribute to employability and higher education. The intensive effort made is to ensure the devices and the related skills are in place. Also, developing an ICT capacity that makes information gathering, research, lesson delivery, and interaction easier for both students and teachers is an important requirement that LFIS need to have in place as modern learning institutions.

Buildings and education technology constitute the physical conditions of the learning environment. The other part of the equation is made up of soft (non-physical) factors: leadership, management, and teacher training. Schools that are well-led and well-managed and have teachers that are well-trained are likely to offer a better learning environment than those with poor leadership, management, and teacher training.

Many of the proprietors of LFIS have no prior skills and experience of leading and managing people as well as running businesses. Yet they employ teachers and other support staff and run their schools as social enterprises. In order for LFIS to function effectively, they need to create strong and competent leadership and management capacities. These determine staff productivity, school profitability, and sustainability.

Under normal circumstances, the quality of education is determined by the level of training the teachers possess. What is taught and how it is transmitted determine what the children receive, learn, and internalize. The quality of education is often as poor or as good as the quality of teacher training. Most of the teachers in LFIS do not have formal teacher training qualifications. The main reasons why the quality of education is high in such schools is the on-the-job training given to teachers, the ordered environment maintained by proprietors, and personal attention given to students. Combined with lower teacher absenteeism, less school days and school years, and formal training, these attributes can produce even better learning outcomes.

All the above-mentioned expansion and improvement efforts cost money. The LFIS sector needs huge investments in their effort to expand and improve infrastructural facilities, build state-of-the-art learning technology, engage compatible devices, build leadership and business management capacities to engage highly trained teachers, and thereby take the sector's contribution to the education of the poor to a much higher level.

Edify mobilizes funding from individuals and foundations that are deeply committed to the education of the poor and are generous in sharing their wealth and transmits the funding to LFIS to help them expand their educational facilities, including technology, to improve their leadership, management and accounting abilities, and teacher training skills. This will create access to more poor children and improve the quality of education they receive.

However, the financial and technical assistance Edify and other similar organizations provide in support of the LFIS sector is far from being adequate. It is just a scratch on the surface. Yet the world mobilizes huge amounts of money for educational purposes. Pearson, for example, records that $75 billion in aid money has been dedicated to education over the last seven years.[15] This money is channeled through government agencies and often goes only to support public education. Only 2 percent of global education fund is estimated to be allocated to LFIS.

Without sounding like we're anti-public education, we propose that the world mobilizes and allocates funding specifically geared toward supporting the LFIS sector too. As shown above not only does the sector play an important role in meeting the education gap, but it also provides better quality education. Most of the children educated in these schools are from families living in poverty in rural and marginalized areas. They are equally entitled to benefit from the grant donated by the international community as those in public schools. To ensure this is done, we propose a Global Fund for LFIS (GFL) be established.

The GFL could start with $100–$200 million managed by a lean autonomous body. The money could come from the international contributions in relation to the realization of the EAL, MDGs, GPE, and SDGs objectives. The other option is that bilateral and multilateral donor agencies as well as national governments place a certain percentage of their education budget in the fund.

The fund can then start working with countries where there is a higher concentration of LFIS and channel the funding through national and international NGOs that are already in the field. The relevant NGO will administer the funding on the basis of credible proposals from the field and be accountable to the fund.

Creating the Global Fund as a source for LFIS to meet part of their financial constraints will help them create more and better educational opportunities for accessing and receiving quality education by the poor. The international community should accept and embrace the support to LFIS as part of the global effort to enhance education, not as a help to individuals to selfishly enrich themselves but to expand and improve access to the quality education poor children deserve. The proprietors are small social entrepreneurs and deserve to receive capital aid as part of the national SME development effort as well.

The international donor community should view the work of LFIS as a key business solution to the global education crisis as it viewed microfinance as a tool for poverty alleviation during the last quarter of the twentieth century. As it did with microfinance, the donor community should support the LFIS sector to move from the experimental stage to maturity. In other words, the LFIS sector should have a share of the global and domestic education budget that has traditionally been channeled through the ineffective public systems.

Conducive Environment for LFIS to Grow

One of the other main constraints LFIS face in going forward and educating the poor is the lack of favorable regulatory frameworks. In most cases, government policies, standards, and practices are not always conducive to the healthy, effective functioning of LFIS.

1. *Many national governments put conditions that are often contextually unrealistic.* For example, in slum areas where settlements are densely built and land/space is extremely difficult to acquire, governments demand that schools have large classrooms and sports fields. They also demand they employ trained teachers and pay salaries equivalent to what the governments pay their teachers. These are difficult to meet as LFIS charge low fees and earn low incomes. The only option would be raising school fees, which would push parent's expenses high and inhibit many poor students from coming to school. As a result, many LFIS are closed down by the government or operate as unrecognized schools. In both scenarios the poor suffer.

2. *LFIS in many countries find the process of getting official license and registration long and painstakingly difficult, cumbersome, and costly.* During inspection exercises, education bureaucrats often threaten proprietors or take spontaneous measures to close schools down, claiming they do not meet government standards. Such scenarios often create much temptation for corruption, which involves bribery and illegal practices. In some countries, the school inspector shows up at the LFIS and simply asks the proprietor, "Do you have the envelope of cash for me?" If a bribe is given, the inspector leaves.

If a bribe is not given, the inspector then harasses the proprietor with real or invented infractions of school regulations. This problem could partly be addressed by engaging NGOs to participate in the inspection of schools, and governments are encouraged to do so.

3. *The expansion and growth of LFIS is constrained partly because land, particularly in urban areas, is often expensive or unavailable.* Further, getting title deeds is difficult as a result of national and traditional land policies, which often disfavor the poor and low-income people such as LFIS proprietors. If an entrepreneur submits *bona fide* architectural plans for a school, the government will give the land for the school, provided the entrepreneur completes significant construction and educates at least eighty students within three years on that land, and in accordance with the architectural designs. If the entrepreneur meets the standard, the government will transfer title of the land free and clear to the entrepreneur. If construction is not completed and a school educating the children is not in place, the government will take back the land and offer it to another entrepreneur. Unfortunately, the government charges a land transfer tax of approximately 40 percent of the value of the land. It is sometimes hard for entrepreneurs to come up with the cash to pay the 40 percent up front. National governments should endeavor to address the land problem that constrains LFIS from expanding their educational facilities.

4. *Lack of capital is another major constraint faced by LFIS.* Governments can do at least four things to ease the capital constraint:

- Governments can provide interest-free loans to microfinance institutions to make loans to LFIS. Governments can also absorb 50 percent of all loan losses equally with the microfinance institutions. In other words, from the first dollar of default, the government would bear 50 cents and the institution would bear 50 cents. This will encourage MFIs to serve LFIS with the capital they need to expand and increase their services.

- Governments can require all banks to have 10 percent of their loan portfolio accessible to LFIS at affordable rates.
- Governments can provide 50 percent subsidies for education technology equipment purchased by schools. When a school borrows money to purchase computers or mobile learning devices, the school will only be required to repay 50 percent of the amount to the microfinance institution or bank that makes the loan.
- Governments can rent or sell failing public schools to LFIS proprietors at reasonable rates.

5. *LFIS find internet connectivity difficult and expensive.* Given the future orientation of online learning as demonstrated during the COVID season, this problem will have profound effects on the functioning of LFIS. It will constrain their ability to provide e-based learning and put them at a disadvantage. Governments can provide free or heavily subsidized internet connectivity so students can learn how to use the internet to increase their learning. Electricity supply is the other serious problem LFIS are faced with since it is expensive and unreliable. Students will also be able to do projects with students in the West online. In this way, students will learn from other cultures and develop twenty-first-century skills such as collaboration, learning to find facts, synthesizing facts, producing,

and creating with the facts. Websense or other software that blocks children from going to inappropriate sites should be used.

The conclusion here is that LFIS are operating in an environment that is generally inimical to full and accelerated growth, thereby limiting their ability to educate more children living in poverty. Governments should appreciate that it is in the national interest to create a favorable environment for LFIS by:

- Making access to land, capital, education technology, and connectivity easier.
- Allocating textbooks.
- Offering training opportunities for teachers teaching in LFIS.
- Making registration and licensing processes transparent, expedient, and less costly.
- Making policies and standards public and understood by LFIS.
- Training more teachers to make it easier and cheaper for LFIS to employ qualified teachers.

National governments should realize their protection, collaboration, and support—and not their disruptive intervention, bureaucratic red tape, and mistrust—that will create an enabling environment for LFIS to play their complementary role more effectively and make an even greater national contribution.

Creating a Culture That Appreciates and Respects Teachers

Teaching is one of the noblest jobs one can have. Jesus came to teach all He knew from His Father. Whatever knowledge He had,

He passed it on to others so they would teach and mold others. He told His disciples (students) they would do greater things than He because the Holy Spirit would be with them. So a student is taught to teach (directly or indirectly) others—and through their teaching mold others into better people.

Teachers want to teach children in and outside classrooms new things, new ways, new and thoughts and to spark their imaginations to accomplish great things for themselves and for society and to become change agents. It is difficult to build a transformed nation without educated citizens, and it is difficult to educate citizens without educated teachers. Citizens think as they are taught and act as they think.

Teaching is the source of ideas and actions. As every battle is won or lost in the mind, those who mold the mind hold the key to the door of development and transformation. And these are none other than teachers. It is not the school building, the computer lab, or the sports field, which are all important ingredients of quality education; rather, what the teacher does in the classroom determines what kind of men and women will be leading future generations.

Yet in many developing countries, the role of teachers does not receive the appreciation and respect it deserves. People selected for training often come from among the less successful academically, and the quality of training is generally poor. Moreover, salaries and benefits are relatively lower than other professions even with comparable degrees. In most cases, teaching facilities and staff rooms are poor or non-existent. Salaries are paid irregularly, and management, supervision, and feedback systems are discouragingly poor. Their contribution is not viewed with appreciation and respect, not even by their own employers. As salaries are low and irregular, teachers have a low standard of living and have to supplement their incomes. In some societies, even parents and students do not appreciate and respect teachers. All these are indicators of little or no appreciation and respect for the profession of teaching. In short:

> While teachers may be educating the future leaders of the world and molding young minds, they often don't get the respect they deserve for doing a hard, time-consuming and sometimes frustrating job. Education may not be a glamorous profession in the strictest sense, but it does garner more respect—and often more benefits—in certain parts of the world than others."[16]

According to the 2013 Global Teacher Status Index published by Varkey GEMS Foundation, "China, South Korea, Turkey, Egypt, and Greece respect their teachers more than all other European and Anglo-Saxon countries. Israel and Brazil featured at the lower end of the Index Status."[17]

The lack of respect for the teaching profession, no doubt, affects the enthusiasm and performance of teachers in negative ways and vice versa. One key factor in expressing respect for teachers is the value attached by the education system to the level of training teachers. Although it no longer is the case, the key to Finland's impressive educational performance, for example, is that selection is rigorous and competitive and only the top students are recruited to train as teachers. According to research conducted by Amanda Ripley, getting a placement in a teacher training college in Finland is as difficult as getting admission to MIT and other prestigious universities. She says, "In Finland, *all* education schools were selective.

Getting into a teacher-training program there was as prestigious as getting into medical school in the United States."[18]

When teaching and teachers are respected by the education system itself through its selection process, remuneration standards, and regulatory practices, the perception and culture change dramatically. Top students choose to enroll in teacher training colleges, and children aspire to becoming a teacher just as much as they dream about becoming a doctor, an engineer, a pilot, an architect, or a lawyer.

This in turn changes the quality and quantity of teachers being trained in training colleges and eventually of the teachers in schools. LFIS are likely to benefit from such a development because there will be an increase in the supply of qualified teachers in the market. Furthermore, with more qualified and respected teachers in the market, a favorable condition for an overall improvement in the quality of education is created.

Edify does everything possible not only to train teachers but also to create a culture in which teaching is appreciated and valued by proprietors, students, parents, and the teachers themselves. It is time that those countries where the perception of teachers is low follow the example of the countries that give the respect to teachers that they deserve. Training teachers is necessary but not sufficient for delivering quality education. This must be accompanied with a wide range of measures that positively impact public attitudes and the overall teaching environment and reward system.

Establishing Public-Private Partnerships

The LFIS sector in general, and Christian LFIS in particular, has proven to be successful in many areas related to education:

establishing and keeping discipline, ensuring security and safety, attracting girls, retaining students in schools, attaining a high level of teachers' presence and commitment, establishing good teacher-student relationships, achieving academic scores, securing active parental participation, and forming good moral characters.

These are all good aspects of a quality education with which the world of government schools is struggling. The LFIS sector is generating several ways of improving the content and quality of education and offers a lot of opportunities to learn. It will, therefore, be advisable to pay close attention to how LFIS do business and draw lessons that government schools can apply in improving their educational practices to the benefit of children being educated there instead of ignoring them and dismissing them as "competitors" or "profit-makers." National governments, donor agencies, UNICEF, and GPE should endeavor to look into this and appreciate the lessons to be learned and then formulate implementation strategies for translating the concept of learning from LFIS into practice.

The key measure would be the establishment of public-private partnerships. The partnerships could then promote mutual learning and trust through constructive practices, including exposure visits, twinning of schools, and regular discussion forums. Doing business this way means exercising the eighth goal of the MDGs: partnership development.

Embracing LFIS as a Business Solution

As a business solution, the LFIS sector is likely to be the way that the millions of children in the world currently receiving no education or a poor education can be reached sustainably and effectively. The timing in education finance is analogous to the early 1970s when ACCION and Opportunity International were the only players in microfinance, and Professor Mohamad Yunus was just getting started. Although there are not as many LFIS as there are microfinance clients, these schools probably serve as many impoverished children as the microfinance industry currently serves adults.

Prior to the overwhelming and convincing evidence generated by the microfinance industry, the poor were regarded as "unbankable." The general perception was the poor would not be able to do business and repay loans and therefore were not creditworthy. The false perception was dealt a blow when various microfinance institutions emerged and started lending to the poor for various economic activities and proved that the poor nearly always paid back and did so at a higher rate than the rich.[19]

After the 1990s the microfinance industry began receiving global recognition, and private investors started investing millions in making the sector evolve into a multibillion-dollar industry. Until microfinance proved to be a profitable and serious business, the funding of the industry during the first twenty years of its life depended heavily on official grants. The sector was small, commercial investors were skeptical, and there was little expectation it would grow into a multibillion-dollar industry, let alone win a Nobel Peace Prize.[20] Even its prominent pioneer, Laureate Mohammad Yunus, was taken by surprise. He never anticipated what microfinance has become today. In his own words:

> When I started my initiative that led to the creation of Grameen Bank, my ambition was small and simple—to help the poor people in Jobra, a village in Bangladesh. I thought if I could give them access to a small amount of money maybe

> their lives could change for the better. I never imagined the
> scale of impact that idea would have today.[21]

Understandably, microfinance institutions and private investors are cautious about investing in new products. Although many microfinance institutions aimed to enhance the education of children through micro-enterprise and student fee loans, giving loans to school proprietors to expand/build educational facilities was not common for a long time in the industry's history. The main reason was group lending was the most predominant lending methodology and dealt with small loan sizes and short loan cycles.

By its very nature, school business is an SME that involves higher loan sizes and longer terms. To many MFIs, loans to school proprietors constitute a new product that requires new skill sets and institutional arrangements. As a result, MFIs tend to view the new product as risky and non-profitable; therefore, they have a reluctance to enter into ventures—although this seems to have changed a bit with the conversion of some MFIs into regulated banks and deposit-taking institutions.

The experience of Edify and other organizations investing in education finance has proven the opposite: Edify's experience with implementing MFIs has demonstrated that lending to school proprietors is not only socially desirable as it contributes to the goal of increasing education, which MFIs seek to achieve, but it's also financially profitable.

Just as microfinance is to material poverty, LFIS are a business solution to the education crisis that has been long dependent on international handouts. This does not mean the LFIS model is a panacea and the only way of educating all the children of the developing world, nor do we suggest all the schools should convert to LFIS. But it is an option to children and parents who do not have other choices and are looking for better options. The LFIS sector offers a good business solution to the education of a large number of children living in poverty in a more sustainable and independent manner. The government sector has failed and is failing to cope with the increasing demand for education, and the LFIS sector must be provided with the necessary support to undo the damage done to education by the supply deficit caused by government failure.

Another international example in this regard is the move taken by Pearson, the UK-based company. In 2012, Pearson launched a fund, the Pearson Affordable Learning Fund, initially capitalized with US $15 million, to invest in low-fee education. The first investment of this fund was Omega Schools in Ghana, a chain of low-cost private schools (previously Edify had a key investor through its loans). Pearson also invested through a separate fund in Bridge International Academies in Kenya. Pearson also operates a chain of these schools in India. (These are not LFIS.)[22]

Scale follows capital injection. Increased private investment and lending by the microfinance industry in the LFIS sector is highly likely to make huge contributions to the scaling up of the sector, thereby creating greater opportunities for more children to go to school and receive a quality education. And this can happen when the LFIS sector is embraced as a business solution to the education crisis by private investors in general and impact investors in particular.

On the basis of its twelve years of experience, Edify can testify that LFIS are reliable borrowers and business partners. Edify encourages private investors who have not considered the LFIS sector to look seriously at the LFIS sector and start participating. And for those who are already involved, they should increase their investment in the education of children living in poverty. The market is huge, the return is good, the cause is noble, and the time is now.

Boosting LFIS Capital Base

Edify is not a microfinance institution. However, during its twelve years of service, it has provided loan products and services through partnerships with various financial intermediaries, including commercial banks, deposit-taking MFIs, and those with only lending licenses. Edify capital has been loaned to such organizations at concessionary rates for on-lending to Edify partner schools, according to the terms and conditions of each and every lending partner with contextual variations. There is a solid experience that the engagement of MFIs in the provision of financial services to LFIS has boosted their capital base and helped them increase their physical capacity to create more access to education. It has been of great mutual benefit to both parties. With regard to the MFIs, lending to LFIS, is an opportunity for:

Business expansion. By expanding their client base from traditional micro-entrepreneurs to small-scale businesses such as LFIS, MFIs expand their market base and thereby grow their businesses and profit-making objectives. Compared to micro-entrepreneurs who are often scattered and difficult to reach, LFIS are mainly based in urban and peri-urban areas, which makes them easily accessible. They are also relatively better organized and have better record keeping and accounting. They are also more recognized by law and easier to deal with as legal entities. In other words, recruitment, delivery, and monitoring costs to be incurred are relatively lower than would be the case with most micro-entrepreneurs, particularly new recruits. Engaging in the provision of credit to LFIS is therefore a profitable and desirable opportunity for MFIs business expansion and growth.

Social development ministry. Education is one of the key weapons of social and personal transformation. It is the great equalizer. Engaging with schools to create access to quality education among children living in poverty will open a new field for social development, thereby broadening the ministry of MFIs in the transformation of lives.

Wealth generation and poverty alleviation. Conventionally, MFIs have engaged in wealth generation through enterprise development based on the production and distribution of physical goods and services. Engaging with LFIS means funding education-based social businesses, which generates wealth by producing employable citizens who build economies, communities, and nations. By strengthening the capital base of school owners, MFIs are likely to employ more paid teachers and staff, build more infrastructure, and buy more supplies, which boost both forward and backward connections and promote wealth generation and improved standards of living.

Christian ministry. As shown in previous sections, the main purpose of LFIS is not only to educate children according to the curriculum laid by national government and promote academic excellence in ways that students have greater opportunity for higher education and employability. It is also to shape their character according to the values and principles of Jesus Christ through the provision of a Christ-centered education. Engaging in the provision of credit services among LFIS is highly likely to create an opportunity for Christian MFIs to participate in the spiritual transformation and character formation of future citizens in the schools, thereby meeting their part of their Christian mission.

Monitoring, Evaluating, and Assessing Impact

This section particularly refers to those engaged in supporting LFIS. Very often there is a tendency to count the number of training events and analyze the content of training and think that is all that matters for satisfaction and success. That is self-deception.

Generally speaking, change does not happen without improving existing skills or acquiring new skills. And this happens either through on- or off-the-job training. However, training alone will not make improvements. The newly acquired skills have to be applied properly. For this to happen, monitoring and evaluation exercises accompanied by mentoring, and coaching become critical. Edify endeavors to move toward realizing this goal.

Organizations such as Edify, which fund and facilitate the training of school proprietors, administrators, and teachers, must build an M&E capacity to ensure that proper pre- and post-training follow-ups are undertaken to ensure trainees are helped to translate training outputs into the desired tangible outcomes of improving the quality of education, academic performance, and character formation.

In this regard, Edify equips and engages loan officers to closely monitor trained proprietors while transformation officers and coaches monitor trained teachers. The monitoring exercise is not only to assess whether acquired skills have been translated into practice or not. It is also to provide on-the-job feedback to make any improvements that need to be made. In this way, monitoring becomes another form of training, an opportunity for continuing the classroom training in the field where skills are put into practice. This is an important intervention, and the loan officers and transformation officer need to be equipped with better skills to discharge their responsibilities effectively.

Moreover, Edify has also learned while monitoring and coaching done by its field officers is necessary, it is not sufficient and long-lasting. These staff members are external and visit the schools only occasionally. They have no authority over those being monitored and cannot hold them to account in the event they have been found wanting. In their capacity as owners and employers, the proprietors are there every day of the week, every week of the month, and every month of the year. They are also the ones who gain when teachers apply the newly acquired skills well and lose when they don't, incurring opportunity and real costs when teachers are being trained. They therefore constitute the best monitoring forces. They need to have a proper understanding of the content and objectives of every training in advance so they can select the right people prior to the training event and equip them with the knowledge of monitoring tools to provide effective supervision after the training.

At another level, further vigorous impact assessments of the LFIS sector will be beneficial in generating evidence-based knowledge and lessons that will be of significant use in improving business designs and strategies for a better performance.

However, while impact assessment is a necessary component for improving performance and quality (excellence), its effectiveness and usefulness is determined not by the activity in itself but by the indicators and tools applied and the way this is executed.

Effective and fruitful impact assessment require a proper baseline survey, clearly defined and measurable indicators, a bottom-up approach involving genuine participation at all stages of the process, follow-up strategies and plans, human and technical capacity, and budget allocation. Most of all, a genuinely participatory impact assessment requires grassroots participation, not only as informants but also as contributors to the designing and planning of the evaluation process and users of the final outcomes.

Impact assessment is neither an audit inspection nor is it a routine to meet donor requirements. It is a serious development activity undertaken to reflect on past or ongoing programs and to draw lessons for improving and directing future strategies and activities to achieve maximum outcomes for the benefit of the poor. An organization becomes effective and successful when it learns from its experience, and this occurs when it allows monitoring, evaluation, and impact assessment to happen.

While this is a necessary component of any genuine development process, it is not sufficient. More important is that the monitoring, evaluation, and impact assessment capacity and culture are internal. In other words, the LFIS should be at a stage where they do not only recognize and embrace the phenomenon of monitoring and evaluation as an integral part of an effective education/school system, but also they are able to undertake it themselves on a sustainable basis. This is an outcome Edify seeks to achieve and encourage others likewise.

Networking Toward a Global LFIS Movement

Many LFIS operate more in isolation than in partnership with one another. There are associations of independent private schools in some countries, but they are often weak and not fully representative. In both cases, the LFIS do not enjoy the benefits and opportunities that networking brings.

Good networking helps LFIS to share information, experience, and knowledge, as well as enhance innovation and creativity that lead to the overall improvement of education in schools. It also can serve as a forum for discussing common concerns and for finding common solutions. As LFIS work together to achieve commonly agreed goals related to the sector, networking generates openness, unity, and strength. This develops a sense of belonging and identity among the LFIS, empowering them to exert pressure on governments through lobbying and advocacy on any policy changes they wish to be made in support of their sector.

Three levels of networking should be developed here: the first one relates to the creation of national networks of LFIS in developing countries. Those LFIS that do not have national associations should create one, and those that already have associations but are not properly functioning should revitalize them. Through such associations LFIS can network and cooperate effectively and efficiently to strengthen their overall role in the education sector.

The second level of networking concerns the establishment of a global LFIS network jointly created by national networks and supporters in developing and developed countries. Establishing a global LFIS network will bring the various service providers (fundraisers and program implementers) closer, thus enabling them to speak the same language and exert global lobbying and advocacy to create an influence in favor of the sector. It will also be a catalyst for knowledge sharing, efficiency, and innovation.

The third level of networking relates to the networking between the global LFIS network and other international groupings that are of relevance to the sector. This could relate to the global LFIS representatives participating and speaking on behalf of the LFIS sector at conferences and meetings organized by relevant UN agencies, World Bank, EU, AU, Commonwealth, USAID, DFID, etc. The global LFIS association could also undertake lobbying and advocacy activities, develop industry standards, facilitate research, and engage in building the global knowledge and profile of the LFIS sector.

A united and effective networking across the globe is likely to engender a powerful global movement. This strengthens the voice of the LFIS sector, empowering it to exert influence on education policies and funding at international, regional, and national levels in favor of the poor and marginalized who deserve access and a quality education.

Edify is already facilitating the formation of national associations in the countries where it is operating and would be willing to engage with interested service providers and actively participate in the organization of the first international conference with the aim to establish the global LFIS network, which will serve as the linchpin of the ensuing global movement.

Innovation, Innovation, and Innovation

We live, learn, teach, and work in a world that is different from even ten years ago. This world is the internet world, inhabited by what Tony Wagner calls the "innovation generation," as many of the youth "have extraordinary latent for—and interest in—innovation and entrepreneurship, likely more than any generation in history."[23]

Undoubtedly, education has been and is a great catalyst of innovation throughout history. The emphasis, focus, strategy, and investment given to the role of innovation by the education system and the way students' capacity is built determine the extent to which it is enhanced.

This presents a huge challenge to education, schools, and teachers of our time: the innovation generation and non-innovation one. The new versus the old. The old education/teaching tradition and practice obsessively measures student success by academic scores, appreciates silent listening and right answers, and tends to stifle curiosity, imagination, provocative questions, and experimentation. For the old tradition, all that matters is the level of exam results scored by students.

The views of schools, teachers, and parents with regard to the role of schools and education seem to contradict the views of the youth. In the words of Wagner:

> [The innovation generation are] swimming against the tides of tradition. A lot of parents still harbor hopes that their children will pursue prestigious careers and be economically better off than they are. Too many teachers and employees still reward the "old school" behaviors of deference to authority and striving for "success," conventionally defined—and count on carrots and sticks for motivation. The result is that many in the Innovation Generation are skeptical of adult authority and the institutions that their elders have presided over. School is a game the Innovation Generation knows they have to play to get "credentialed," but they do it with as little effort as possible.[24]

The old tradition doesn't creatively embrace difference and disruptive learning. It rather wants to contain uniformity and tradition at any cost and only fails to discover the interests of students and unleash their potential accordingly, but it also discourages and buries them even when they are obvious. And even less is done to help students discover the process they should take to know what they are interested in. In this way, schools, teachers, and parents kill creativity and innovation and long-term development. Dr. Robert Sternberg says, "Creativity is a habit. The problem is that schools sometimes treat it as a bad habit. . . . Like any habit, creativity can either be encouraged or discouraged."[25]

While it recognizes the importance of academic scores in education and works toward enabling LFIS to achieve that, Edify also seeks to help them put on the new culture of educating students: creating access to education technology and instituting a habit of creativity. An environment in which students are passionate about being different in their thinking without any form of inhibitions, which allows curiosity and imagination and innovation to flourish.

In the LFIS it supports, Edify promotes a culture of innovation in which students are taught, encouraged, and empowered to constantly ask questions, imagine things, experiment ideas, and not only excel in academic subjects. The schools and teachers also have to create time and space in order to enable them to excel in team-building, collaborative problem solving, communication skills, caring, loving, serving, honesty, perseverance, and transparency, all of which are critical for innovation and whole-person success. Edify believes that only through a culture of innovation will the youth be able to develop into highly curious and highly imaginative citizens and build nations that are conducive places for human flourishing.

The education world must not dogmatically treat good schools and quality education in terms of academic scores but also put innovation, creativity, critical thinking, and empowerment high on the education agenda at all levels. Students don't have to be in universities and colleges to be taught to think creatively and do creative things. They should start already at pre- and primary levels, and efforts should be made to create an innovation culture. According to Wagner, such culture constitutes teamwork, interdisciplinary problem-solving, intrinsic incentives, exploration, play, and empowerment, which all enhance expertise, critical thinking skills, and motivation.[26] We must take heed that education doesn't put all its eggs in the basket of academic scores pretending this is all that matters. We have to let education stimulate and not stifle innovation.

Embracing the Two-in-One

All education has hitherto primarily focused on academic excellence measured by test scores and pass rates. Employment, career development, promotions, and rewards have tended to be based more on the basis of performance and less on character.

As a result, education has targeted making sure students single-handedly study and work hard to achieve as high scores as possible to be competitive and successful in fulfilling their career aspirations. Aspects of personal development related to emotions, feelings, behavior, and attitudes that constitute the person's overall character are often sidelined as not equally important. Consequently, little attention is given to enhance the development of such traits among students as part of the classroom-based lesson. Sometimes the two are even treated as opposites contradicting each other.

Christian LFIS see education as consisting of two inseparable and necessary components: performance (academic excellence) and character (discipleship). Education is about the development of the whole person and about who they become. A person who performs well and does not have diligence, resilience, self-control, integrity, and faith is bound to fail in achieving the desired goals of a holistic life. Likewise, a person with good character (values and principles) will struggle in life if they cannot perform (skills and competence).

The desired abundant life is not achieved with the one or the other. In fact, a Christ-centered character is likely to boost performance (academic and non-academic alike). Both need to exist simultaneously in one person. The equation is therefore not one-in-one, i.e., performance or character in a person, but two-in-one, i.e., both performance and character in a person. The good character referred to here is a Christ-centered character rooted in the values and principles of Jesus Christ that include love, humility, justice, honesty, integrity, accountability, and sacrifice. A Christ-centered education is about raising future leaders who are equipped to build flourishing Godly nations.

The education offered by Christ-centered LFIS recognizes this and seeks to achieve both academic and character excellence in every student and beyond their school. In that way, each student leaves school with the mind of Christ (character) and academic excellence (performance) and joins the labor force or the higher education sector ready to generate wealth, create jobs, lead, and serve by burying such malpractices as fraud, corruption, bribes, and any form of dishonest gains.

Quality education should be concerned not only with what students know but also with who they become as citizens. The

Christ-centered education facilitated by Edify strives to produce citizens who are resilient, optimistic, persistent, trustworthy, loving, just, diligent, accountable, and committed to serve and not to be served.

Moreover, every academic subject is taught from two perspectives: the secular and Christ-centered worldviews. This increases the breadth and depth of learning and knowledge received by the students and prepares them to become better citizens with the responsibility to build better nations.

With this in mind Edify seeks to impact significantly all the children who will ever attend a school from the time that Edify starts working with that school. Although a loan to build more classrooms increases access for more children to attend a school, the learning and the values imparted in all of the classrooms, both present and in future, are what really matter. A Christ-centered education, offered by Christian LFIS, is inherently capable of producing future adults and peers who care about worthy accomplishments, including academic achievements. A study in the US showed "religiously involved youth tend to score higher than other adolescents on school achievement, social success, confidence in self, and personal maturity."[27]

The two-in-one education outcome that can be achieved only through Christ-centered value education is a prime condition for building nations where corruption, inefficiency, selfishness, and injustice become things of the past or are dealt with swiftly and constructively. In the words of Mary Joan Iwenofu, "Religious and moral education has a positive impact on national development, it shapes the nation to a greater development, especially when persons are formed to respect human dignity, care about the welfare of others and demonstrate integrity and social responsibilities, reflect on moral issues and seek peaceful resolution of conflict."[28]

It is therefore important the international community acknowledges and supports the work of Christian LFIS and does not dismiss them or distance itself by claiming the religious aspect is "a concern" or "religion is a private matter." In fact, in this day and age of terrorism, the education of Christ-centered values and principles in schools is paramount and should be received as an integral part of the anti-terrorism campaign.

Christian LFIS should be appreciated, celebrated, and supported for producing citizens of high academic and character standards and not made to feel unaccepted, marginalized, and relegated to mere "religious entities." That is what they are not. They are academic institutions that produce future citizens who are equipped with excellent professional skills and character traits that are key for healthy living and nation building.

Christian LFIS supported by Edify do not just do "religion." They do a Christ-centered education, and this is as important as learning academic subjects rooted in secular values. A Christ-centered education teaches children about loving God, loving and serving one another, self-control, accountability, faithfulness, humility, diligence and hard work, transparency, accountability, responsibility, forgiveness, reconciliation, and all character traits necessary for building healthy, peaceful, harmonious, and prosperous individuals, families, communities, and nations.

Christian LFIS are, therefore, not only about making performing and diligent citizens, but they are also about producing performing and transformed citizens: two-in-one. To use the words of Nelson Mandela, Christian LFIS produce men and women of "good head and good heart," which "are always a formidable combination." They bring forth citizens who abhor hatred and embrace love, which is the source of human flourishing and nation building. Mandela was a good example. (Although he never confessed his faith publicly, Mandela was educated in a mission school and was surrounded by influential Christian personalities like Desmond Tutu.) In setting the format for post-apartheid South Africa's future, he did not practice hatred, war, bitterness, and revenge against his former oppressors and tormentors. Instead, he chose love, forgiveness, peace, and reconciliation. His approach saved South Africa from further bloodshed and destruction. He was able to take the forgiveness-reconciliation course partly because he was educated in a Wesleyan Mission school during his formative years where he learned to love his enemy, love his neighbor, and forgive those who transgress against him. He was also surrounded by influential Christian personalities like Desmond Tutu who prayed with him in and out of prison. That is probably why Mandela could say, "People are taught to hate and they can learn to love."

Edify believes a Christ-centered education offered by Christian LFIS will produce many future "Mandelas" and MLKs, which the world, and Africa in particular, needs so badly. Citizens with not only human knowledge but also supernatural wisdom since Africa and the world need people with both knowledge and character.

Moreover, the world should also recognize many of the LFIS in developing countries are faith-based entities. It is therefore important and beneficial to the education community that Christian LFIS are recognized as major contributors to holistic education and given a share of all the support national governments and members of the international community can offer without any prejudice. Seeing a Christ-centered education as "a concern" should be erased from the minds of all players involved in education so they can embrace Christian LFIS without any biases.

This is not how education started historically and the present attitude should not be allowed to pervade and color the view of secular donors, academics, and practitioners. Let us not forget that most of the learning institutions in Western Europe and America prior to the nineteenth century that gave birth to the education of our time, including the greatest universities with the greatest influence on society, were established and operated by Christians. The top ten universities of the world were founded by Christians for the purpose of providing education rooted in Christ-centered values. The motto of Harvard University once read: "Truth for Christ and the Church" although this has now been changed to just "Truth." The motto of Yale University reads: "Light and Truth" (written in Hebrew). The motto of Oxford University reads: "The Lord is my Light" (Psalm 27). The motto of Cambridge University reads: "Here we receive light and sacred draughts." The list can go on and on.[29]

Christian LFIS today are doing exactly what their predecessors did, and which some have continued to this day, though some others have drifted away because of secular pressures and opposition. These entities, founded and operated by low-income and often lowly educated Christian women and men in low-income communities to educate low-income children, are doing a noble service to society by sacrificing their time, emotions, and meager resources more than the bureaucrats and elites who are busy turning over every stone to enrich themselves.

Why are they doing this? The answer is that Christian LFIS are inspired by Christ-centered values and principles to love and serve their neighbor. They are doing what UNESCO, EAL, and MDGs are doing: educating and preparing children for a better future. The difference is LFIS are doing so using the two-in-one approach. Such schools must not be sidelined as only "religious." Instead, they should be honored for what they are doing and supported to do even more. They are not doing anything odd.

APPENDIX 1

Christian Transformation and Training Officers Appreciated for Their Contributions

Allan Lopez

Annet Mbabazi

Chris Mulisa

Claudia Sawadogo

David Kabre

Deborah Sekyi

Jackie Mutoni

Joel Mumbya

Jose Perez

Joseph Ssekajja

Joshua Muzinda

Justine Mutoni

Katherine Aguayo

Leandro Peguero

Leo Mayson

Mariatu Koroma

Michael Kamara

Mihiret Abera

Mike Adu Carol

Sem Haokip

Thangboi Haokip

Yerlina Torres

Yvonne Deiba Ewudzie

APPENDIX 2

Edify Lending Partners

Burkina Faso   Micro Aid – http://www.microaid.bf

Dominican Republic   Esperanza Internacional – https://esperanza.org
Aspire – http://www.coopaspire.com
Amezerano Community Banking – https://www.acb.rw

Ethiopia   Vision Fund – https://www.visionfund.org

Ghana   Sinapi Aba Trust Savings and Loans – https://sinapiaba.com
Fidelity Bank Ghana Limited – https://www.fidelitybank.com.gh/

Guatemala   Foundation for Assistance to the Small Business – http://fundacionfape.org.gt

Liberia   Foundation for Women – https://www.foundationforwomen.org

Peru	Adventist Development and Relief Agency – https://www.adra.org.pe
Rwanda	Goshen Finance – https://www.goshenfinance.rw
Sierra Leone	A Call to Business – http://acalltobusiness.co.uk/sierra-leone
Uganda	Hiinga – https://hiinga.org

APPENDIX 3

Edify Training Partners

1. Association of Christian Schools International - https://www.acsi.org
2. Association Evangelique d'Appui au Developpement - http://www.aead.net
3. Agape Development Initiatives, Sierra Leone
4. Evangelical Students and Graduate Union of Ethiopia - https://www.evasue.net
5. Inter-Generational Transformation Ministry - https://www.facebook.com/Istministry/
6. MALD Educational Support - https://www.maldeducation.com
7. Ghana, Seeds of Empowerment - https://www.seedsofempowerment.org
8. Awana - https://www.awana.org
9. Foundation First Charitable Trust - https://foundationfirsteducation.org
10. University of San Diego - https://www.sandiego.edu
11. EdTech Innovations Limited - https://edtechinno.com/
12. Creative Writing Academy - https://www.cwa.edu.gh/
13. Bible League Ghana - https://bibleleagueghana.org/
14. Certified Ghana - https://certifiedghana.com/

15. Guatemala Prospera - https://www.guatemalaprospera.org/
16. Efecto Mostaza - https://efectomostaza.com/
17. Especialidades 625 - https://e625.com/
18. The Learning Group - http://thelearningroup.com/
19. Asociación de Distrito de Alto Rendimiento - http://dar.org.gt/
20. Asociación de Centros de Cuidado Infantil Diario y atencion preescolar - https://m.facebook.com/Acipre-108660281492267/about/?ref=page_internal&mt_nav=0
21. Missionary Ventures - https://mvi.org/
22. Cornerstone Leadership Academy - https://cornerstoneschoolsafrica.org
23. International Leadership Institute - https://iliteam.org/about
24. Desarrollo Cristiano del Peru - https://desarrollocristiano.pe
25. World Reader- https://www.worldreader.org
26. Acreduca - https://www.facebook.com/acredita.educacionsac
27. Asociación de centros comerciales del Peru - http://accep.org.pe/
28. Sinergia - https://sinergiaflt.org/equipo/
29. La Asociación Pro Enseñanza y Desarrollo Integral - https://aprendird.org/
30. Apacienta Mis Ovejas, Dominican Republic
31. Creativity Lab - http://creativity.rw/
32. RWA TECH Hub - http://rwatechhub.ac.rw/
33. Aquila Consult - https://aquilaconsult.net/
34. Educators International - https://educatorsinternational.org.uk/
35. Bridge2Rwanda - https://www.bridge2rwanda.org/
36. DevLink Consult - https://www.facebook.com/DevLink-Consults-Ltd-336484269887626/
37. Amani Initiative - https://www.amaniwestnile.org

38. New Hope International - https://www.newhopeinternational.net/
39. Scripture Union - https://scriptureunion.org/
40. Christian Schools Owners Association - https://nacsu.org/
41. ICT Teachers Association of Uganda - https://www.ictteachersug.net/
42. University of San Diego School Leadership Training, https://www.sandiego.edu
43. Dr. Paul Kim: Stanford Mobile Inquiry-Based Learning Environment - https:gse-it.standford.edu/smile

APPENDIX 4

Pictures of LFIS

Ghana

Sierra Leone

Dominican Republic

Peru

Burkina Faso

Liberia

Rwanda

Guatemala

NOTES

Chapter 1

1. United Nations, Universal Declaration of Human Rights, Article 26, 1948.

2. UNESCO, World Declaration on Education for All, 1990, unesco.org/ark:/48.

3. www.globalschoolsforum.org/page/aboutus, accessed on June 18, 2021.

4. https://www.globalpartnership.org/results/education-data-highlights, accessed on June 18, 2021.

5. https://www.unicef.org/press-releases/new-global-tracker-measure-piandemics-impact-education-worldwide, accessed June 21, 2021.

6. https://en.unesco.org/covid19/educationresponse, accessed on June 21, 2021.

7. Paula Cordeiro et al., "Responses to COVID-19 from Non-State School Leaders in Latin America, Sub-Saharan Africa, and India: A Call for Educational Equity," https://www.frontiersin.org/articles/10.3389/feduc.2021.618323/full, accessed on June 21, 2021.

8. Although different from country to country, the number of children enrolled in primary schools increased by 40 million. Between 1999–2008, for example, an additional 52 million children were enrolled in primary school. In Sub-Saharan Africa, net enrollment increased from 58 percent in 1999 to 74 percent in 2007. The

number of out-of-school children has decreased from 108 million at the end of 1990s to 61 million today. Primary completion rates have risen from 84 percent to 94 percent since 1991. Gender parity in primary enrollment has improved significantly in the regions that began the decade with the greatest gender gaps. Government expenditure on education increased very significantly in most developing countries.

9. http://www.huffingtonpost.com/desmond-tutu/facing-the-future-global_b_544449.html.

10. Ibid.

11. "Sustainable Development: Knowledge Platform," United Nations, 2015, https://sustainabledevelopment.un.org/post2015/transformingourworld/publication.

12. "Press Release: World Leaders Commit to Tackling Global Education Crisis," *Sustainable Development Goals*, United Nations, September 20, 2017, www.un.org/sustainabledevelopment/blog/2017/09/press-release-world-leaders-commit-to-tackling-global-education-crisis/.

13. https://en.unesco.org/news/617-million-children-and-adolescents-not-getting-minimum-reading-and-math.

14. UNESCO, Understanding Education Quality, 28.

15. https://www.trtworld.com/magazine/covid-19-reveals-digital-divide-as-africa-struggles-with-distance-learning-37299.

16. https://en.unesco.org/covid19/educationresponse/consequences.

17. https://www.newvision.co.ug/news/1521006/covid-19-education-interventions-favour-wealthy.

18. https://www.trtworld.com/magazine/covid-19-reveals-digital-divide-as-africa-struggles-with-distance-learning-37299.

19. https://en.unesco.org/covid19/educationresponse/consequences.

20. https://en.unesco.org/covid19/educationresponse/consequences.

21. "Food, Agriculture, and Decent Work," ILO & FAO Working Together, www.fao-ilo.org/fao-ilo-youth/en.

22. https://www.unicef.org/press-releases/third-youth-surveyed-globally-unicef-say-their-education-not-preparing-them-skills.

23. http://data.uis.unesco.org/Index.aspx?queryid=156.

24. Makonen Getu, interview with two LFIS proprietors, Bukaywa Primary School, Vihiga Country, Western Region, Kenya, 2008.

25. Op. cit.

26. https://www.un.org/en/sections/issues-depth/population/index.html.

27. Maria T. S. Schleicher, "Achieving Education for All, World Economic Forum 2000," UNESCO Thematic Studies, http://www.ehow.com/about_6164071_population-growth-affects-educational-system.html.

28. Justin Line, http://mostlyeconomics.wordpress.com/2012/01/09/how-to-ensure-demographic-dividend-does-not-become-a-demographic-bomb/.

29. Ibid.

30. "Global Education Monitoring Report Press Release," UNESCO, April 9, 2020.

31. UNESCO Press Release, July 13, 2020, en.unesco.org/news/covid-1.

32. https://www.transparency.org/cpi2018#summary.

33. Jean-Marie Hyacinth Quenum, "The Root Cause of Widespread Corruption in Sub-Saharan Post-Colonial Nation-States," *Asian Horizon*, 6, no. 1 (March 2012): 103–108.

34. "Transparency International Report," *Exporting Corruption,* 2020, https://www.transparency.org/en/projects/exporting-corruption.

35. https://www.un.org/press/en/2015/gaef3438.doc.htm.

36. "UEFA Global Monitoring Report," UNESCO, 2015.

37. "Transparency International, Global Corruption Report," Education, 2013.

38. Jean-Marc Bernard, "Facing Education Challenges," GPE Secretariat.

Chapter 2

1. Geoffrey Walford and Prachi Srivastava, "Examining Private Schooling in Less Economically Developed Countries: Key Issues and New Evidence," in *Private Schooling in Less Economically Developed Countries: Asian and African Perspectives,* Oxford Studies in Comparative Studies, ed. Prachi Srivastava and Geoffrey Walford (Providence, RI: Symposium Books, 2007).

2. Colin Bagnay, "Cinderella or Ugly Sister? What Role for Non-State Education Provision in Developing Countries," in *Private Schooling in Less Economically Developed Countries: Asian and African Perspectives,* Oxford Studies in Comparative Studies, ed. Prachi Srivastava and Geoffrey Walford (Providence, RI: Symposium Books, 2007).

3. Igor Kitaev, "Education for All and Private Education," in *Private Schooling in Less Economically Developed Countries: Asian and African Perspectives,* Oxford Studies in Comparative Studies, ed. Prachi Srivastava and Geoffrey Walford (Providence, RI: Symposium Books, 2007).

4. James Tooley, who is a professor and vice-chancellor at University of Buckingham, United Kingdom, is a pioneer researcher and a leading advocate of low-fee independent schools. Through his two books, *The Beautiful Tree* and the Gold award-winning *Educating*

Amaretch, and other publications, James has put the long-neglected sector on the education map of the world.

5. Pauline Dixon, "Why the Denial? Low-Cost Private Schools in Developing Schools and Their Contributions to Education," *Econ Journal Watch* 9, no. 3 (2012): 186–209.

6. James Tooley, "Educating Amaretch: Private Schools for the Poor and the New Frontier for Investors," (IFC, Washington DC, n.d.).

7. Colin Bagnay, "Cinderella or Ugly Sister? What Role for Non-State Education Provision in Developing Countries," in *Private Schooling in Less Economically Developed Countries: Asian and African Perspectives,* Oxford Studies in Comparative Studies, ed. Prachi Srivastava and Geoffrey Walford (Providence, RI: Symposium Books, 2007).

8. https://data.worldbank.org/indicator/SE.PRM.PRIV.ZS.

9. James Tooley, *The Beautiful Tree* (Washington, DC: Cato Institute, 2009), 246.

10. The World Bank put this figure at 58 million in 2018. It is difficult to know the true figure. According to Tooley, part of the reality is that many children whom the officials believe are out of school are actually in low-fee independent schools (unrecognized ones and off the government radar).

11. Ross Baird, "Private Schools for the Poor: Development, Provision, and Choice in India," A Report for Gray Matters Capital, May 2009.

12. Interview with the director of Dignitas, a US-based NGO operating in Mathare Valley, Nairobi.

13. https://data.worldbank.org/indicator/SE.PRM.UNER.FE.

14. http://www.uis.unesco.org/Education/Documents/unesco-world-atlas-gender-education-2012.pdf.

15. In Ghana, for example, about 750,000 of the country's teenagers get pregnant every year. Shirley Asiedu-Addo, "Teenage Pregnancy Impacts on Girls' Education," *Daily Graphic*, June 8, 2013.

16. http://www.newsmax.com/Stossel/Education-Blob-Learning-schools/2012/07/05/id/444491.

17. "UN Human Development Report," 2010, 39.

18. Hanushek E. A. et al., "Education and Economic Growth," *Education Next* 8, no. 2 (Spring 2008): 62–70.

19. Ibid.

20. www.ghanabusinessnews.com/2013/07/06/ghanas-education-system-is-in-crisis-prof-adei/. Stephen Adei is former rector of Ghana Institute of Management and Public Administration and a professor at the Pentecost University College in Accra.

21. Ibid.

22. http://econweb.ucsd.edu/~kamuralidharan/papers/Workingpercent20Papers/Thepercent20Aggregatepercent20Effectspercent20ofpercent20Schoolpercent20Choicepercent20(4percent20Octoberpercent202013).pdf.

23. Ibid.

24. http://www-wds.worldbank.org/external/default/WDSContentServer/WDSP/IB/2013/09/17/000442464_20130917141021/Rendered/INDEX/810760BRI0E2P00Box0379828B00PUBLIC0.txt.

25. Tooley, *The Beautiful Tree*, 246.

26. http://en.wikipedia.org/wiki/Critical_thinking.

27. Hanushek et al., 62–70.

28. James Tooley and Pauline Dixon, *Private Education Is Good for the Poor: A Study of Schools Serving the Poor in Low-Income Countries* (Washington, DC: Cato Institute, 2005), 3.

29. http://opinionator.blogs.nytimes.com/2013/05/08/where-private-school-is-not-a-privilege/?_php=true&_type=blogs&_r=0.

30. World Conference on Education for All, Jomtien, 1990.

31. "Our Common Future," Population and Human Resources, 17, www.un-documents.net/ocf-04.htlm.

32. "Rich World, Poor World: A Guide to Global Development," Center for Global Development, 2002.

33. Nelson Mandela, quoted in Reginald McKnight's *Wisdom of the African World,* New World Library, 1996.

34. Horace Mann, 1848.

35. "Educating for a Sustainable Future: A Transdisciplinary Vision for Concerted Action," 1997, http://www.unesco.org/education/tlsf/mods/theme_a/popups/mod01t05s01.html#edu.

36. http://www.unfpa.org/gender/empowerment2.htm.

37. "Education for All Global Monitoring Report," UNESCO, 2011.

38. Paul Collier and Anke Hoeffler, "Greed and Grievance in Civil War," *Economic Papers* 56 (4): 563–95.

39. "All Children Learning Report," GPE, 2012–2013.

40. Allison Anderson and Lauren Greubel, "Upfront Newsletter," Brookings Institute, February 2013, http:www.brookings.edu/research/opinions/2013/01/16-africa-.

41. Edify Annual Report, 2011.

42. Interview with James Tooley, January 2014.

43. Guy Ellena, http://www.tradeinvestafrica.com/feature_articles/148954.htm.

44. James Tooley, *Really Good Schools: Global Lessons for High-Caliber, Low-Cost Education* (The Independent Institute, 2021).

45. The overwhelming majority of Edify partner schools are registered and pay government taxes.

46. Bob Lupton, *Toxic Charity: How Churches and Charities Hurt Those They Help and How to Reverse It* (New York: HarperCollins Publishers, 2011).

47. Dambisa Moyo, *Dead Aid: Why Aid Is Not Working and How There Is a Better Way for Africa* (London: Allen Lane Penguin Group, 2009).

48. This is in contradiction to the increasingly growing recognition of the role LFIS play in complementing the educational efforts made by national governments.

49. Chris Crane, *A Dream and a Coconut Tree: Transforming Education for the Poor* (EMT Communications, LLC, 2021).

Chapter 3

1. http://practicalaction.org/docs/technical_information_service/school_buildings_in_developing_countires.pdf.

2. Op. cit.

3. www.ia.-sb.org/schoolFacilities.aspx?id=560.

4. http://www.epa.gov/iaq/schools/pdfs/student_performance_findings.pdf.

5. Chris Crane, "Notes for Improving Observations and Reflections on Accra," February 9, 2012.

6. http://www.theguardian.com/teacher-network/2013/apr/25/changing-classroom-environment-improve-learning.

7. University of San Diego, School of Leadership and Education Sciences, Proprietors' Training, Affordable Private Schools, Ghana, Module 3: "Facilitator's Guide," 25.

8. http://practicalaction.org/docs/technical_information_service/school_buildings_in_developing_countires.pdf.

9. Ibid.

10. Emma Patchett, "'The Curse': The Impact of Sanitation on Schoolgirls in Developing World," http://www.theguardian.com/journalismcompetition/sanitation-schoolgirls-in-the-developing-world.

11. Learner-Centered Psychological Principles: A Framework for School Reform," http://www.cdl.org/resource-library/articles/learner_centered.php.

12. http://en.wikipedia.org/wiki/Student-centred_learning.

13. Linda Galindo.

14. University of San Diego, School of Leadership and Education Sciences, Proprietors' Training, Affordable Private Schools, Ghana, Module 4: "Recruiting, Selecting & Developing Quality Teachers."

15. Makonen Getu, *Transforming Microfinance: A Christian Approach* (Oxford: Regnum Publishers, 2013).

16. For further details, see Edify Annual Report, 2012.

17. http://hlc.org.in/?page_id=540.

18. http://www.teachamantofish.org.uk/changing-the-world. See also http://teachamantofish.org.uk/documents/TEACH-A-MAN-TO-FISH_ANNUAL-REPORT-AND-FINANCIAL-STATE-MENTS-11-12.pdf.

19. Sidhar Sundaram, "Infinite Visions—The Aravind Eye Care Experience," http://www.aravind.org/aravindnews/files/aug2012/InfinteVisions.pdf.

20. http://rwandafriends.wordpress.com/sonrise-school/; http://www.tfcanglican.org/pages/page.asp?page_id=186100.

21. http://en.wikipedia.org/wiki/Blended_learning and http://www.testden.com/partner/blendedpercent20learningpercent20forpercent20independentpercent20schools.PDF.

22. http://www.testden.com/partner/blendedpercent20learningpercent20forpercent20independentpercent20schools.PDF.

Chapter 4

1. Martin Berkowitz, "Understanding Effective Character Education," *Expert Perpsectives,* 330, https://wicharacter.org/wp-content/uploads/ExpertPerspectives-Dr-Marvin-Berkowitz.pdf.

2. Thomas Kuhn, *The Structure of Scientific Revolutions* (Cambridge: Cambridge University Press, 1970), 175.

3. Stephen Covey, *The Seven Habits of Highly Effective People* (New York: Simon and Schuster, 1989), 23.

4. N. Wolterstoff and C. College, *The Transforming Vision* (Downers Grove, IL: InterVarsity Press, 1984), 32.

5. http://infed.org/mobi/the-potential-of-role-model-education/.

6. A. A. Bucher, "The Influence of Models in Forming Moral Identity," *International Journal of Educational Research* 27, no. 7 (1997).

7. Ibid.

8. Unfortunately, there are also situations where children take role models for "bad" and "wrong" things and end up becoming "bad" and doing "wrong" things.

9. Klaus Issler, *The Formation of Christian Character: Living into the Life of Jesus* (Intervarsity Press, 2012), 16.

10. Larry Nucci, *Moral Development and Character Formation* (Chicago: University of Illinois Press, 1997).

11. Issler, *The Formation of Christian Character*, 28.

12. Op. cit., 33, 145.

13. J. L. Brown and C. A. Moffett, *The Hero's Journey: How Educators Can Transform Schools and Improve Learning* (Alexandria, VA: ASCD, 1999), 1.

14. http://blogs.naz.edu/ethics/2010/04/to-educate-a-man-in-mind-and-not-in-morals-is-to-educate-a-menace-to-society-----the-odore-roosevelt.html.

15. The character list consists of sixty-six different traits. See http://charater-in-action.com/character-traits-make-a-whopping-difference/.

16. http://www.goodreads.com/author/quotes/23924.Martin_Luther_King_Jr_.

17. Jean-Marie Hyacinthe Quenum, "The Root Cause of Widespread Corruption in Sub-Saharan Post-Colonial Nation-States" *Asian Horizons* 6, no. 1 (March 2012): 103–108.

18. "Transparency Report," https://www.transparency.org/en/press/2019-cpi-efforts-stagnate-in-g7#.

19. Interview with Technology Ubiquity Counseling and Clean Environment in Education.

20. William Jeynes, 2003.

21. "Why Should Christians Care About the Environment?" Geneva College, http://www.geneva.edu/page/why_care.

22. Ann Mooney, Chris Oliver, and Marjorie Smith, "Impact of Family Breakdown on Children's Well-Being," Research Report, No DCSF-RR113, Institute of Education, University of London, 2009, 2, http://dera.ioe.ac.uk/11165/1/DCSF-RR113.pdf.

23. Luis Sena, program coordinator, Esperanza, Santo Domingo.

24. Jon Saphier et al., "The Skillful Teacher," RBT Research for Better Teaching, Inc., 2008.

25. Harro Van Brumelen, *Walking with God in the Classroom: Christian Approaches to Teaching and Learning* (Alta Vista College Press, 1998), 40.

26. David Freeman, Biblical Integration Training Module, London, 2019.

27. Craig Bouvier, *Christian Educators Journal,* http://www.cejonline.com/article/discipline-to-discipleship-a-new-path-for-school-discipline/.

28. Donavan L. Graham, *Teaching Redemptively: Bringing Grace and Truth into Your Classroom* (Purposeful Design Publications, ACSI, 2009), 9.

29. AMO (Apacienta Mis Ovejas) is a Christ-centered curriculum designed in 2002 by Elizabeth Youmans, head of Chrisalis International in Orlando, Florida, for at-risk children around the world. It has been translated into Spanish, Portuguese, French, Romanian, Korean, and Burmese. APRENDI is a local training organization established in 2008 to "promote holistic development and values teaching in schools located in poor communities."

30. ACSI (Association Christian Schools International) has its international headquarters in Colorado Springs but operates in Ouagadougou as a local organization and is a member organization of local Christian schools. It provides training to school leaders and teachers. ACSI and Edify have a memorandum of understanding to serve in partnerships globally.

31. The name Awana is derived from the first letter of Paul: "Approved workmen are not ashamed" (2 Timothy 2:15). Awana

was established to help churches, parents, and other interested parties in discipling children and youth to know, love, and serve God by training leaders, teaching the gospel among children and youth, and providing curricula (training plans and materials) globally. It operates in all Edify countries in Africa as well as India.

32. AEAD (Association Evangelique d'Appui au Development) is a local organization based in Ouagadogou. Although it is involved in various socioeconomic projects, AEAD promotes education in general, and girls education in particular, church planting, and training of church leaders. In partnership with Edify, AEAD has developed a contextualized CCE training manual consisting of twenty-five different lessons. The manual is distributed and taught in the Edify-supported schools by AEAD facilitators in consultation with the Edify CTTO and school proprietors.

33. CLA stands for Cornerstone Leadership Academy and is headquartered in Kampala, Uganda, providing a two-year training of servant leadership and Christ-centered character development to young leaders. Its models and tools are used by Edify Liberia, Rwanda, and Uganda in training, leaders, teachers, and students. The three countries also partner with Awana.

34. ADI (Agape Development Initiatives) is involved in the provision of professional and servant leadership skills.

35. ISTM is Integrated Spiritual Transformation Ministry and is involved in training leaders, teachers, and students while EVASUE (Evangelical Students and Graduate Union of Ethiopia) engage in discipleship training.

36. CSI (Character Solutions International-India) and DAI (Development Associates International) are both involved in servant leadership and biblical integration training.

Chapter 5

1. Mercy N. Fodje, "The Impact of Technology to Education in the Developing Countries," 1, http://www.icte.org/T99_Library/T99_194.PDF.

2. "The Future of Mobile Learning: Implications for Policy Makers and Planners," UNESCO, 2012, 7–8, http://unesdoc.unesco.org/images/0021/002196/219637e.pdf.

3. http://ict-adv-disadv.blogspot.fi/.

4. UNESCO, 2013.

5. UNESCO, 2012, 10.

6. Charles Kenny, quoted in Annie Kelly.

7. Vikashkumar Jhuree, "Technology Integration in Education in Developing Countries: Guidelines to Policymakers," *International Journal*, 2005, 6, 4 (2005): 468.

8. Michael Trucano et al., "Ten Trends in Technology Use in Education in Developing Countries That You May Not Have Heard About," *Edutech*, June 26, 2012.

9. UNESCO, 2013.

10. Ibid.

11. http://www.gsma.com/publicpolicy/wp-content/uploads/2012/04/africamobileobservatory2011-1.pdf.

12. https://www.bing.com/search?q=global+expenditures+in+edcuation+by+2030&cvid=a302281acb584ec3a83db621a8a4e5d8&FORM=ANSPA1&PC=LCTS.

13. Lishan Adam et al., "Transformation-Ready: The Strategic Application of Information and Communication Technologies in Africa," Education Sector Study Final Report prepared for the African Development Bank, the World Bank, and the African Union, ICT Development Associates Ltd, December 2011.

14. Ibid.

15. Aleph Molinari, "Let's Bridge the Digital Divide," TED, 2012, cited in David Hulegaard.

16. https://internetworldstats.com/stats.htm.

17. https://www.worldbank.org/en/programs/all-africa-digital-transformation#:~:text=Thepercent20Digitalpercent20Economypercent20Initiativepercent20forpercent20Africapercent20percent28DE4Apercent29percent20aims,topercent20investpercent20percent2425percent20billionpercent20betweenpercent20nowpercent20andpercent202030.

18. Chris Crane, internal paper, August 1, 2013.

19. Ibid.

20. David Risher, Worldreader, www.worldreader.org, October 7, 2020.

21. http://www.readwrite.com/author/david-risher, August 22, 2011. Kade is the capital of Kwaebibirem District, Eastern Region, Ghana.

22. Ibid.

23. Cited in Annie Kelly.

24. Annie Kelly, "The Impact of Technology Sector on Children," *The Guardian*, June 17, 2013.

25. Jerry Chih-Yuan Sun and Susan E Metros, "The Digital Divide and Its Impact on Academic Performance," *US-China Education Review* (2011): 153–161, http://ict-adv-disadv.blogspot.fi/.

26. Jhuree, 468.

27. Luis Osin, "Computers in Education in Developing Countries: Why and How?" 3.

28. Valley Christian School was named the most innovative school in the US a few years ago by Intel, which considered approximately seven thousand applicants for this prestigious award

29. Seth Weinberger, "Future Learning," http://www.youtube.com/watch?v=NmrEZlxMito.

30. Lishan Adam et al.

31. http://www.impactalliance.org/ev_en.php?ID=49157_201&ID2=DO_TOPIC. CDI (Committee for the Democratization of Information Technology) was established in Brazil in 1995 with a mission to "mobilize and transform communities through information technology and communication for greater citizenship and quality of life." http://www.cdi.org.br/.

32. CDI, 2012.

33. Jhuree, 468.

34. Lishan Adam et al.

35. Ibid., 22.

36. Lewins quoted in Shalni Gulati, "Technology-Enhanced Learning in Developing Nations: A Review" *The International Review of Research in Open and Distance Learning* 9, no. 1 (2008).

37. Edify database, February 2020.

38. Fiagbor, paper presented at the Rwanda National Leadership Conference on Education Technology.

39. Ibid.

40. Paula Cordeiro and Andy Johnson, "Education Interrupted: Edify's Roadmap to Continuing Learning During the 2020 Pandemic," Edify, 5.

41. Ibid., 29.

42. https://markets.businessinsider.com/news/stocks/global-education-technology-market-to-reach-341b-by-2025-1027892295#.

Chapter 6

1. INTRAC, Most-Significant-Change(1).pdf-read-only, 1, 2017.

Chapter 7

1. AMO is a Christian training program published by Chrysalis International that "lays Christ and His Word as the foundation for renewing minds and cultivating Christian character and conscience" and serves schools "in their role to disciple the rising generation for Christ." https://training.amoprogram.com/about/mission.

Chapter 8

1. "Global Education Monitoring Report," UNESCO, https://gem-report-2017.unesco.org/en/chapter/accountable-governments/.

2. Ibid.

3. ISO 21001 is the international standard published by the International Organization for Standardization.

4. Ministerio de Educación: Propuesta de Metas educativas e Indicadores, 2021, http://www.minedu.gob.pe/pdf/propuesta-de-metas-educativas-indicadores-2021.pdf.

5. Ministerio de Educación – Ley Nº 26549, Ley de los Centros Educativos Privados, http://www.minedu.gob.pe/normatividad/leyes/ley_26549.php.

6. Ministerio de Educacion: Reglamento de las Instituciones Privadas de Educación Básica y Educación Técnico Productiva, http://www.minedu.gob.pe/normatividad/reglamentos/RegInst-EducPrivadas.php.

7. Cronología de la pandemia de COVID-19 en Perú, https://es.wikipedia.org/wiki/Anexo:CronologpercentC3percentADa_de_la_pandemia_de_COVID-19_en_Perú.

8. Diario Gestión, https://gestion.pe/peru/unos-300000-esco-lares-peruanos-desertan-en-medio-de-la-pandemia-noticia/.

9. Banco Central de Reserva del Peru, Programa Reactiva Peru, https://www.bcrp.gob.pe/docs/Publicaciones/Reporte-Infla-cion/2020/setiembre/ri-setiembre-2020-recuadro-5.pdf.

10. Diario Gestión, https://gestion.pe/peru/coronavirus-peru-cin-co-mil-colegios-privados-ya-no-abririan-sus-puertas-el-2021-esti-ma-asociacion-de-escuelas-particulares-nndc-noticia/.

Chapter 9

1. http://tedxtalks.ted.com/video/TEDxGlasgow-Pauline-Dix-on-How-P, 2012.

2. "World Teachers Day Fact Sheet," https://unesdoc.unesco.org/ark:/48223/pf0000374450.

3. Ibid.

4. Jordan Naidoo and Olav Selm, "Making Education a Priority in the Post-2015 Development Agenda: Report of the Global Thematic Consultation on Education in the Post-2015 Development Agenda," UNESCO, 2013, 5. These statistics should be read with caution as they might not, for example, include children registered in unregistered independent schools.

5. http://dspace.cigilibrary.org/jspui/bitstream/123456789/29540/1/Hiddenpercent20Assestspercent20-percent20Southpercen-t20Africaspercent20Low-Feepercent20Privatepercent20Schools.pdf, 49.

6. Stefan Schimer, Jeff McCarthy, and Ann Bernstein, "Promoting School Choice for the Poor: Practical Ideas from International Experience," The Centre for Development and Enterprise, 2012, 4.

7. Ibid.

8. Ibid.

9. http://www.economist.com/news/middle-east-and-africa/215 96981-paid-private-schools-are-better-value-money-free-sort-class-room?zid=304&ah=e5690753dc78ce91909083042ad12e30.

10. Ibid.

11. Ibid.

12. Ibid.

13. Ibid.

14. Pauline Dixon, "Why the Denial? Low-Cost Private Schools in Developing Countries and Their Contributions to Education," *Economic Journal Watch* 9, 3 (September 2012): 186–209.

15. http://www.affordable-learning.com/what-is-affordable-learn ing.html#sthash.7QsrYMbk.dpbs.

16. Staff writers: The 10 Best Countries for a Teacher.

17. Peter Dolton and Oscar Marcenaro-Gutierrez, "Varky GEMS Foundation Global Teacher Status Index," (October 2013), 14. The twenty-one countries covered by the study included Israel, Brazil, Czech Republic, Italy, Japan, Germany, Switzerland, Portugal, Finland, Spain, France, UK, USA, Netherlands, Singapore, Egypt, New Zealand, South Korea, Turkey, Greece, and China listed here in the order of lowest to highest scores.

18. Amanda Ripley, *The Smartest Kids in the World and How They Got That Way,* 85.

19. Asif Dowla and Dipal Barua, *The Poor Always Pay Back: The Grameen II Story.*

20. For a detailed historical account, see David Roodman, "Microfinance Due Diligence," 2012, and Makonen Getu, "Transforming Microfinance: A Christian Approach," 2013.

21. http://edition.cnn.com/2013/11/15/opinion/yunus-microfinance-grameen-bank/.

22. http://www.theguardian.com/global-development/2012/jul/03/pearson-invest-private-education-africa-asia. See also http://pearsonschools.in/aboutus.html.

23. Tony Wagner, *Creating Innovators: The Making of Young People Who Will Change the World* (New York: Scribner, 2012), 18.

24. Ibid., 17.

25. Robert Sternberg, quoted in Wagner, 17.

26. Op. cit., 58.

27. Patrick Fagan, "Religious Practice and Educational Attainment: How Worship Influences Academic Success," 5, http://www.ncfpc.org/FNC/1010S2-Fagan.pdf.

28. http://search.tb.ask.com/search/GGmain.jhtml?searchfor=mary+joan+iwenofupercent2C+religious+and+moral+education+and+its+impact+on+national+development&st=kwd&ptb=913FADF7-80C9-4EF2-A3B1-ACEB7D80F475&n=780b-833c&ind=2014020412&p2=^Y6^xdm005^YYA^g-b&si=CN-bi7e5srwCFZShtAodBTsA-g, 5.

29. Charles Malik, *A Christian Critique of the University* (Downers Grove, IL: Intervarsity Press, 1982).

ABOUT THE AUTHORS

Makonen Getu, PhD

Makonen serves as vice president of Christian transformation in Edify. Prior to that he spent the majority of his career in international development working for United Nations Development in Lesotho, Swedish International Development Cooperation Agency in Zambia, World Vision International in Zambia and Australia, and Opportunity International in Zimbabwe and United Kingdom. He has also worked as a lecturer at the University of Stockholm and Oxford Centre for Mission Studies and has published several books and articles on topics related to economic development, microfinance, transformation, and low-fee independent schools. Makonen holds a PhD in Economic History with a degree in International Economic Development from the University of Stockholm and a Diploma in Clinical and Pastoral Counselling Skills from The Institute of Counselling, Glasgow Caledonian University. Makonen has been married to Lea since 1983, and they have twin daughters, one son, and one grandson.

Christopher A. Crane

Christopher Crane cofounded Edify with Tiger Dawson in 2009, which makes microfinance and SME loans and provides training to ten thousand schools that educate three million children living in poverty in twelve developing nations. He was CEO for eight years and is now chairman. From 2002–09, Chris was CEO of Opportunity International, a Christian microfinance organization, with operations in twenty-eight countries with 1.5 million active clients. Chris acquired COMPS InfoSystems in 1992 and served for eight years as CEO of this digital commercial real estate database company with 400 employees. Chris was named Ernst & Young Entrepreneur of the Year in the software/internet category in San Diego in 1999. He earned an MBA from Harvard Business School.

Bettina Gomez-Garcia

Bettina Gomez-Garcia is chief strategy officer and vice president for Latin American Programs. Bettina is passionate about community transformation and is an education advocate. She believes that education breaks the poverty cycles, and a Christ-centered education transforms nations. She has a background in the academic and business sector, working as a dean and professor for executive education and in the corporate sector designing, planning, and executing strategies to fulfill corporate objectives with a sustainable achievement. She is married to Luis, and they have two daughters.

Printed in Great Britain
by Amazon

82974461R00200